Primo Levi and Ka-Tzetnik

Yochai Ataria

Primo Levi and Ka-Tzetnik

The Map and the Territory

Translated by Shmuel Sermoneta-Gertel

palgrave
macmillan

Yochai Ataria
Tel Hai Academic College
Upper Galilee, Israel

ISBN 978-3-030-76742-6 ISBN 978-3-030-76743-3 (eBook)
https://doi.org/10.1007/978-3-030-76743-3

This Palgrave Macmillan imprint is published by the registered company Springer Nature Switzerland AG.
The registered company address is: Gewerbestrasse 11, 6330 Cham, Switzerland

Because what is, is. What we are, we are. And both are impossible.
Robert Antelme, The Human Race (1992, 65).

In the end we ourselves demand explanations of ourselves, until in the end we succeed in annihilating everything around us, ourselves included, or in other words explain ourselves to death.
Imre Kertész, Kaddish for an Unborn Child (2004).

It is shame. We are men, we belong to the same human family that our executioners belong to. Before the enormity of their crime, we feel that we, too, are citizens of Sodom and Gomorrah, and cannot be exempted from the charge that an otherworldly judge, on the basis of our own testimony, would bring against all humanity.
Primo Levi, 'The Deported. Anniversary' (2015, 1128).

For Ori,
Your every breath is proof that humanity is not lost, that there is still hope for the human project.

Acknowledgements

I am indebted to so many people that I am at a loss to explain the precise contribution that each has made towards the realization of this book, for which I offer my sincere apologies. I would like to thank the following individuals (by no means an exhaustive list), who helped and advised me along the way—reading, commenting, and enlightening me: Yechiel Szeintuch, Manuela Consonni, Omer Bartov, Berel Lang, Amit Kravitz, Rivka Brot, Gil Anidjar, Yossi Guterman, Avihu Ronen Dan Laor, Dina Porat, Mooli Lahad, Debbie Eylon, Keren Dotan, and Yemima Ben-Menahem. All mistakes are of course my own.

I would especially like to thank Amos Goldberg, for the ongoing dialogue, intellectual openness, and, above all, the courage to express a different and unique point of view.

I am also grateful to David Shimonovich for his editing of the Hebrew edition of this book. Over the years, David has become my closest collaborator and confidant—probably the only person familiar with my unrefined self—my early drafts. Thank you, David, for being who you are. I also wish to thank Aviya Ben David, who prepared the book for translation. My profound thanks to Shmuel Sermoneta-Gertel, for his exemplary translation from Hebrew to English. Thank you, Shmuel, for preserving my voice and for being a translator, an editor, and, in many ways, a colleague. I would like to express my appreciation to Beth Farrow, Rachel Daniel, and Madison Allums, at Palgrave Macmillan, for their excellent editorial work.

I am grateful to the Tel-Hai Academic College and the Ka-Tzetnik Foundation for their financial support for the translation of this book. Finally, I would like to thank the librarians at the Tel-Hai Academic College, for their invaluable help in obtaining every book and article I requested.

Contents

List of Figures

Introduction: The Map and the Territory

In *The Drowned and the Saved*, Primo Levi recalls the cynical warning of the SS soldiers:

> No matter how this war ends, we have won the war against you. *No one will be left to testify, but even if one of you does survive, the world will not believe you.* There might be suspicions, discussions, historical research, but there will be no certainty, *because we will destroy both you and the evidence.* And even if some evidence should remain and some of you do manage to survive, people will say the events you describe are too monstrous to be believed: *they will call them exaggerations of Allied propaganda, and they will believe us, who will deny everything, and not you. We are the ones who will dictate the history of the concentration camps.*[1] (Levi 2015, 2411)

Levi and Ka-Tzetnik try, each in his own unique way, to testify and to recount events that often appear beyond the realm of possibility. Both writers have had a significant impact on the development of Holocaust discourse in academic, political, and social contexts, albeit from ostensibly contrasting perspectives: whereas Levi is famously associated with the concept of the 'grey zone', Ka-Tzetnik is identified with that of 'another planet'.

Apart from *a shared sense of urgency to tell their stories*, it seems that the two men could not have been more different. Levi's writing is considered self-aware, ironic, reserved, and precise, while Ka-Tzetnik's writing is perceived as unaware, kitsch-filled, and bordering on the pornographic. Levi's texts, written in the first person singular, appear to allow the trauma to be worked through, while Ka-Tzetnik writes in the third person singular and obsessively relives the past, ostensibly impeding any healing process. Levi draws upon his memories, while Ka-Tzetnik is unable to distinguish between his nightmares and hallucinations and reality. Levi was somewhat estranged from Judaism, while Ka-Tzetnik, born Yehiel Feiner, studied at the Yeshiva of Lublin.[2]

Levi is widely appreciated by researchers, while Ka-Tzetnik has, in recent decades, become a kind of punchbag for scholars of Holocaust literature and psychoanalysis. Dan Miron (1994, 202), for example, winner of the 1993 Israel Prize for Hebrew literature, argues that Ka-Tzetnik failed to faithfully convey the complexity of the human experience. Miron explains his position as follows:

> The same, constant, inner cry that seems to have enabled him to raise the cry of Auschwitz more volubly than others also diminished its spiritual force. Thus, while his stories of Auschwitz may be deafening, the true roaring thunder of the horror is in fact more tangible and present in the hushed tones of other writers.[3] (214)

Contrary to the prevailing trend in Holocaust literature studies, I will try to show that Ka-Tzetnik—perhaps precisely because of his perverted style—*at times* succeeds where Levi fails. According to Bartov (1997, 52), 'Ka-Tzetnik does what Levi ultimately reproaches himself for having been unable to accomplish, namely, he writes from the point of view of the drowned, the Mussulman, the living skeleton who no longer has a consciousness.' In this book, I will attempt to substantiate this claim and take it a step further.

The main thesis of the book is that a deeper understanding of the central elements of the Holocaust requires both Levi and Ka-Tzetnik. While Levi draws the map, Ka-Tzetnik describes the territory. Levi provides the broader picture, the various minutiae of daily life in the camp, cases in which a Kapo showed signs of humanity, moments at which he himself felt that he was losing parts of his own humanity, while Ka-Tzetnik continuously crashes against the gazes of those who 'left him behind on their way to the crematorium' (Ka-Tzetnik 1977, 63)—just as he did when he took the stand at Eichmann's trial.

I will argue that neither perspective is sufficient in and of itself: both are necessary, as well as the interplay between them. In order to maintain an anchor of some sort in the face of repeated collapse, we would do well to grasp Levi as we read Ka-Tzetnik; and, in order to feel the gaping abyss beneath the clear, precise phrasing, we would do well to grasp Ka-Tzetnik as we read Levi. The result is *understanding rooted in feeling, feeling based on understanding*. The interplay between Levi and Ka-Tzetnik, the possibility of reading them together yet separately, allows us to engage sincerely and profoundly with Levi's question, 'if this is a man'. We would thus do well not to rely exclusively on Levi or to cast Ka-Tzetnik aside, but rather to follow the advice of Kohelet: 'Take hold of this, and from this, too, withdraw not your hand.'

In order to illustrate these assertions, I will focus on core issues addressed by Levi and Ka-Tzetnik—for example, the Muselmann, the possibility and necessity of testifying, the nature of traumatic memory, the question of people's humanity, the victims' sense of having been tainted, the possibility of giving voice to the dead, and collaboration with the perpetrators.

Another goal of this book is to question one of the leading theories in trauma studies today—that there is a clear dichotomy between acting out and working through: processes of acting out represent the post-traumatic subject's uncontrollable and unconscious repetition of traumatic scenes, while processes of working through represent relative control over the traumatic event and its articulation, with the potential to counteract the force of acting out and the repetition compulsion. Despite the analytical distinction between the two processes, LaCapra (2014, 71) stresses that 'acting out and working through are … intimately linked'.

Levi's writing is widely recognized as a perfect example of working through processes, while Ka-Tzetnik's writing is seen as the epitome of acting out. I will show that both writers, in fact, oscillate between acting out and working through, with numerous examples of both processes in their respective works. To substantiate this claim, I will compare the process that Levi went through, as reflected in his writing—from his first book, *If This Is a Man* (published 1947, see Fig. 1), to his last book, *The Drowned and the Saved* (published in 1986); and the process that Ka-Tzetnik underwent, as reflected in his writing—from his first book, *Salamandra* (Eng. *Sunrise over Hell*), which he began to write, in Yiddish, in 1945 (published 1946, see, Fig. 1), to the last book in the series, *Hatsofen* (published 1987; Eng. *Shivitti*). I will also argue that the generally accepted link between mode of writing and the ability to recover from trauma is unfounded, rooted mostly in the wishful thinking of certain theoreticians, who have adopted a dichotomous and somewhat simplistic approach.

Fig. 1 A shared sense of urgency to tell their stories
Left: Front cover of the first edition of Levi, *Se questo è un uomo* (Italian, 1947). Source: https://upload.wikimedia.org/wikipedia/en/3/3c/IfThisIsaMan.jpg
Right: Front cover of the first edition of Ka-Tzetnik, *Salamandra* (Hebrew, 1946). Source: https://www.kedem-auctions.com/wp-content/uploads/ol/online-12/241_1.jpg

The way in which Levi and Ka-Tzetnik describe the experience of writing their first books is quite similar. In 1976, Levi wrote, in an appendix for the school edition of *If This Is a Man*: 'The need to tell was so strong in us that I began to write the book there … although I knew that under no circumstances would I be able to keep those notes, scribbled any way I could—that I would have to throw them away immediately, because if they were found on me they would cost me my life. But I wrote the book as soon as I returned, in a few months: the memories were burning inside me' (Levi 2015, 167). Elsewhere, Levi writes: 'I came back from the camp with a narrative impulse that was pathological' (2001, 129); and 'I wrote at night or during my lunchbreak. Almost the entire chapter "The Canto of Ulysses" was written in half an hour between 12.30 and 1 p.m. one day. I was in a sort of trance' (162). This is how, by Levi's own account, his best-known work, *If This Is a Man*, came to be. In Shivitti (1989, 110), the final volume of the Salamandra series, Ka-Tzetnik described the writing of Salamandra (Sunrise over Hell) as follows: 'I wrote Salamandra in precisely two and a half weeks. It was my first testimony, written while I was still a skeleton in striped Auschwitz shrouds racing death in a hospital in Italy.' At the time, Ka-Tzetnik believed he did not have long to live: 'I myself knew my days were numbered. I spoke to the Israeli soldier who was nursing me: "Quick. Get me paper and pencil. I vowed to them in Auschwitz, as I stood near their ashes behind the crematorium…. This I must do now, while I still can"' (15).

Overview

The first part of the book is dedicated to the figure of Ka-Tzetnik. Chapter 1 examines the transformation that Ka-Tzetnik underwent over time, as reflected in *Shivitti* (1989). In 1976, Ka-Tzetnik sought treatment for his persistent nightmares, at the clinic of Prof. Jan Bastiaans in the Netherlands. Bastiaans treated his patients with LSD, and *Shivitti* is an account of Ka-Tzetnik's experiences under the influence of the hallucinogenic drug. A dramatic change appears to have come over Ka-Tzetnik during the course of the treatment. He ceased viewing Auschwitz as another planet, another world with different rules, and began to see those who planned and executed the destruction of the Jewish people as ordinary human beings. This transformation is ignored by most scholars, who treat *Shivitti* (*Hatsofen*, The Code) as if it were just another book in the Salamandra series (*Salamandra* [1946; Eng. Sunrise over Hell, 1977], *Beit habubot* [1953; Eng. *House of Dolls*], *Hasha'on* [1960; Eng. *Star Eternal*], *Piepel* [1961; Eng. *Piepel*], and *Ha'imut* [1966; Eng. *Phoenix over the Galilee*]), when it is, in fact, a very different kind of book. In this chapter, I will argue that had Ka-Tzetnik ended his chronicle (the Salamandra series) with *Phoenix over the Galilee*, much of the criticism levelled against him over the years might have had merit. In *Shivitti*, however, the sixth and final book in the series—in some sense, a reflective work on the series and its author—Ka-Tzetnik, as a writer, becomes a complex and interesting figure, no longer merely eccentric and exaggerated, as many seem to believe.

While the first chapter discusses the treatment to which Ka-Tzetnik submitted in order to discover the secret of his nightmares—essentially to determine whether they were rooted in reality or in fantasy—the second chapter grapples with Ka-Tzetnik's ability to tell the difference between the two. Ka-Tzetnik's accounts of historical processes, such as the deportation of the 8000 Jews of Sosnowiec on 12 August 1942, seem entirely accurate, yet, when it comes to his personal experiences, he appears unable to distinguish between reality and fantasy. To substantiate this claim, I will examine the story of Daniella, the sister of Harry (protagonist of the Salamandra series). This story, first told in *Sunrise over Hell* and at greater length in *House of Dolls*, is one of the most dramatic in all of Ka-Tzetnik's books; a breaking point for readers and for the author himself: 'I behold *Feld hure* branded between my sister's breasts. And *I see myself instantly splitting in two.* ... I ... see the key to my nightmares. It's hidden beneath the brand between my sister's breasts' (Ka-Tzetnik 1989, 98–100).

Ka-Tzetnik wants to know—must know—whether his sister was indeed a prostitute in the service of the Nazis, and whether he actually saw her. Considerable historical evidence, however, would seem to indicate that the story itself is extremely unlikely. Nevertheless, Ka-Tzetnik continued to insist, on various occasions, even fifty years after Auschwitz, that he did not write literature but facts. In this chapter, I will argue that Ka-Tzetnik himself did not know the source of his nightmare, and was unable to make a clear distinction between nightmare and nightmarish reality. Consequently, he was able to experience the nightmare as something that had actually occurred—in fact, in the state that he was in, he could not experience the nightmare as anything but reality.

The third chapter concentrates on Ka-Tzetnik's testimony at the Eichmann trial. De-Nur (lit. 'of fire')[4] made every effort to appear at the trial under his literary pseudonym, Ka-Tzetnik. Only moments before he was supposed to take the stand, however, the prosecutor Gideon Hausner informed him that the judges would not allow him to testify under his pen name, insisting that he must use his real name, Yehiel De-Nur. During his testimony, under Eichmann's gaze, Ka-Tzetnik understood something he had denied up to that moment—that he himself had lived through those experiences, that the stories he had written were his story. This is when trauma—the moment at which victims realize what has happened and that it has happened to them—struck with full force. At that moment, with the words of the court president ringing in his ears, with Eichmann's gaze upon him, the camera cut away for an instant and De-Nur collapsed.

In order to survive, Ka-Tzetnik created (unconsciously) a far more aggressive defence mechanism, detaching himself entirely from his past, thereby losing contact with his original memories. His previous defence mechanism had allowed him to maintain contact with his personal experiences in the camps, through the figure of Ka-Tzetnik. After the Eichmann trial, however, he became completely detached, with his books serving as his only remaining connection to his past. As it turns out, Ka-Tzetnik was not alone in this. Levi too had similar problems:

> My story is entirely anomalous, because between that experience and me stand a certain number of books that function as artificial memory. Had I not written *If This Is a Man*, I would probably have forgotten many things. … I have given a large number of interviews, and all of this interposes itself between the authentic experience and the present. (Spadi 2003, 29)

Chapter 4 focuses on the Muselmann, described by Levi (2015, 85) as the epitome of evil: 'If I could encompass all the evil of our time in one image, I would choose this image, which is familiar to me: an emaciated man, head bowed and shoulders bent, on whose face and in whose eyes no trace of thought can be seen.' The Muselmann is the threshold between the human and the inhuman, between the living being and the dead object. Ka-Tzetnik and Levi agree that the Muselmann is the ultimate witness. Therefore, in order to understand Auschwitz, we must first understand the world of the Muselmann—the cipher and the gatekeeper of Auschwitz. Levi and Ka-Tzetnik, each in his own way, seek out the voice of the Muselmann. This chapter will show how the Muselmann marks the limits of Levi's writing—contrary to Agamben's (1999, 59) view that '[Levi] is the only one who consciously sets out to bear witness in place of the *Muselmann*.' The manner in which Levi writes about Auschwitz prevents him from giving voice to the Muselmann, and, in that sense, the Muselmann indeed exists on another planet. In *Piepel* (1961), Ka-Tzetnik tells the story of Moni (Harry's brother), a sex slave to the Kapos who, when he is no longer attractive to them, becomes a Muselmann. As we shall see, despite a heroic effort to enter the world of the Muselmänner, Ka-Tzetnik crashes again and again, in his attempts to find their voice. Together with Moni, Ka-Tzetnik finds himself on the verge of 'Muselmannity', unable to represent the Muselmann's inner world. In this chapter, I will suggest that the gap between Levi and Ka-Tzetnik may be described in the following terms: while Levi defines the limits within which testimony is still possible, without attempting to penetrate the lacuna, Ka-Tzetnik crashes against the Muselmann's doors. I will also argue that any attempt to understand the Muselmann, the lacuna of Auschwitz, requires both Levi and Ka-Tzetnik. On the one hand, while Levi draws the map and defines the boundaries, providing an objective picture of the situation, it is a bird's-eye view, an accurate description but always from the outside. Ka-Tzetnik, on the other hand, may fail to describe the Muselmann from within, but his repeated and inevitable failures, in and of themselves, afford some measure of understanding. Ka-Tzetnik's tormented efforts to come as close to the limit as he can recreate the territory of the crushed soul in the concentration camp. The map alone does not give us the necessary proximity, while the territory engulfs us and does not allow us to get our bearings. The combination of the two affords us a greater, albeit imperfect understanding of the Muselmann.

Chapter 5 explores the emotional price paid by survivors who attempt to describe the experience of prisoners in the concentration and extermination camps. In this context, I will examine the writings of Jorge Semprún, a member of the French Resistance sent to the Buchenwald concentration camp in 1944. According to Semprún (1997, 127), survivors who insist on telling their stories, who refuse to offer 'simple eyewitness accounts', pay a heavy price: life itself. Semprún stresses that the experience of a survivor who seeks to write about death from within the silence, or, alternatively, about life from within death, is not one of relief. On the contrary, Semprún is aware of the stark contrast between himself and Levi on this point: 'While writing may have torn Primo Levi from the past, assuaging the pain of memory … it thrust me back into death, drowning me in it' (250). For Semprún, the process of writing was one of re-enacting (acting out) the extermination process. So too Ka-Tzetnik, who burnt his writings and rewrote them again and again—in this sense, Ka-Tzetnik is an example of someone who uncontrollably re-enacted the trauma in his writing. In this too, however, Ka-Tzetnik underwent a fundamental change as he wrote *Shivitti*: 'The number on the top of this page of manuscript has just jumped out at me. I can't believe my eyes: I've filled dozens of folio pages with my tiny letters without even realizing the newness of what I'm doing: I am writing in the first person!' (Ka-Tzetnik 1989, 70). This is a change that those who embrace the working through approach, as opposed to acting out, would do well to consider. The fact that this change is ignored by many scholars reinforces the idea of the dogmatic and tendentious reading of Ka-Tzetnik.

The final chapter in this part of the book addresses the well-known characterization of Ka-Tzetnik as being addicted to kitsch and death. It is interesting to discover that Ka-Tzetnik is not the only one addicted to kitsch. Hitler himself was not only addicted to kitsch—cream cakes with strawberries, films of burning cities, and so forth—but an expert at creating kitsch, on an unprecedented scale. In his book, *Reflections of Nazism: An Essay on Kitsch and Death* (1984), Friedländer claims that Hitler understood the power of juxtaposing kitsch and death, of combining these two ostensibly opposing vectors into a single force. Hitler was enchanted by death, which he promoted and glorified by means of the lowest and the most dangerous kind of kitsch. In this chapter, I will argue that it was precisely Ka-Tzetnik's use of kitsch that affords him profound insight into the nature of the Nazi regime, penetrating even 'the most hidden, darkest, and most repulsive recesses of the human psyche' (Bartov 1997, 53).

Thus, surprisingly and shockingly, what initially appeared to be a weakness in Ka-Tzetnik's writing is actually a point of strength, enhancing his ability to describe the concentration and extermination camps.

The second part of the book focuses on the question of Levi's suicide. Primo Levi died on 11 April 1987, at 10:05, in Torino, in the house where he was born and lived nearly his entire life. Levi's suicide has led scholars in a range of disciplines to ask themselves whether they may have misunderstood him and whether his writings should be revisited. Chapter 7 will review the various ways in which scholars have related to Levi's suicide.

Chapter 8 examines the dialogue between Levi and Jean Améry—both Auschwitz survivors, who even shared the same barracks for a time. While Levi's suicide was a scandal, Améry's was perfectly reasonable, almost necessary. Améry was up to his neck in resentment, representing the pitiful state of the survivor, forever trapped in victimhood. Levi associated Améry's suicide with his identity problem, as well as his tendency to 'trade blows'. In an attempt to explain Levi's suicide, some have suggested that Levi too underwent a transformation in his final book, *The Drowned and the Saved*, and that like Améry, he came to 'trade blows' with the German people. In this chapter, I will show that this argument is unfounded, and that the Italian Levi's struggle with the German people is nothing like that of Améry, who was himself German. Although attempts to compare the suicides of Améry and Levi may be interesting, even enlightening, they do not reveal the reason for Levi's suicide. I will try to shed some light on the subject, by examining the circumstances of Levi's death.

Chapter 9 addresses the specific method by which Levi chose to end his life. As a chemist, Levi could easily have taken poison, yet he resorted to far more violent means. In this chapter, I will examine Levi's suicide through the prism of Camus's novel *The Fall*, suggesting that Levi's suicide lies on the boundary between leaping and falling—between the young woman's leap from the bridge and the protagonist Clamence's endless fall. I will try to show that Levi, in his suicide, evokes the fall of European man. This explanation is insufficient, however, as Levi did not merely fall—a passive process, in contrast to the active process of leaping. Semprún describes a similar experience, which may afford some insight into Levi's suicide. Semprún began to write *L'Écriture ou la vie* (Eng. *Literature or Life*) on the Saturday of Levi's suicide, exactly forty-two years after his own liberation from the Buchenwald concentration camp. In the book, Semprún tells how, on 5 August 1945, he fell off a train, just as it was about to enter the station. Semprún (1997, 209–10) is unsure of what exactly happened: 'But had I fallen from this ordinary, crowded commuter train, or had I deliberately thrown myself onto the tracks? Opinions differed; I myself had no conclusive view of the matter. ... But *perhaps voluntary death is a kind of dizziness*, nothing else.' We soon learn that Semprún, as he stood on the train platform, did not know where he was and, for a moment, felt like he was on the train headed for Buchenwald. Buchenwald is Semprún's reality. Sometimes he dreams that he is not there, but he always wakes up to discover that at least some part of him has remained a prisoner at Buchenwald. The first chapter of the third and final part of *Literature or Life* is entitled 'The Day of Primo Levi's Death'. In this chapter, Semprún discusses the last page of Levi's *The Truce*:

> Nothing can stop the course of this dream, says Levi; nothing can relieve the secret agony it causes, even if you turn to a loved one, even if a friendly—or a loving—hand is held out to you. ... Nothing, ever, will deflect the course of that dream. ... Nothing is true except the camp, all the rest is but a dream, now and forever. Nothing is real but the smoke from the crematory of Buchenwald, the smell of burned flesh, the hunger, the roll calls in the snow, the beatings. (235–6)

In this sense, it would seem that the survivor never actually leaves the concentration camp: the camp is reality and life afterwards merely a dream. I would thus suggest that when Levi fell/leapt, he may not have been entirely aware of where he was or, more precisely, when he was. The leap is an attempt to awaken from the nightmare, but it is only after the fall (if one survives, as Semprún did) that it becomes clear that one is not asleep, but awake. A leap meant to awaken the survivor from the dream, that is, reality outside the concentration camp thus looks like suicide.

Chapter 10 explores the topic of the grey zone. Levi asserts that the world of the camps cannot simply be 'reduced to two blocs'. Indeed, according to Levi (2015, 2431–2), one of the crushing blows upon entering the camps was the 'concentric aggression at the hands of the very persons in whom you had hoped to find future allies'. Breaking the dichotomous model of *good* and *evil* and entering the grey zone, which has 'undefined contours' and 'both separates and connects the two opposing camps of masters and servants' (2435), requires great emotional strength and extraordinary analytical ability. In this chapter, I will examine various types of collaborator: the Kapo, the Sonderkommando, and the Judenrat member. I will also examine the case of Reserve Police Battalion 101 of the German Order Police, responsible for the mass execution of Jews, liquidation of ghettos, guarding the trains on which the Jews were deported to the extermination camps, manhunts and massacres against Polish partisans, and other atrocities. Reserve Police Battalion 101 is the subject of an important debate among Holocaust scholars, which may be encapsulated as follows: the 'ordinary people' explanation (Christopher Browning) versus the 'ordinary Germans' explanation (Daniel Goldhagen). Levi, who wrote that the SS 'were made from the same cloth as us, average human beings, of average intelligence and average malice' (2566), would probably have sided with the former. As we shall see in this chapter, the grey zone offers an explanation, if only a partial one, of the way in which people act in the impossible situation in which total power is exercised.

In Chap. 11, I will argue that Levi himself was trapped in the grey zone—at no time more so than during the six-month period (beginning in the spring of 1982) in which he translated Kafka's *The Trial*. As he worked on the translation, Levi increasingly found himself identifying with Kafka's protagonist, Joseph K. Translating *The Trial* exacted a heavy price from Levi, who appears to have fallen into depression (and not for the first time) towards the end of that same year. In this chapter, I will suggest that the moment Levi accepts the ending of *The Trial* not only as the most logical outcome, but also as the only possible outcome, his time begins to run out. It is not that this mode of thinking was new to Levi, but having translated *The Trial*, he could no longer repress what he had known at least since his imprisonment in the concentration and extermination camps. After having translated *The Trial*, it seems that Levi had no choice but to confront Kafka, as he could no longer escape the Kafkaesque world: true, his death was certain, but maybe, he could die like a *man* and not like a *dog*. Contrary to K., who 'could not completely rise to the occasion', Levi could rise to the occasion, defeating Kafka in the internal struggle between the two figures, the doppelgängers, and complete the task himself.

Chapter 12, the final chapter of the second part of the book, deals with Levi's efforts to understand, recount, and explain. In order to recount, Levi first had to understand—a need that, over the years, became not only an existential necessity, but a malignant presence as well. In this chapter, I will argue that within the obsession to explain lies a mortal danger, or, if you will, what appears, at first sight, to be a process of working through is in fact a process of acting out (from the perspective of those who accept this approach). In Levi's case, the need to provide explanations came at a particularly high price. Levi's main difficulty was not his inability to explain Auschwitz, but his inability to explain Lorenzo, who, in a situation in which humanity had collapsed, did the impossible—preserved his humanity:

> An Italian civilian worker brought me a piece of bread and the remains of his ration every day for six months; he gave me an undershirt of his, full of patches; he wrote a postcard on my behalf to Italy and brought me the reply. For all this he neither asked nor accepted any reward, because he was good and simple, and did not think that one should do good for a reward. … However little sense there may be in trying to specify the reasons that I, among thousands of others like me, was able to stand up to the test, I believe that I owe it to Lorenzo if I am alive today; and not so much for his material aid as for his having constantly reminded me by his presence, by his natural and plain manner of being good, that a just world still existed outside ours, something and someone still pure and whole, not corrupt, not savage, unconnected to hatred and fear: something difficult to define, a remote possibility of good, but for which it was worth surviving. (113–15)

Indeed, there would appear to be no room for people like Lorenzo in the Kafkaesque world, and even in the real world, Lorenzo was unable to survive. He died in 1952, and Levi named his two children after him. In this chapter, which concludes the second part of the book, I will suggest that Levi could not bear his failure to explain Lorenzo.

Listen Intently

Levi's suicide remains a mystery, and this book will not change that. We find it hard to accept that the Levi of *If This Is a Man* and *The Periodic Table* took his own life. When considered in light of Ka-Tzetnik's collapse at the Eichmann trial, the fact that Levi committed suicide, throwing himself from the third-floor landing, raises new questions and opens new horizons of thought regarding the message he wished to convey by his final act. Ka-Tzetnik's collapse at the Eichmann trial exhorted us to listen to the witnesses. The collapse came seconds after Ka-Tzetnik said, in the first person singular and the present tense, as if transported back to Auschwitz: 'I see them, they are staring at me.'[5] This was something the court could not tolerate. It is thus incumbent upon us to complete the task and listen fully to the witnesses—to everything they are willing and able to tell.

One of the questions raised by Levi's suicide is whether we ever really listened to him in his lifetime. The answer is not unequivocal. In the final part of *The Drowned and the Saved*, Levi presents a sample of his correspondence with German readers, which reflects the fact that many Germans, as empathetic as they may have been, still found a way of rejecting guilt and avoiding responsibility. Others, like Müller, director of the laboratory at Auschwitz where Levi worked, chose to 'touch up' their pasts. In a letter to Levi, Müller made the preposterous claim that 'the entire Buna-Monowitz factory ... had been constructed with the intention of "protecting the Jews and helping them to survive"' (935).

What then did Levi wish to convey by his suicide? I believe that Levi too wished to enjoin us to listen to the survivors, the witnesses. Indeed, Levi's lifelong anxiety that the survivors would not be listened to began while he was still at Auschwitz:

> They are all listening to me and it is this very story that I am telling: the three-note whistle, the hard bunk, my neighbor whom I would like to move but am afraid to wake because he is stronger than I am. I also speak at length about our hunger and about how we are checked for lice, and about the Kapo who hit me on the nose and then sent me to wash because I was bleeding. It is an intense pleasure, physical, inexpressible, to be at home, among friendly people, and to have so many things to recount, but I can't help noticing that my listeners do not follow me. In fact, they are completely indifferent: they speak confusedly among themselves of other things, as if I were not there. My sister looks at me, gets up, and goes away without a word. A desolating grief now rises in me, like some barely remembered pain of early childhood. It is pain in its pure state, untempered by a sense of reality or by the intrusion of extraneous circumstances, the kind of pain that makes children cry; and it is better for me to swim up to the surface once again, but this time I deliberately open my eyes, to have a guarantee in front of me that I am in fact awake. My dream stands before me, still warm, and although I'm awake I'm filled with its anguish. And then I remember that it's not just any dream, and that since I arrived here I have dreamed it not once but many times, with hardly any variations in setting or details. I am now fully awake and I remember that I recounted it to Alberto and that he confided, to my amazement, that it's also his dream and the dream of many others, perhaps of everyone. Why does it happen? Why is the pain of every day so constantly translated, in our dreams, into the ever repeated scene of the story told and not listened to? ... While I ponder this, I try to take advantage of the interval of wakefulness to shake off the anguished remnants of the preceding sleep, so as not to compromise the quality of the next sleep. I sit up, crouching in the darkness; I look around and *listen intently*. (57)

Primo Levi asks us to listen to the survivors, and that includes Ka-Tzetnik. In this sense, the renewed reading of Ka-Tzetnik's works proposed in the present volume is, I would like to think, a response to Levi's plea that we listen to the survivors. I find the very same plea in Ka-Tzetnik's collapse at the Eichmann trial: he too asked us to listen to the witnesses. It is my sincere hope that this book is a step in that direction.

Notes

1. Unless otherwise noted, all emphases, throughout the book, are mine.
2. As we shall see, although there is some truth in this dichotomous approach, it is not entirely accurate. To some extent, it stems from myths that Levi and Ka-Tzetnik themselves cultivated. For example, Levi's connection to Judaism before the Holocaust was stronger than he describes. Similarly, both Levi and Ka-Tzetnik had literary ambitions before Auschwitz—that is to say that they were not 'born', as writers, at Auschwitz.
3. Unless otherwise noted, all translations of non-English sources are the translator's own.
4. 'A river of fire [*di-nur*] streamed forth before Him; thousands upon thousands served Him; myriads upon myriads attended Him; the court sat and the books were opened' (Daniel 7:10).
5. De-Nur's testimony at the Eichmann trial is available in English at https://www.nizkor.org/session-068-01-eichmann-adolf/

References

Agamben, Giorgio. 1999. *Remnants of Auschwitz: The Witness and the Archive*. Trans. Daniel Heller-Roazen. New York: Zone Books.

Antelme, Robert. 1992. *The Human Race*. Trans. Jeffrey Haight and Annie Mahler. Evanston: The Marlboro Press/Northwestern.

Bartov, Omer. 1997. 'Kitsch and Sadism in Ka-Tzetnik's Other Planet: Israeli Youth Imagine the Holocaust'. *Jewish Social Studies* 3 (2): 42–76.

Friedländer, Saul. 1984. *Reflections of Nazism: An Essay on Kitsch and Death*. Trans. Thomas Weyr. New York: Harper & Row.

Ka-Tzetnik 135633. 1961. *Piepel*. Trans. Moshe M. Kohn. London: Anthony Blond.

———. 1977. *Phoenix Over the Galilee*. Trans. Nina De-Nur. New York: Pyramid.

———. 1989. *Shivitti: A Vision*. Trans. Eliyah Nike De-Nur and Lisa Herman. New York: Harper & Row.

Kertész, Imre. 2004. *Kaddish for an Unborn Child*. Trans. Tim Wilkinson. New York: Vintage Books.
LaCapra, Dominick. 2014. *Writing History, Writing Trauma*. Baltimore: Johns Hopkins University Press..
Levi, Primo 2001. *The Voice of Memory: Interviews 1961–1987*, eds. Marco Belpoliti and Robert Gordon. Trans. Robert Gordon. New York: New Press.
Levi, Primo. 2015. *The Complete Works of Primo Levi*, ed. Ann Goldstein. Various translators. 3 vols. New York: Liveright.
Miron, Dan. 1994. 'Between Books and Ashes' (Hebrew). *Alpayim* 10: 196–224.
Semprún, Jorge. 1997. *Literature or Life*. Trans. Linda Coverdale. New York: Viking.
Spadi, Milvia. 2003. *Le parole di un uomo: Incontro con Primo Levi*. Rome: Di Renzo.

PART I

Ka-Tzetnik

CHAPTER 1

Shivitti (*Hatsofen*: The Code)

Salamandra (1946; Eng. *Sunrise over Hell*, 1977) was one of the first books about the Holocaust to appear in Hebrew, and is certainly one of the best known. It is an extreme work by any standard, and many subsequent books on the subject of the Holocaust may very well have been understated precisely in reaction to this work. The Salamandra series—comprising *Salamandra* (1946; Eng. *Sunrise over Hell*, 1977), *Beit habubot* (1953; Eng. *House of Dolls*, 1955), *Hasha'on* (1960; Eng. *Star Eternal*, 1966), *Piepel* (1961; Eng. *Piepel*, 1961 [*Atrocity/Moni*, 1963]), and *Ha'imut* (first published as *Kaḥol me'efer*, 1966; Eng. *Phoenix over the Galilee*, 1969 [*House of Love, 1971*])—thus remains an anomaly in the landscape of Holocaust literature.

Had Ka-Tzetnik concluded his chronicle with these five books, much of the criticism against him in recent decades might have had merit. The sixth book in the Salamandra series, however, *Hatsofen* (1987; Eng. *Shivitti*, 1989), which is, in a certain sense, a reflective work on the series and on the author himself, made Ka-Tzetnik the writer a far more complex and interesting figure, no longer merely eccentric and excessive, as many would have it.

Y. Ataria, *Primo Levi and Ka-Tzetnik*,
https://doi.org/10.1007/978-3-030-76743-3_1

1.1 Block Poetics and the Danger of Identification with the Murderer

Goldberg (2013a, 62) eloquently describes what are perceived to be the two possible voices of the survivor:

> One approach embodies addiction to the plenitude of pain, and its representation in a virtually unmediated text, while the other approach constitutes the dilution and diversion of pain by means of subtle humour. The rhetorical mode of the first approach is pathos, and that of the second is irony. The poetics of the first strategy I will call 'block poetics',[1] because it represents the plenitude of pain that has not been worked through. The poetics of the second strategy I will call 'fissure poetics', since it strives—linguistically, narratively, and figuratively—to open a fissure in the heavy block of pain and suffering, and to wrest it from its complete control.

These two approaches evoke LaCapra's (1996, 1998, 2014) definitions of 'acting out' and 'working through'. According to LaCapra, acting out constitutes an uncontrollable and unconscious return of the post-traumatic subject 'haunted or possessed by the past and performatively caught up in the compulsive repetition of traumatic scenes—scenes in which the past returns and the future is blocked or fatalistically caught up in a melancholic feedback loop' (2014, 21). Working through, on the other hand, constitutes a process whereby the traumatic event is somewhat controlled and even represented—if only in part. This process 'may counteract the force of acting out and the repetition of compulsion' (22), because it allows one to create a distinction between the present moment and the traumatic event: 'One is both back there [in the traumatic event] and here at the same time, and one is able to distinguish between (not dichotomize) the two' (90). Note, however, that despite the theoretical distinction between these two processes, acting out and working through are intimately linked[2]:

> I would emphasize that the relation between acting-out and working-through should not be seen in terms of a from/to relationship in which the latter is presented as the dialectical transcendence of the former. I have noted that, particularly in cases of trauma, acting-out may be necessary and perhaps never fully overcome. Indeed, it may be intimately bound up with working through problems. (1996, 205)

The Nazi machine was not merely functional, but also included considerable sadistic elements. This point is especially important in the present context, because the moment sadism is involved, the process of working through becomes far more problematic and less likely to take place. The Nazi ideology was body-oriented in the most radical possible way (Neumann 2002), and in this sense, the machine in Kafka's story (2000) 'In the Penal Colony' offers a nearly perfect representation of the Nazi idea: the need to mark the body, thereby transforming it into an imagined object that is a source of enjoyment (*jouissance*). A critical element is the enjoyment that the executioner derives from the machine's operation, which is 'complete, boundless, excessive, unrestrained, and sadistic' (Goldberg 2013a, 62). While pleasure exists within certain decreed boundaries, enjoyment begins precisely where bounded pleasure ends. It is an 'addictive, excessive emotion that seeks to violate every law, with ever-increasing intensity', which, 'if not restrained, will inevitably cause suffering, to the self or others, ultimately aspiring to death'. The sadistic act may be said to pertain 'to the realm of enjoyment rather than pleasure. It aspires to utter enjoyment, based on the objectification and suffering of the other, effectively affording all of the power of enjoyment to the sadist' (66–7). In the course of this process, the victimizer annihilates the victim, but, at the very same time, needs the victim, as the perverted, sadistic torturer's only source of enjoyment. Consequently, when the victim seeks to describe her or his experience as the object of enjoyment, they encounter an acute problem. Words represent nothing, but become the expression of suffering itself, as the word is seared into the flesh. Thus, when the victim seeks to describe the experience, it is not a description but rather a recreation of the traumatic event: 'In this case, the words are part of the pain, rather than linguistic signifiers that signify it' (71).

Many scholars (Amir 2019; Glasner-Heled 2005; Miron 1994) tend to relate to Ka-Tzetnik as a figure that represents block poetics—the victim who incessantly recreates the Nazi torturer's enjoyment:

> The most radical example of this kind of excessive expression is the poetics of Ka-Tzetnik—the boundless, instantiating poetics of the scream, which transposes the excess of sadistic sacrificial reality, and the suffering it entails, to the text. The text itself thus becomes excessive and continues to act upon the reader with near immediacy. The emotional effect of the text is not a product of the information it conveys, but of the nauseating physical suffering it concentrates within itself. This is what I call 'block poetics'—blocks of

> words filled to overflowing with screaming and extreme emotion. … Despite its ethical quality, this strategy would appear to fall short of its goals—to the extent that these are communicative and therapeutic. It does not communicate physical suffering, in the sense of making it accessible to the reader's consciousness, but draws it into the narrative or judicial text. It renders the suffering present rather than communicating it! Nor does it unravel its all-embracing plenitude or open a crack or fissure in it, to ease the narrator's suffering. In some way, it even continues to act on the same plane as the murderer's sadism. Just as the murderer's enjoyment is complete, so too the victim is wholly enveloped in her or his screaming body—self, voice, and text constituting a single continuum of physical pain, of memory seared into the body, of words that are nothing but a scream of suffering. Since a text of this kind is a continuation of the sadistic sacrificial act, the danger is that it may replicate the power relations embodied in that very act, whereby the suffering subject, denied access to enjoyment, will seek enjoyment, albeit unconsciously, through the murderer—that is through identification with the murderer. This type of text believes completely in the plenitude and eternity of the murderer and in the murderer's ability to monopolize all enjoyment. … In the context of the poetics of rendering present (block poetics), the victim's only path to enjoyment may thus require identification with the murderer. (Goldberg 2013a, 71–3)

The totalitarian Nazi regime—the laws of which were Hitlerian fantasy and the reality of which was arbitrary death for the Jews—penetrated the victims' inner world in the deepest sense, marking their bodies and searing their souls. On 18 May 1941, Warsaw ghetto diarist Chaim Kaplan wrote, 'Unconsciously, we accept its ideology and follow in its ways. Nazism has conquered our entire world' (Goldberg 2017, 214–15). That is to say that no part of Jewish life, external or internal, was free of it. Goldberg explains that the Nazi persecution of the Jews did not merely elicit feelings such as rage, sorrow, or the desire for revenge, but was also destructively turned inwards, against the victim's own self-image. Deprived even of their language, they existed in a kind of 'linguistic grey zone', in which every word and image in the language of the Jews was inexorably bound to that of the Nazis. Under these conditions, when the victims employed images—of animals, for example—they were not images at all, but the actual reality of the Warsaw ghetto: 'figurative language was cancelled, and the Jews became animals even in their own language' (Goldberg 2012, 366). In this situation, the victims' language lost its metaphorical dimension, thereby reducing their existence to the purely biological.

The only way in which words can be used in such circumstances is through the Kafkaesque machine that inscribes them on the body itself: 'Here the Nazi mark is affixed to the body of the Jewish victim, leaving no gap into which words might be directed in the constant search for new words to express changing, living self-perception and desire, thereby constituting identity' (Goldberg 2017, 249). Every word in the victim's world is affixed to the body and derives from the body, devoid of any complexity beyond corporeal reality. Words thus become expressive; they become an integral part of the pain, rather than mere linguistic signifiers. They become part of the 'thing itself' (253–4). Corporeal reality is then all that remains, and the Jew becomes a lifeless object. Under such conditions, body-disownership, that is, a sense of hostility towards one's own body, may develop.[3]

Similarly, Amir (2019, 51) asserts that 'one of the greatest dangers lurking in the territory of excess is the danger of collusion', while Glasner-Heled (2005, 190) stresses that one of the central motifs in the work of Ka-Tzetnik is the Jewish victim's attraction to Germanness, so that even Ka-Tzetnik himself cannot help but see the distinguished-looking bearded Jew (Ka-Tzetnik 1978, 37) through German eyes. Glasner-Heled also argues that

> Ka-Tzetnik's writings effectively present an explicit indictment of the Jews themselves, perceived as bearing responsibility for the catastrophic proportions of the Holocaust they suffered. Although Ka-Tzetnik condemns the Nazis in no uncertain terms and spares no detail in describing the horrors they perpetrated, he places the 'settling of accounts' firmly within the Jewish world, in which the Nazis become almost 'irrelevant'. The rage, the enmity, and the doomsday revenge fantasies that Ka-Tzetnik places in the mouths of his protagonists are all directed against Jewish characters, and not against the Nazis. (193)

Miron (1994, 220–1) offers a more violent thesis. He believes that Ka-Tzetnik burns his book of poetry (second-rate poetry, according to Miron) as a kind of self-revenge:

> Not only in a similar fashion to his loved ones, paralleling their destruction by fire, but also because they were killed, and as retribution for their deaths. That is to say that De-Nur identifies the book with his relatives and with himself, but also exacts revenge from the book for the deaths of his relatives and for himself. He punishes it and consigns it to the flames, in the manner

> of 'an eye for an eye': just as they were destroyed by fire, so to you shall be destroyed by fire. ... De-Nur learns from the murderers what must be done to De-Nur. He is swept into the terrible identification of the victim with the murderer.

According to Lyotard (1988, 8), 'the "perfect crime" does not consist in killing the victim or the witnesses (that adds new crimes to the first one and aggravates the difficulty of effacing everything), but rather in obtaining the silence of the witnesses, the deafness of the judges, and the inconsistency (insanity) of the testimony'. The problem lies not in this or that article by Miron or some other scholar, but in understanding the deeper significance of the approach he represents. In his article, Miron does not reveal Ka-Tzetnik's unconscious, but rather his own unconscious as an interpreter. By making Ka-Tzetnik, an admittedly extreme figure, into a madman, he himself takes part in the perfect crime. I therefore accept Miron's conclusions:

> What we have before us is an example of a deep pathology, in which we may and indeed must take an interest, not because we seek to reveal the secret of the tormented individual, as famous and influential as that individual might be, but because this pathology threatens all of us collectively and nests within us, as a culture-bearing society.... We are all liable to be swept up by the syndrome of identification with the murderer, by internalizing something of the murderer's belligerence and ruthlessness, combined with a disdain for the weak in and of themselves, that is, in and of ourselves. (222)

The question arises, however, who really identifies with the Nazi murderer? *Is it Ka-Tzetnik or the interpreters who derive enjoyment from Ka-Tzetnik's immolation?* By way of example, I would call attention once again to Glasner-Heled (2005, 170), who describes Ka-Tzetnik's writing as extreme, emotionally and intellectually unrestrained, and insensitive to the complexity of Holocaust representation. While Miron ignores Ka-Tzetnik's transformation in *Shivitti*, Glasner-Heled addresses the work and recognizes that it indeed reflects a change in Ka-Tzetnik's worldview. Ultimately, however, she dismisses the change, arguing that it in fact provides further proof of her central thesis, that Ka-Tzetnik was motivated by identification with the aggressor:

> In my estimate, it does not represent a significant and dramatic shift in the views of Ka-Tzetnik on the Holocaust, but is, rather, the natural continuation

> of tendencies that characterized him from the outset.... It is not only the voice of a new insight regarding the banality of evil that emerges from the later text, but another voice as well: the voice of identification with the aggressor. ... Ka-Tzetnik thus places himself alongside the aggressor. (195)

From a theoretical perspective (as opposed to the perverted discourse towards which we have veered), these scholars appear to locate Ka-Tzetnik within the category that Amir (2016, 622–3) termed the excessive-psychotic mode of testimony:

> The excessive-psychotic mode, on the other hand, is a much more illusory one. Here the traumatic object becomes an addictive and gratifying object in its own right, an object whose totality actually replaces a functional sense of being. ... Testimony in this case involves the traumatic memory becoming ... an object that refuses transformation and to which the obstinate adherence becomes malignant. Adherence to the excessiveness of suffering and the traumatic object's imperviousness to new meanings or any other processes of change turn traumatic repetition into a thing in itself (*Das-Ding*). One of the great hazards in working with trauma is, indeed, that analysis may take a psychotic-excessive form, with the traumatic object becoming an object of *jouissance* (pleasure), which, under the cover of being subject to analytic work, actually blocks it. ... The excessive testimonial mode is a mode that forms, through the consummate totality of the traumatic object, an illusion of union without lack, union that allows a lingering in the Real—at the cost of relinquishing the formation of both subject and subjectivity. The deceptiveness of this testimonial mode is related to its intensive linguistic characteristics: Although the register of the Real precedes language and in many ways also opposes it, the overt manifestation of the excessive-psychotic mode is not an absence of language. On the contrary, it often presents articulate and well-developed language, with a wealth of rhetorical features. But underneath the rhetorical cover this is a language that attacks, rather than produces, linking.

To the extent that these approaches may be said to have something in common, they all seem to be rooted in psychoanalytical discourse. Without completely dismissing Ka-Tzetnik's importance as one who managed, in his own unique way, to reveal significant insights into concentration camp life, all reach the same conclusion, albeit with varying degrees of delicacy and sophistication: at the heart of Ka-Tzetnik's writing lies an uncontrollable identification with the victimizer and a repetition compulsion that produces sadistic enjoyment inimical to the therapeutic process.

Miron (1994) shows how easy it is, even for someone engaged in trauma discourse, to relate to the victim in a judgemental fashion and ultimately attempt to silence them. Miron would appear to be a radical example of the process whereby an interpreter cannot help but identify with the victimizer, thereby completing the process of annihilation.

In short, these scholars view Ka-Tzetnik as having been motivated by processes of acting out that create a block poetics (the excessive-psychotic mode of testimony) and receive expression in writing that is all emotional excess and *jouissance*. Even if these observations are correct to some extent, I believe that Ka-Tzetnik's writings must not be reduced to perversion and identification with the executioner, especially in the light of the final book in the Salamandra series, *Shivitti*.

Bartov (1997, 45) describes the personal process that Ka-Tzetnik went through, with the publication of *Shivitti*:

> Volume 6, *Ha-tsofen* (The Code, or Shivitti), is apparently a purely autobiographical account of the author's treatment for depression by a Dutch psychiatrist using controlled doses of LSD, and it ends in a mystical kabbalistic vision whereby Ka-Tzetnik's initial perception of Auschwitz as "another planet" is radically reversed and his mind is liberated from its haunting memory by accepting that Auschwitz was and remains an integral part of the human experience.

Bartov further remarks that 'in the long run one must credit Ka-Tzetnik/Dinur with a tremendous achievement, whose ultimate peak was reached in the last volume of the sextet, after 40 years of solitary struggle' (67). Without ignoring the flaws in Ka-Tzetnik's writing, Bartov recognizes the unique insights he offered—'the bizarre and startling mixture of kitsch, sadism, and what initially appears as outright pornography, with remarkable and at times quite devastating insights into the reality of Auschwitz, the fantasies it both engendered and was ruled by, and the human condition under the most extreme circumstances imaginable' (45). This explains, at least to some degree, why the writing of Ka-Tzetnik, despite its shortcomings, continues to fascinate us. Bartov wonders, however, why these same methods work on scholars:

> I should say at the outset that my own second encounter with Ka-Tzetnik, and this time with his complete works rather than the fragments I read in my youth, revealed that my memory—and, I suspect, that of other members of my generation—of what he was all about, indeed, my internalized under-

> standing of his representation of the Holocaust, was largely false. And yet what I found just as troubling was that those elements of the work which had fascinated so many youths born in Israel between the late 1940s and early 1960s have retained that quality which makes it impossible to put down these volumes even as I now realize, and rebel against, what it is about them that makes them so gripping: namely, their obsession with violence and perversity. Ka-Tzetnik is the kind of writer who under different circumstances would have appealed mainly to a juvenile readership; his prose is mediocre, and his ability to reconstruct human relations, to infiltrate the minds of his protagonists, and to enter the sphere of the emotions with any degree of subtlety is at best limited. Love, loyalty, tragedy, even loss are all treated with dramatic brush strokes, often accompanied by bombastic exclamations; sexual relations between lovers are described in an almost embarrassingly adolescent manner. In short, parts of this sextet, when read in isolation from the rest, would have earned this writer a not particularly prominent place on the shelves of an average teenager's library, and would have been forgotten immediately after they were read. But these books treat the sphere not of the normal but of the depraved. And it is precisely because they are written by an author who lacks the gifts of a great writer (and himself claims not to be a writer at all, but merely a chronicler) yet is determined to apply his limited literary abilities to an experience that lacks any precedent either in history or in representation, that the result is so striking, baffling, outrageous, and yet devastating. (45–6)

Based on *Shivitti*, the final volume of the Salamandra series, I will consider the transformation that Ka-Tzetnik underwent over the years, and why *Shivitti* demands a rereading of Ka-Tzetnik.

1.2 Ka-Tzetnik's Transformation

Ka-Tzetnik went to Prof. Bastiaans's clinic in the Netherlands in 1976, to undergo treatment with LSD, for the nightmares that visited him night after night. *Shivitti* is (ostensibly, at least) an account of Ka-Tzetnik's experiences under the influence of the hallucinogenic drug.

On an ethical, philosophical plane, Ka-Tzetnik's main insight in *Shivitti* is that Auschwitz was not 'another planet'—contrary to his assertion at the trial of Adolf Eichmann in 1961, which shaped and perhaps continues to shape (if only by negation) Holocaust discourse in Israeli society. In *Shivitti*, Ka-Tzetnik (1989, 10) asks: 'God, who created Auschwitz?' The answer is not simply that the Germans created Auschwitz but that, in other circumstances, the roles might have been reversed, with the prisoners becoming jailers and vice versa: 'I am terrified of that S.S. man—he is me' (61). The great secret (*Hatsofen*—The Code) is that Auschwitz was created by humans, and we are not immune to becoming mass murderers—just like the Germans.

When the trucks deliver their load to the factory, that is, the Muselmänner to the gas chambers and the crematoria, there was always an S.S. officer, 'who by this planet's law and perfect order, must stand where he is to oversee the departure of both truck and load' (7). In the early morning, however, 'unfinished sleep is still on his face'—he is cold, tired, even bored:

> This dawn is cold, and he keeps both hands in the pockets of his black greatcoat. He stands there watching the noiseless flow of a river of skeletons of the open gate of the barracks to the open maw of the track. And his mouth opens wide in a long yawn. … All I know about this German is that on a cold morning like this he'd certainly prefer snuggling under the covers of his warm bed without having to get up this early because of some load that has to leave for the crematorium. (9–10)

At this point, Ka-Tzetnik expresses the impossible insight—impossible because it is almost self-evident:

> If this is so, then he could have been standing here in my place, a naked skeleton in this truck, while I, I could have been standing there instead of him, on just such a cold morning doing my job delivering him and millions like him to the crematorium—and like him, I, too, would yawn, because like him I'd certainly prefer snuggling under the covers of my warm bed on a cold morning like this. (10)

In an interview broadcast on Israeli television ('*Zeh hazman*', 30 May 1988), De-Nur said:

> Auschwitz was not another planet, as I had previously thought. Auschwitz was not created by Satan or by God, but by humans. … Hitler was not Satan. … He was a man. … That means that Auschwitz was not created by Satan or by God. I saw man; I saw him when he sent me to the crematorium.

This insight gives Ka-Tzetnik no peace, as it undermines the concept of humanity or, more precisely, the idea that only humans of a certain kind can become genocidal Nazis. It is worth putting this insight into a broader theoretical framework.

Although the Holocaust cannot be understood in a reductive, simplistic fashion, Goldberg (2013b) argues, in his introduction to the Hebrew edition of Zygmunt Bauman's *Modernity and the Holocaust*, that 'modernity is an all-important (if not all-explaining) key to understanding the Holocaust, and the Holocaust is essentially a modern historical event, "created" from shockingly modern building blocks' (33). *Modernity and the Holocaust* (Bauman 2008) begins with the harsh statement: '*The Holocaust was born and executed in our modern rational society, at the high stage of our civilization and at the peak of human cultural achievement, and for this reason it is a problem of that society, civilization and culture*' (x; emphasis in the original). That means that Treblinka, Kapo, Muselmann, Sonderkommandos, Einsatzgruppen—every last one was a product of civilization and a testimony to progress or, in the words of Robert Antelme (1992, 219), 'This extraordinary sickness is nothing other than a culminating moment in man's history'.[4]

The question of whether anyone can be certain that she or he would not act like the Nazis preys on Ka-Tzetnik's mind, forcing us to confront the question of what it means to be human. Of course things would be so much simpler if we knew the answer to this question, but there is nothing deterministic, for good or ill, about the concept of 'human nature'. There is no gene for evil (although people will undoubtedly keep looking for one) or more active area of the brain in the wicked, and it is hard to say who may have a particularly high potential to become a mass murderer. As Primo Levi explained in *The Periodic Table* (*Il sistema periodico*, first published in 1975), we know of no chemical substance that renders neutral matter 'good' or 'bad'. The truth of the matter is that there would appear to be some of each in all of us: 'It became known very soon that these men, whenever they took their uniforms off, were in no way evil. They behaved much like all of us' (Bauman 2008, 151): or, in Levi's (2015, 2568) words at the close of his final book, *The Drowned and the Saved*:

> By "torturers" they mean our former guardians, the SS, and in my opinion the term is inappropriate: it implies deformed individuals, born bad, sadistic, flawed at birth. Instead, they were made from the same cloth as us, average human beings, of average intelligence and average malice: with some exceptions, they were not monsters, they had the same faces as us, but had been brought up badly.

Christopher Browning (2001, xviii) wrote that the very same people who 'carried out the massacres and deportations, like the much smaller number who refused or evaded, were human beings' and, therefore, 'I must recognize that in the same situation, I could have been either a killer or an evader—both were human.'[5] These elements may exist and even coexist, without contradiction. Bauman (2008, 7) offers an even more radical possibility:

> We suspect (even if we refuse to admit it) that the Holocaust could merely have uncovered another face of the same modern society whose other, more familiar, face we so admire. And that the two faces are perfectly comfortably attached to the same body. What we perhaps fear most, is that each of the two faces can no more exist without the other than can the two sides of a coin.

More than anyone, Ka-Tzetnik is identified with the essentially reassuring concept of Auschwitz as 'another planet'. If the murder and abuse could only have occurred *there and then* and could only have been perpetrated by Germans, then we are safe—not only from its happening to us again, but also from becoming the murderers ourselves. As we have seen in *Shivitti*, Ka-Tzetnik came to share Levi's understanding that the Holocaust was perpetrated by ordinary people and, what is more, that the Holocaust cannot be relegated to there and then, as the grey zone is here and now—a result of the human condition, especially, one might add, in the circumstances created by modernity.

When the 'grey zone' is compared to 'another planet', the former appears to present a far more complex picture. Take the concept of 'law', for example. On the other planet, there are relatively clear laws—different from those on our world, but clear to its inhabitants—and those who disobey them are put to death. In the grey zone, on the other hand, it is unclear which laws apply and how one should relate to them. The grey zone is a zone of changing laws, rather than other laws.

In the short story 'In the Penal Colony', Kafka describes a machine that, over the course of twelve hours, engraves the transgression of the condemned (who are ignorant of the judgement or the crime of which they have been accused) into their flesh. At the sixth hour, the condemned begin to decipher the judgement, with their bodies:

> And how quiet the man becomes at the sixth hour! Even the stupidest man is now enlightened. It starts around the eyes. From there it spreads out. A look that might lure you into joining him under the harrow. Nothing else happens, the man simply begins to decipher the writing.... You've seen that it's not easy deciphering the script with your eyes; but our man deciphers it with his wounds. (Kafka 2000, 205)

The process is overseen by an officer who is the last representative of the former commander. The former commander, however, is no longer alive, and all that remains of him are the machine itself and a leather portfolio containing the designs for the various judgements: 'designs hand-drawn by the former commander' (197). The designs are fed into the machine: 'Up there in the draftsman you'll find the gear unit that controls the movements of the harrow; now this unit is regulated according to the design prescribed by the judgment. I still use the former commander's drawings.' When the traveller tries to decipher one of the designs, all he can see is 'a crisscross of labyrinthine lines covering the paper so densely that the blank gaps were barely discernible'. The officer urges him to read the designs but he is unable to do so, despite the officer's insistence that they are 'quite legible'. The traveller replies that the design is 'very intricate ... but I can't decipher it' (203). The question arises whether the laws themselves were not imaginary to begin with. Therein lies the difference between the other planet and the grey zone. On the other planet, laws exist. They may be twisted or unknown, but they do exist. In the grey zone, on the other hand, the laws are not merely unclear. There is no certainty that they even exist at all (this issue will be discussed at length in Chaps. 10 and 11, in the second part of the book).

The idea of the grey zone is especially disconcerting, because it means that there is no way to determine what it is in human nature (a chemical additive or process) that will cause someone to collaborate or to act in a given way. We know how we entered the grey zone—we were chosen or decided to act of our own accord to become functionaries—but we do not know how we will behave once we are there, or what we will be like when we leave.

From an ethical, philosophical perspective, this insight regarding *ordinary people* in the modern era is harder to accept than the horrors of Auschwitz themselves. As Ka-Tzetnik (1989, 10) put it, 'All at once an additional horror seizes me, one I've not yet known'. In a moment of insanity, or perhaps extreme clarity, Ka-Tzetnik wonders:

> Am I the one, the one who's created Auschwitz? It's much worse than that he—the German facing me with the death's skull insignia on his cap, his hands deep in the pockets of his black S.S. coat—could have been in my place. It's that I—and this is the paralyzing horror—I could have been there in his place! (11)

The horror lies in the understanding that there is no difference between dispatcher and dispatched; both are players in the same game. To put it in terms of Kafka's (2000) 'Before the Law', one might say that there is no difference between the man from the countryside and the gatekeeper. At the moment of annihilation itself, 'two of us, dispatcher and dispatched are equal sons of man' (Ka-Tzetnik 1989, 11). It is in that moment, in that encounter between 'dispatcher and dispatched', that their complete equality is revealed. Both are human, inhabiting the same earth—and therein lies the horror:

> And I was anxious to see the face of Satan, creator of Auschwitz, but instead I suddenly saw my own face imposed over the frenzied snakes … on my head an S.S. cap, the death skull emblem above the visor … and I yawned and yawned and kept looking at that S.S. man, now just one more naked skeleton, amid a mass of naked skeletons being hauled off to the burning. (21–2)

Everything leads to the complex and sobering conclusion that we created Auschwitz:

> Long ago I was a seeker of solitude, distancing myself from human contact and interference, so that I could be alone with Auschwitz. But nowadays Auschwitz has lumbered its way to everyone's doorstep. Wherever there is humankind, there is Auschwitz. It's wasn't Satan who created the Nucleus, but you and I. We did! (107).

Notes

1. Goldberg (2013a, 92–3, n. 2) borrows the metaphor of the block from Deleuze and Guattari's (1986) analysis of Kafka.
2. For a more extensive discussion, see Ataria (2017).
3. For a more extensive discussion, see Ataria (2016a, b, 2018, 2020) and Ataria and Gallagher (2015).

4. Anteleme himself had been a prisoner at the Buchenwald concentration camp and at a forced labour camp near Bad Gandersheim. As allied forces approached, he and the other prisoners were sent on a death march towards Dachau.
5. It is interesting that even scholars, engaged in so-called academic research, do not fail to observe—on a personal note, in the first person singular—that one of the insights they draw from their work is that they too could, under certain circumstances, become mass murderers.

References

Amir, Dana. 2016. When language meets traumatic lacuna: The metaphoric, the metonymic, and the psychotic modes of testimony. *Psychoanalytic Inquiry* 36 (8): 620–632.

———. 2019. *Bearing witness to the witness: A psychoanalytic perspective on four modes of traumatic testimony.* Milton Park: Routledge.

Antelme, Robert. 1992. *The human race.* Trans. Jeffrey Haight and Annie Mahler. Evanston: The Marlboro Press/Northwestern.

Ataria, Yochai. 2016a. I am not my body, this is not my body. *Human Studies* 39 (2): 217–229.

———. 2016b. Post-traumatic stress disorder: A theory of perception. *Body, Movement and Dance in Psychotherapy* 11 (1): 19–30.

———. 2017. *The structural trauma of western culture: Toward the end of humanity.* New York: Palgrave Macmillan.

———. 2018. *Body disownership in complex posttraumatic stress disorder.* New York: Palgrave Macmillan.

———. 2020. Investigating the origins of body-disownership: The case study of the Gulag. *Journal of Phenomenological Psychology* 51 (1): 44–82.

Ataria, Yochai, and Shaun Gallagher. 2015. Somatic apathy: Body disownership in the context of torture. *Journal of Phenomenological Psychology* 46 (1): 105–122.

Bartov, Omer. 1997. Kitsch and sadism in Ka-Tzetnik's other planet: Israeli youth imagine the Holocaust. *Jewish Social Studies* 3 (2): 42–76.

Bauman, Zygmunt. 2008. *Modernity and the Holocaust.* Cambridge: Polity Press.

Browning, Christopher R. 2001. *Ordinary men: Reserve police battalion 101 and the final solution in Poland.* London: Penguin.

Deleuze, Gilles, and Félix Guattari. 1986. *Kafka: Toward a minor literature.* Trans. Dana Polan. Minneapolis: University of Minnesota Press.

Glasner-Heled. 2005. Whom does Ka-Tzetnik represent (Hebrew). *Dapim: Studies on the Holocaust* 19: 167–200.

Goldberg, Amos. 2012. *Trauma in first person: Diary writing during the Holocaust* [Traumah beguf rishon: Ketivat yomanim bitekufat hasho'ah]. Or Yehuda: Kinneret, Zmora-Bitan, Dvir and Heksherim Institute, Ben Gurion University.

———. 2013a. Body, *jouissance*, and irony in representations of suffering during the holocaust period (Hebrew). In *Pain in the flesh: Representations of the body in sickness, suffering, and jouissance* [Ke'ev basar yadam: ḳovets ma'amarim al haguf haḥoleh, hasovel, hamit'aneg], ed. Orit Meital and Shira Stav, 62–100, Critical Mass series. Or Yehuda: Ben Gurion University and Kinneret, Zmora-Bitan, Dvir.
———. 2013b. Introduction to *modernity and the Holocaust* [Moderniyut vehasho'ah], by Zygmunt Bauman. Trans. Yaniv Farkas. Tel Aviv: Resling.
———. 2017. *Trauma in the first person*. Trans. Shmuel Sermoneta-Gertel and Avner Greenberg. Bloomington: Indiana University Press.
Kafka, Franz. 2000. *The metamorphosis, in the penal colony, and other stories*. Trans. Joachim Neugrochel. New York: Scribner.
Ka-Tzetnik. 1978. *Sunrise over hell*. Trans. Nina De-Nur. London: Corgi.
———. 1989. *Shivitti: A vision*. Trans. Eliyah Nike De-Nur and Lisa Herman. New York: Harper & Row.
LaCapra, Dominick. 1996. *Representing the Holocaust: History, theory, trauma*. Ithaca: Cornell University Press.
———. 1998. *History and memory after Auschwitz*. Ithaca: Cornell University Press.
———. 2014. *Writing history, writing trauma*. Baltimore: Johns Hopkins University Press.
Levi, Primo. 2015. *The complete works of Primo Levi*. Ed. Ann Goldstein. Various translators. 3 vols. New York: Liveright.
Lyotard, Jean François. 1988. *The differend: Phases in dis*pute. Trans. Georges Van Den Abbeele. Manchester: University of Minnesota and Manchester University Press.
Miron, Dan. 1994. Between books and ashes (Hebrew). *Alpayim* 10: 196–224.
Neumann, Boaz. 2002. *The Nazi Weltanschauung: Space, body, language* [Re'iyat ha'olam hanatsit: Merhav, Guf, Safah]. Haifa: Haifa University.

CHAPTER 2

The Secret of Ka-Tzetnik's Nightmare

Ka-Tzetnik' last book, *Shivitti* (*Hatsofen*—The Code, 1989) is about Ka-Tzetnik's terrible nightmare: 'being called by my own name, waiting naked to see eyeball to eyeball the most horrifying of all my fears—the secret revealed; the secret of the nightmares that had visited me night after night these last thirty years' (Ka-Tzetnik 1989, x). Indeed, in this book, the final volume of the Salamandra series, Ka-Tzetnik confronts his nightmares, that is, his uncertain encounter with Daniella: 'No! No! I cry inside. I won't go! I won't see the specter of my nightmares! No! No!' (97). This chapter examines Ka-Tzetnik's attempt to confront his most terrifying secrets, through the story of Daniella and the story of the coal bin.

2.1 Ka-Tzetnik's Deposition and His Ability to Distinguish Between Fact and Fiction

Yechiel Szeintuch's book on Ka-Tzetnik includes the preliminary deposition that Yehiel De-Nur gave to the police before testifying at the trial of Adolf Eichmann: a summary of the testimony he intended to give at the trial itself. The deposition includes a list of fifteen topics on which Ka-Tzetnik declared himself willing to expand at the trial. Topic number twelve refers to his having hidden in a coal bin on a van, thereby saving his life.[1] It goes without saying that we have no way of determining whether this event actually occurred. We may presume, however, that had such a

Y. Ataria, *Primo Levi and Ka-Tzetnik*,
https://doi.org/10.1007/978-3-030-76743-3_2

means of escape indeed existed, we would almost certainly have heard of other, similar cases.

In the deposition, taken by Chief Inspector Goldman,[2] there is no information regarding De-Nur's marital status, his father's name, his profession, or his religion. The document does not even include the time and place at which the testimony was given, and the witness's name is listed not as Yehiel De-Nur, but as Ka-Tzetnik. On the one hand, this may reflect De-Nur's desire to conceal his 'true identity'. On the other hand, however, when it comes to testifying to Holocaust experiences, De-Nur himself may cease to exist, leaving only Ka-Tzetnik. Both explanations may be true, as they are not mutually exclusive, but neither explains why that was the name written on the official form. Ka-Tzetnik, which means concentration camp prisoner, is the name of the murdered victims and, from the moment De-Nur chooses (to the extent that it was a conscious choice) to be Ka-Tzetnik, he is able to testify, at least in theory, on behalf of every victim. It is thus no coincidence that De-Nur referred to himself simply as Ka-Tzetnik, without the number 135633.[3]

As noted above, Ka-Tzetnik's police deposition, which is a summary of the testimony he intended to give at Eichmann's trial, includes the story of the coal bin. It is a story that defies imagination, raising the question of whether Ka-Tzetnik was able to distinguish between fantasy and reality. This is a critical question, as much of the criticism of Ka-Tzetnik rests on the premise that he was perfectly aware of the difference and intentionally fabricated some of his stories. If he lacked the capacity to distinguish between fact and fiction, however, he cannot be accused of intentional fabrication.

In order to determine whether Ka-Tzetnik was able to distinguish between fantasy and reality, we must first examine his final book, *Shivitti*, in which De-Nur was, in his own words, 'as Ka-Tztenik as I could be'. Ostensibly, when returning to Auschwitz in an LSD-induced trance, all blocks and barriers should have been removed, allowing his primary experience to emerge—if such an experience ever existed.

On 15 November 1995, De-Nur told Szeintuch that in *Shivitti*, he was as Ka-Tzetnik as he could be, because the LSD 'shot' him back there, making him entirely Ka-Tzetnik and not Yehiel De-Nur (Szeintuch 2003, 70). Furthermore, in his 'Afterword and Foreword' to *Shivitti*, Ka-Tzetnik recounts that he merely transcribed his trances. If so, the fact that the descriptions of the trances include a number of doubtful incidents poses a problem, as some of these incidents appear in his books as real stories rather than imaginary events. I would therefore suggest that at least in some of his trance states, De-Nur returned to his books rather than to his primary experiences. When there was no primary experience to begin with, all that remains is second-order experience, that is, the books that Ka-Tzetnik himself wrote.[4]

Indeed, in some cases, Ka-Tzetnik appears not to know whether a specific incident actually happened to him or whether it was a story he had heard somewhere. What is more, I would suggest that Ka-Tzetnik did not always know the source of his stories—whether rooted in reality or the product of his nightmares. I would thus argue that the great secret revealed in *Shivitti* (*Hatsofen*—The Code) is *the witness's inability to rely on his own memories*—memories that were 'encoded' even for Ka-Tzetnik himself.

This raises the question: can Ka-Tzetnik's books be considered historical sources? If he himself could not distinguish between fact and fiction, the answer is obvious. Nevertheless, Szeintuch (2009) argues, rather convincingly in some cases, that large parts of Ka-Tzetnik's books can be considered historical documents to all intents and purposes. Two possible explanations for this are:

1. We know that after the war, De-Nur met with many survivors, whom he questioned at length about their experiences and, on the basis of their testimonies, was able to produce historical documents. This is certainly true of the description of the Warsaw ghetto uprising in *Sunrise over Hell.*
2. Ka-Tzetnik represents many different figures, of whom Yehiel Feiner was one. When Feiner emerges, the experiences conveyed are of the first order—including precise accounts of historical events.

In his account of the Warsaw ghetto uprising, for example, Ka-Tzetnik does not deny the fact that he was not present at the event itself and attributes the information he provides to those who were survivors he met along the Bricha route.[5] We may thus deduce that in other cases, the information that Ka-Tzetnik provides is of the first order. His description of the deportation of the 8000 Jews of Sosnowiec on 12 August 1942, for example, is a first-order account. By way of corroboration, Szeintuch cites the testimony of Chaya-Ita Goldblum, from Sosnowiec, better known as Prof. Judith Sinai (1925–2013). In *Sunrise over Hell*, she appears as Lilka, sister of Harry Preleshnik's wife Sanya (Preleshnik is the main character in the Salamandra series). It seems that Ka-Tzetnik and Chaya-Ita Goldblum stood near one another during the deportation,[6] and their descriptions of the event are similar.[7]

Avihu Ronen (1989), in his dissertation on the Jews of Zaglembie, strengthens the argument that large parts of Ka-Tzetnik's books may be treated as historical, documentary sources. Ronen writes the following about *Salamandra* (*Sunrise over Hell*):

> This book, one of the most important literary works written on the Holocaust in general, is based on the experiences of Yehiel De-Nur … in the city of Sosnowiec during the Holocaust. It is, however, not merely a literary document, but a historical one as well. When compared to other testimonies and documents, it is readily apparent that most of the events described in the book indeed happened—*often precisely as Ka-Tzetnik describes them*. Indeed, apart from the change of names and a degree of creative licence, particularly with regard to the experiences of the book's protagonist, this work is a historical document for all practical purposes. (chap. 2, n. 29)

Indeed, in his deposition before the Eichmann trial, De-Nur reveals that he documented life in the ghetto:

> I walked in the direction of the Centrale to see them with my own eyes, because in that period I took notes on the events in the ghettos in the vicinity, and even received information from one of the Centrale's heads, Bohm, who knew that I was writing everything down with the purpose of leaving a memoir (Szeintuch 2009, 28–9).

Now that we have understood that Ka-Tzetnik may be trusted as a historical witness, the question of his reliability when describing his own experiences becomes all the more compelling. Moreover, in light of the accurate historical accounts he provides, we are faced once again with the question of the fabricating author, that is, one who is able to distinguish between reality and fantasy but intentionally chooses to create fiction.

2.2 He Was Empty of Himself

A distinction should be made between descriptions of historical background and those of subjective experience, but was Ka-Tzetnik able to tell the difference between fact and fiction, between autobiographical experiences and imaginary events? Did he have the capacity to choose the character in whose name he wrote—whether his own or one he had invented? The following examples may offer some insight into the matter.

Ka-Tzetnik describes his mother marching to her death in the gas chambers, although Feiner, according to the testimony of Jehoshua Eibeshitz, had lost his mother in childhood (no later than 1928).[8] Similar questions arise with regard to Ka-Tzetnik's role in the Sonderkommando: 'Harry was employed in the Sorting Department, examining those asphyxiated by the gas, searching the dead mouths for gold teeth and marking with a black cross, on the chests, corpses for the plier-workers to deal with' (Ka-Tzetnik 1978, 240). According to Szeintuch (2009, 350), however, there is no evidence that Ka-Tzetnik was ever a member of the Sonderkommando.[9]

This case might have remained just another story, had De-Nur not said the following to Szeintuch, in a conversation that took place on 22 October 1997:

> It is true that *I* was not present during the Warsaw ghetto uprising but, as *I* wrote in the introduction, my female protagonist Sanya was there, and *I* looked into her. … After the war, *I* asked many people what she had done there, everywhere, because *I* didn't know, because *I* was not there, and *I* wanted to know everything about her. What *I* wrote about the train to Auschwitz is also true: suddenly the opportunity arose [to board a train purportedly headed for Switzerland] and she (Sanya) took it. That is how she came to Auschwitz and that is how *I* encountered her and recognized the [beauty] mark on her face. (Szeintuch 2003, 125)

At first glance, this excerpt teaches us that Ka-Tzetnik, at least in some cases, clearly distinguished between reality and fantasy ('because *I* was not there') and that he sometimes relied on the testimonies of others ('After the war, *I* asked many people what she had done there'). The excerpt also entails an impossibility, however, because in the very same conversation with Szeintuch, Ka-Tzetnik recounts: 'and that is how *I* encountered her and recognized the [beauty] mark on her face'. Yet, it is not entirely clear who the 'I' that encounters Sanya is. It is important to remember that, in such interviews, De-Nur generally sought to heighten and maintain a clear boundary between De-Nur and Ka-Tzetnik. Nevertheless, he often vacillated between the two personas, to the point that it is sometimes hard to tell who is speaking: Ka-Tzetnik or De-Nur.

When De-Nur, in his conversation with Szeintuch, describes the encounter with Sanya, is he explaining how his protagonist, Harry, came to find Sanya, that is, the episode's narrative logic? It is by no means clear that this is the case and that it is not De-Nur himself who found her, as he explicitly states, 'and that is how *I* encountered her'. Moreover, the pronoun 'I' appears in an earlier sentence as well—'I asked many people'—which clearly refers to De-Nur, during the course of his journey to Palestine along the Bricha route. If we decide, however, that it is De-Nur who is recounting his experiences as Feiner-Ka-Tzetnik-Harry, in the first person singular, then his description of the 'encounter' with Sanya indicates that he found the gassed body of his beloved—that is an actual event, not an imaginary one. And if this is true, then De-Nur-Feiner was a member of the Sonderkommando, for which, as noted above, there is no evidence whatsoever. Another solution, of course, is that of the fabricating author. This solution is somewhat simplistic, however, and, more importantly, fails to understand the essence of Ka-Tzetnik's personality.

I would like to suggest that De-Nur's use of the pronoun 'I' is not the same as the ordinary concept of 'I'. In *Phoenix over the Galilee* (*Ha'imut*),[10] De-Nur (1977, 80) explains: 'All, all, brother Jews! He was alive in each one of them now. He was each one of them. And they were all alive within him. He alone was not within himself. He was empty of himself.' This passage is key to understanding the figure and writing of Ka-Tzetnik.[11] If the concept 'I' is nothing more than empty parentheses or quotation marks, always there to frame other content, then such descriptions begin to make sense, and we may be a step closer to resolving the mystery of Ka-Tzetnik, which finds its ultimate expression in the story of Daniella.

2.3 Daniella

The story of Daniella in *House of Dolls* is one of the most dramatic in all of Ka-Tzetnik's books, a watershed for readers and for the author himself. Unlike Ka-Tzetnik's story of hiding in the coal bin, the story of Daniella—Harry's sister,[12] in the Salamandra series—is not among the fifteen topics listed in the deposition he gave to the police. In 'Curriculum Vitae', published in a teachers' guide, Ka-Tzetnik (1993, 208) wrote[13]:

> The day after my escape from the death march, as I walked from Auschwitz to the Land of Israel, with the shroud of Auschwitz still wrapped around my Muselmann skeleton, my legs carried me, of their own accord, back to the white, dead ghetto, blanketed in snow. I had hidden [before the second transport to Auschwitz] two sacred objects there, in the ghetto, behind me: Monia's work,[14] and Daniella's diary from the German 'House of Dolls'.

From the ghetto, I carried them with me through the ruins of Europe, across the obliterated frontiers of cities and countries. Until I came to the river in Austria that demarcated the border between the Russian and Allied occupation zones. The surface of the water was stained with the blood of those who, near me, had been shot by the Russian border guards. I plunged to the bottom of the river, and Monia's work, shining glory of the human spirit, was lost in the depths.

This is how Daniella's diary—on which *House of Dolls* was based (ostensibly)—survived the war. We may further deduce that the diary was written in the camps and somehow came into Ka-Tzetnik's possession. In this context, it is worth recalling Ka-Tzetnik's nightmares. In a telephone conversation with Szeintuch (2003, 71) on 15 November 1995, De-Nur said: 'I could not sleep at night, because I did not know and was not sure whether I had seen Daniella there or not. That is why I sought treatment, and the moment that I reached that stage, in the fifth session, I left treatment.' The fifth treatment in *Shivitti* did not resolve the mystery, however, and in fact made things worse:

I lift my eyes to the voice in heaven and I behold my sister in the flash of sunrise, a nimbus crowning her head. A circle of angels serenade her. Jewish maidens dead by their own hands, eluding delivery to the Gestapo. They sing 'Welcome, our sister'.... But my sister is a sad saint. I cry up: 'Danni! I gave you my word to bring you to the Promised Land!' But my sister—a sad saint. I behold *Feld hure* branded between my sister's breasts. And I see myself instantly splitting in two. ... I stare at myself, dragged by the feet back to the block and see the key to my nightmares. It's hidden beneath the brand between my sister's breasts. (Ka-Tzetnik 1989, 98–100)

The above description is not much different from the one found years earlier in *House of Dolls*:

Out of a corner emerges a nude woman. She moves like a sleepwalker. The windows shades shut out the sun like a beast blocking off the light with its glossy yellow pelt. Everything is drenched with yellow. What's that? What's that scratching between the woman's breasts? The letters tumble about before his eyes. He can in no way to put them together. The digits beneath them leap up among the letters and jumble up with them. [...] The blue eyes of the woman hook into his brain. How did these eyes get here? Where did they suddenly float up from? What are Daniella's blue eyes doing here? '*The loveliest couple in the world, Pa and Ma.*' Dani's voice ... The eyes

> scream … Her mouth gapes … It's Daniella's voice screaming to him. He hears. He clearly hears. 'HARRY!!! HARRY!!!' (Ka-Tzetnik 1955, 235)

It is hard to see any important new revelation brought on by the LSD treatments, which leads to the question, why did De-Nur need them? What, if anything, did he discover at Prof. Bastiaans's clinic, and why did he decide to leave after the fifth session? Was it because the problem was solved, and he 'discovered' that the encounter with Daniella was nothing more than a nightmare he had dreamt, or, conversely, that the meeting actually took place? A third possibility is that, after the fifth session, he understood and came to terms with the fact that he would have to live with not knowing—hence the Hebrew title of the book he wrote about the experience, a decade later: *Hatsofen*—The Code.

These questions may be answered in a number of different but not mutually exclusive ways. The first answer is that De-Nur himself was unable to determine whether the encounter with Daniella was real or not, and he hoped that, with the help of LSD, any mental blocks would be removed, allowing him to relive the experience. In this case, if we assume that De-Nur's written account accurately reflects his treatment and we compare the information it provides to the details found in his earlier books, it appears that the LSD treatment did not take him beyond what he already knew.

Another possible answer is that, after the Eichmann trial (1961), at which he testified as Yehiel De-Nur, Ka-Tzetnik and Yehiel Feiner/De-Nur (which, for the sake of simplicity I will treat as a single figure) fused together, causing De-Nur to lose access to Ka-Tzetnik (i.e., the primary experiences of Yehiel Feiner). It is in fact De-Nur's detachment from the figure of the writer Ka-Tzetnik that allows him to write as Ka-Tzetnik. During the course of his famous testimony at the Eichmann trial, under Eichmann's gaze, the doppelgängers {[De]-(Nur)}/{([Ka]-(Tzetnik)}, were fused together. When compelled to declare to the world and, no less importantly, to himself, that he, Yehiel De-Nur, is none other than Ka-Tzetnik, the fundamental separation that, on the one hand, allowed him to function as De-Nur and, on the other, afforded him access to his memories—through the figure of Ka-Tzetnik—was lost.[15] It seems that at the moment of his collapse at the trial, the two figures quickly and aggressively fused, shattering the dissociative defence mechanism in which De-Nur had found refuge. Under these circumstances, De-Nur (I call him De-Nur at this stage for the sake of convenience, although our ability to identify the man testifying with any single persona is by no means clear) was forced to erect new barriers, in order to detach himself from the world of Ka-Tzetnik. As a result, De-Nur lost access to Ka-Tzetnik's memories.

This may explain the deterioration or significant change in the style and content of Ka-Tzetnik's writing after the Eichmann trial. *Phoenix over the Galilee*, for example, written after the trial, is very different from *Sunrise over Hell*, *House of Dolls*, and *Piepel*, written before. De-Nur's interest in undergoing LSD treatment thus becomes somewhat clearer. Perhaps he was seeking, through LSD, to revive Ka-Tzetnik, that is, to regain access to his memories.

The possibility that De-Nur found it hard to determine whether an event had actually taken place or was only a story he had invented and which became real in his inner world is consistent with this renewed detachment between the figures. De-Nur, forced to seek a new path to his memories, 'encoded' within the figure of Ka-Tzetnik, turned to the only real source memory he had left: his books or, more accurately, Ka-Tzetnik's books. In such circumstances, there are no first-order events, merely second-order representations of the events themselves—floating signifiers that become the *real thing*, the books replacing the original memories. In terms of map and territory, one might suggest that, once drawn, the map became the territory itself. The problem in Ka-Tzetnik's case is that the map may never have represented any actual territory in the first place—that is to say that the map was disconnected a priori from the territory and was, in this sense, more drawing than chart. Indeed, this appears to have been De-Nur's problem after the Eichmann trial. He himself did not know what his books represented: a real territory or a surrealistic drawing. De-Nur, who knew Ka-Tzetnik better than anyone (as only doubles can know one another, while, at the same time, remaining complete strangers), would have understood the distinct possibility that it was in fact a surrealistic drawing. It is therefore my contention that De-Nur hoped, with the help of LSD, to regain direct access to his original memories, allowing him to determine what is true and what is imaginary. With this in mind, it is obvious why Daniella's story is central to the author's inability to distinguish between nightmarish reality and imagined nightmare. Indeed, Ka-Tzetnik's assertion that he *did know and was not sure whether he had seen Daniella there or not* may offer a key to understanding his testimony.

It would be a mistake, however, to attempt to understand the issue of Daniella solely on the basis of Ka-Tzetnik's final work (*Shivitti*). If we wish to get to the root of the problem, we must go back to the first book in the Salamandra series: *Sunrise over Hell.*

> Harry raises his eyes to the sky, a patch caught in the web of bars within the high window. Previously, he used to get up on the chair to peer out, before the nightmare had hit him. The very thought of doing this now horrifies him. Whatever he's been looking at since, raises the chimera before his eyes once more. Reviewed in the full light of the consciousness, it's as clear as day that he couldn't actually have seen his sister Daniella. Not here. Not in reality. For the millionth time he tried to reconstruct the nightmare, retrieve it from the cloudy depths of his mind, trying to convince someone within that he couldn't have seen it except in a moment of black-out. A strand of memory, which he grasps with both hands as he struggles to climb out of the oblivion: it was one day—that was when it began—through the same window that he's looking at now, when he saw that van making for the carrion shed to collect the weekly carcasses for burning. The S.S. driver, catching sight of him, ordered him to come down and take care of loading outside. Then: he remembers himself carrying them, hoisting them one by one into the van. All this, step by step, his mind can follow. Including the moment he had lingered with the dead Zanvil Lubliner, and his inability to tear himself away. That was when the S.S. driver landed him a dizzying blow on the head—Here, the memory strand thins down into a filament of fog. Hands drag him along. The S.S. compound! Here, there is something horrible; and something terrible is happening as in some bottomless, fathomless deep. The fogginess thickens, now contracting to a point in some yellow space in time from which her face, Daniella's face, comes drifting towards him. Now he can see her clearly. Now he can see her, with the horrible Field Whore tattoo just above her breasts. His ears still resound with the reverberations of her scream 'Harry!', his own name which no one else in camp knows. There's no real substance to all this, he knows, neither to the vision his eyes had perceived, nor to the voice as it pierced his ears. Not his little Dani. Not here. Not in the S.S. orgy grounds. The fact nevertheless has persisted in the miasma of his mind from the moment he came to. (Ka-Tzetnik 1978, 142–3)

In such horrific and surreal circumstances, the prisoner loses the ability to distinguish between dream and reality, and matters are vague from the start: 'But what was the connection with this world and the Hereafter [Heb., lit. "the World of Truth"]?[16] With this Afterlife Planet? What was going on here? Life was nothing but a dream here—or, rather, death was' (188). In a place like Auschwitz, everything is possible, so that the prisoner cannot say to himself, 'This could not have happened.' Consequently, the nightmare easily becomes reality itself. Indeed, in his books, Ka-Tzetnik returns time and again to stories such as these. In *Piepel* (1961), for example, Moni hallucinates that he sees his brother Harry:

> All at once Moni began to stare intently. The more intently he stared, the more the head of that one standing in the first row resembled Harry's head. Exactly his brother Harry's head. What a remarkable resemblance! And that one stared back at him. Moni felt a cold shiver run through him. He knew it was impossible. He knew that it could not possibly be Harrik. Harry is in Palestine. (121)

This explanation, premised on the author's inability to distinguish between nightmare and reality, would appear to be at odds with the story of Daniella's diary, which, as we have seen, is pivotal to our understanding of Ka-Tzetnik. Was there a diary or not? Was it pure fantasy or was there really a diary on which Ka-Tzetnik based his story? If there was no diary and the story was made up, the answer is simple. Yet, as Szeintuch (2009, 117) explains, the anonymous woman to whom Ka-Tzetnik dedicated the Yiddish edition of *House of Dolls* (*Dos hoyz fun di lyalkes*, 1955)—described only as 'a daughter of Israel who did not lose her humanity even at the bottom of the abyss'—was in fact Daniella's friend Fella, who survived the Holocaust and immigrated to Palestine in late 1945. According to the dedication, the book was based on diary pages rescued by Fella (as identified by Szeintuch), but it is unclear whether the diary belonged to Daniella and was merely preserved by Fella, or whether it belonged to Fella herself. It is thus entirely possible that the character Daniella Preleshnik—sister of Harry Preleshnik, protagonist of the Salamandra series—was based on Fella, and the title 'The Diary of Daniella Preleshnik' (Ka-Tzetnik 1977, 33) was the product of a conscious decision by Ka-Tzetnik to write a 'Chronicle of a Jewish Family in the Twentieth Century' (subtitle of the Salamandra series in Hebrew), based on the experiences of various families murdered in the Holocaust. In this sense, we may argue that there was an actual diary, from which it follows that the book *House of Dolls* is indeed based on a true story—assuming that the diary constitutes an authentic testimony and that Ka-Tzetnik did not distort it beyond recognition.

Interestingly, the number that appears on the cover of the Yiddish edition of *House of Dolls* (A13652) is Fella's number (as recounted in the book) and not Daniella's (A13653) (Fig. 2.1). Szeintuch (2009)

Fig. 2.1 Feld-Hure
In Ari Libsker's (2008) documentary film, *Stalags*, Naama Shik (director of the e-Learning Department at Yad Vashem's International School for Holocaust Studies), whose research focuses on women in the Holocaust, explains that, due to the Nazi ideology of race, Jewish women were absolutely not used as prostitutes in Block 24 in Auschwitz or in brothels in other camps. Rather, the women forced to serve in these brothels were German and Polish. Nor did any Jewish women serve as so-called front-line prostitutes. Shik stresses that Paul Goldman's well-known photograph (which also appeared on the cover of the Hebrew and other editions of *House of Dolls* [image on the right]) was staged. The number on the chest of the woman in the photo (ostensibly an Auschwitz number) did not exist at Auschwitz. At Shik's request, the photograph was examined by experts at the Auschwitz Museum, who confirmed that it is indeed a fake. The A series of Auschwitz numbers, employed after the arrival of Hungarian Jews at the camp in May 1944, ended around the number A28000. The number in Goldman's photograph (A125701) is thus completely fabricated.
This further complicates matters. We might simply have dismissed it as yet another example of Ka-Tzetnik's barefaced lies, but we are left wondering why this photograph is exhibited in the Israel Museum with the following caption: 'An Auschwitz survivor, A-125701, bares the inscription Feld-Hure [field whore] tattooed on her chest, Nahalal 1945'. Our perplexity only increases when we realize that the image is the work of Paul Goldman—one of the most important photographers in Israel at the time of its founding.
The image on the left appears on the cover of one of the English-language editions of *House of Dolls* (1970). Note that the number in this image, 135633, is identical to Ka-Tzetnik's own number. The number varies, sometimes considerably, in other editions. We do not know what role Ka-Tzetnik played, if any, in the design of these book covers (for an extensive discussion of this matter, see Bos 2018). Nevertheless, the similarity between the numbers (even identical in some cases) raises a number of questions.
Sources: Image 1 (right): http://images.museumsinisrael.gov.il/thmbn_images/54/64/thn_10000x360_TID125965_ITEM_MAIN_PIC_546436.jpg
Image 2 (centre): https://images-na.ssl-images-amazon.com/images/I/51S3NjXUDQL._SL300_.jpg
Image 3 (left): http://o.aolcdn.com/hss/storage/midas/ed8b8c855e659966efc806f9361204fe/203085970/9+joy+division.jpg

considered a number of possible explanations, ultimately concluding that the diary indeed belonged to Fella.

If the diary is authentic, it was probably hidden by Ka-Tzetnik before his deportation to Auschwitz: 'In the corner, beneath a rafter, lay his sister's notebook exactly where he had hidden it, rotten and mildewed, gnawed by rats. Only the title on the first page was still legible: THE DIARY OF DANIELLA PRELESHNIK' (Ka-Tzetnik 1977, 33).[17] If we accept the premise that there was indeed a diary and that *House of Dolls* was based on it, it is hard to see how an actual encounter between Yehiel Feiner (as De-Nur was then called) and Daniella or someone whom Daniella represents could have taken place. We thus return to the same fundamental problem. If there was no encounter, then De-Nur's terrible nightmare was not based on a real event.[18]

2.4 The Coal Bin

In *Sunrise over Hell*, Ka-Tzetnik (1978, 219) tells the following story:

> Mussulmen in their nakedness crawled out of his van, their skulls reverberating with the drum blows of the S.S. Quivers of a unique stubbornness shoved Harry back, to be last among the last for the van exit. The van was now totally evacuated around him. A coal bin—right there, in that corner. Lightning shocks of power giving the mind a shove to look in: empty! Fold up, get inside![19]

In terms of its imaginary nature, the coal bin story is not much different from the story of Daniella or the story about his mother marching to the gas chambers. However, neither of these other stories appear in his pretrial police deposition. The question is, why did Ka-Tzetnik wish to testify to the event in which he was saved? Why was it important to him to testify on this subject, and how was it relevant to the trial?

While each of the other fourteen topics about which he declared himself willing to testify tells us something about Auschwitz, it is unclear how Ka-Tzetnik's coal bin story is relevant to his testimony—not only in relation to Eichmann's responsibility (on which other topics have equally little bearing), but in terms of what it meant, what it felt like to be a prisoner at Auschwitz. Why then did Ka-Tzetnik wish to tell such a dubious story? I believe that it is precisely the story's dubious nature that makes Ka-Tzetnik's insistence on telling it so significant. I would suggest that the importance of this particular story to Ka-Tzetnik stems from the fact that the coal bin was the crucible in which the different figures were forged, fused, and separated.

2.4.1 *The Metaphorical Womb*

Let us begin with Ka-Tzetnik's protagonist: Harry Preleshnik. In *Phoenix over the Galilee* (*Ha'imut*)—which must be treated cautiously, as it was written after the Eichmann trial—Feiner, who calls himself Phoenix at this point, tries to write the book he had sworn to write, but finds himself unable to do so. The turning point comes when the name Harry Preleshnik bursts forth from the depths of his mind:

> Suddenly he was assaulted by the pain of the name Harry Preleshnik, the pain of the world in which that name had existed. A racking pain so horrendous that only a shattering howl would free him of it. The tentacles of terror coiled about him. The name, his very own in the past, was strangling him. And to save himself his hand shot out in reflex for the pen, as, at that moment, the first words screamed themselves out of him onto the page. He saw the letters of the words. They were flaming before his eyes. He connected them: HARRY PRELESHNIK. Then swept on. (Ka-Tzetnik 1977, 68)

Until Harry is born, Ka-Tzetnik is unable to begin writing,[20] but Ka-Tzetnik himself, as a writer, also has a birthdate. To Ka-Tzetnik's mind, Feiner died the day he entered Auschwitz:

> A peculiar scribe was posted by the last long table, a peculiar pen in his hand. He was inscribing, but not on paper; instead, the newcomers one at a time, would extend the left arm, as if letting a tailor measure its length for a sleeve, whereupon the peculiar scribe would dip his peculiar pen into peculiar ink, and, rather than write, would stab the left arm's flesh and numbers would leap out: 135633. The scribe stabbed as he spoke: 'Get this, whoreson, Hymie Cohen isn't your name any longer. You're dead. Name's exactly what this number says on your arm. It's what they call you by when the furnace wants you. Got it?'[21] (Ka-Tzetnik 1978, 191)

This is how he describes it in 'Curriculum Vitae':

> Ka-Tzetnik was born in 1943 in Auschwitz. When the Kapo seared the number 135633 on his left arm, he hissed at him: Here you were born! Your

> name is this number. By this name they will call you to get on the truck to the crematorium. And in the month of February 1945 Ka-Tzetnik escaped the Auschwitz death march. When a Red Army officer asked him, what's your name, he replied, Ka-Tzetnik: my name was burnt along with everyone else in the crematorium of Auschwitz. (Ka-Tzetnik 1993, 203)

And as he handed over the manuscript of *Salamandra* (*Sunrise over Hell*):

> Some time later, the refugee handed the written pages to the [Jewish] Brigade soldier. Eliyahu Goldenberg recalls: I saw the title *Salamandra* at the top of the first page. I turned to him and quietly said to him: You forgot to write the author's name. And he, from his sickbed, began to shout at me, pointing with his hands: Them! They wrote these pages. Those who went to the crematorium! Them, the katzetniks! They wrote this book! Write K. Tzetnik, write! Write! (ibid.)

I would like to suggest that the story of the coal bin is critical to the question which figure was born when, where, and in what circumstances (and at whose expense), and that is why it was so important to Ka-Tzetnik to tell it to the police, as a kind of birth certificate of the various figures. The coal bin is the womb in which the different figures were created: Harry (protagonist of the Salamandra series), Ka-Tzetnik (the writer), and De-Nur (the public figure). No less importantly, the coal bin is the place in which Feiner died. The coal bin is, at once, womb and black hole, a crematorium that is also a birthing chamber. This is reflected in Ka-Tzetnik's poem 'Salamandra', which, according to Szeintuch, was written before the book *Salamandra*:

> I burned in seven crematoria
> without pause, in one place, for seven years,
>
> . . . .
>
> The fire charred my little sister's flesh
>
> . . . .
>
> and my sister burns, my beloved sister burns.
> My mother's suffering face, still and silent
>
> . . . .
>
> a mother blazing, a mother burns.
> My father madly fought the tongues of fire,
>
> . . . .
>
> my father flickered and burned like a Havdala candle.
> Now, world, I crawl out of the fire toward you,

a torch-creature with seven heads, millions of eyes, with a hurrah,
all the gates broken open before me,
I am here, I, the child of the Salamander.[22]

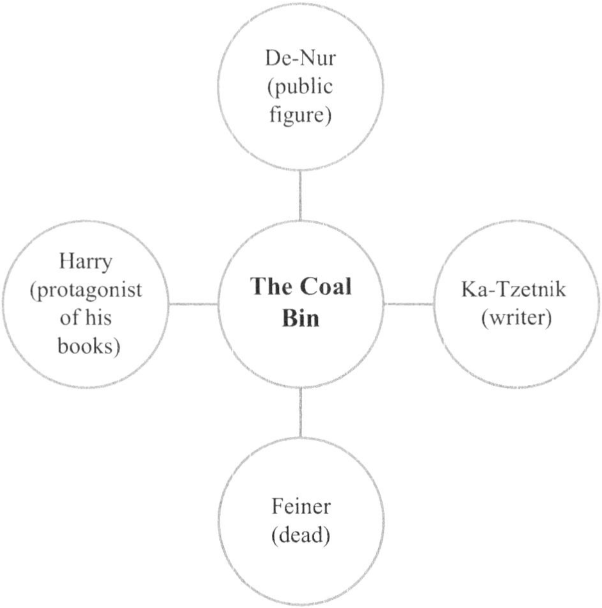

Szeintuch (2009) emphasizes the importance of symbols in Ka-Tzetnik's writings, and the coal bin would appear to be one such symbol. In this bin, his father, mother, and sister were burned, along with millions of other Jews. Szeintuch further stresses the fact that both names, Preleshnik and De-Nur, are related to fire and coal. The coal bin is the crematoria where the Jewish people were burnt, and only the salamander survived. In other words, no one survived Auschwitz. Even those who came out alive were forever altered, recast, and reborn. Ka-Tzetnik is what emerged from the coal bin, broken and covered in soot, forged in Auschwitz.

2.4.2 A Generic Salvation Story

Another possible interpretation is that the coal bin scenario is but one version of Ka-Tzetnik's salvation story, of which there are others—his encounter with Mengele, for example, which he describes in one of his conversations with Szeintuch (2003, 122):

> When I stood before him, he saw the light in my eyes, and I was then more of a Muselmann than any of the Muselmänner. For they lost the flesh on their bones in only three months, and I had already been there two years. Hundreds, hundreds stood behind me, and I was in front of Mengele, and Mengele did not react right away—'to life' or 'to death.' He had to see the light in my eyes, and he lingered ... and then others took advantage of it and moved me to the side of those who went 'to life'.

Such salvation stories appear repeatedly throughout Ka-Tzetnik's books. In *Piepel*, for example, we find the story of Haym-Idl, who was miraculously saved as he waited before the crematorium:

> The Block Chiefs ... set up a shout: 'All engravers step out!' The Block Chiefs stormed through the rows of naked bones in search of the engravers. But many on the list had forgotten their numbers standing here; many had forgotten who they were altogether.... All at once Hayim-Idl finds himself standing outside, apart. Dumbfounded he stands among a handful of other engravers. ... The miracle is too great for him to grasp. He does not have the strength to comprehend it. ... Suddenly it strikes him with a lightning flash: they—are there! And he—is here! He is apart. Outside. ... How and when did the change come about? It would seem to have happened a long, long time ago, in another existence of his. He cannot remember a thing.... He does not know whether he is dying or being born. Wondrous things are happening to him now. ... First Creation. ... He cannot remember whether he has already been in the crematorium. [He cannot remember at all. Yellow fog.][23] He must have been in the crematorium. He remembers seeing the smoke: the smoke of his own body. He remembers feeling himself burn; feeling that he was smoke.... Can it be that he is past the crematorium? (Ka-Tzetnik 1961, 262–3)

2.4.3 The Code

In 'Curriculum Vitae', Ka-Tzetnik (1993) includes the stories of others as well as his own, making it a literary 'collective CV', not limited to the writer's own life and therefore not bound by considerations of biographical accuracy (Szeintuch 2009, 134). Once again, however, things are not that simple—judging by Ka-Tzetnik's own words to Szeintuch, in a conversation that took place on 31 March 1996:

> In the matter of Chaya-Ita Goldblum's testimony regarding the man who came back from Auschwitz [Feiner's return from the labour camps in late

> 1942], I did not know/remember that she had mentioned it. How did she know such a thing?! That I came back from Auschwitz—not Auschwitz, but these camps—was a unique historical event. ... No one came back from there, and everything I wrote in the novel *Salamandra* [*Sunrise over Hell*] is true. It was thanks to Chaya-Ita's sister [Sanya]. (Szeintuch 2003, 99)

Similarly, on 29 November 1995, Ka-Tzetnik told Szeintuch about a meeting with Prof. Hanna Yaoz:

> We met in a cafe, and I told her—I am not a writer; I am a chronicler. What I wrote is the absolute truth, in the sense that it happened to me. How do you come to the conclusion that I write in order to nauseate, when I do not write from the outside, when I wrote that I was there in Auschwitz? How is it possible to write literature about Auschwitz? It is not literature; it is a chronicle. None of those who were in Auschwitz and wrote (and they can be counted on the fingers of one hand) wrote literature. They wrote what they had experienced. ... How absurd to speak of fictional writing, when referring to writers who were in the Holocaust. (Szeintuch 2003, 83)

What was the truth to Ka-Tzetnik? What did he mean when he told Szeintuch that 'everything I wrote in the novel *Salamandra* is true' or 'what I wrote is the absolute truth, in the sense that it happened to me'? Is it all true because the events he describes actually happened to him or to people he knew? More importantly, did Ka-Tzetnik himself make such distinctions? I would argue that he did not, and the reason for this is that in Auschwitz, the possible became the inevitable, so that if something could have happened, it must have happened; and from the perspective of Ka-Tzetnik, the total victim, if it could have happened, it must have happened to him. Every nightmare about Auschwitz is true, and Ka-Tzetnik inevitably experienced it. This is the central message of the Salamandra series: the imaginary and the real are one and the same and, therefore, what could have happened necessarily did.

The story of Ka-Tzetnik's or Harry's birth is the story of life created at a point in time and space in which true and false, reality and dream, were indistinguishable from one another. Under these circumstances, the very concept of fiction was impossible, for what is the point of fiction if one cannot tell fantasy from truth? That is the coal bin. That is why Ka-Tzetnik cannot be considered a fabricating author: his nightmares are true. Had he been a fabricating author, he would have had the ability to distinguish between nightmare and reality. He seems at a loss, however, to say what happened and who was present, and it is this inability to distinguish between nightmarish reality and imagined nightmare that is the essence of the terrible secret in *Shivitti* (*Hatsofen*—The Code). Although, on the conscious plane, the witness knows that it is a nightmare, he cannot prevent it from becoming a memory of a real event.

The reality of Auschwitz is itself a nightmare, in which it is impossible to tell the difference between real and imagined horrors—even in retrospect. Ka-Tzetnik thus struggles to distinguish between what was and what was not there and is ultimately unsuccessful, because the things he experienced, the events he witnessed, the stories he heard at the time and later, as well as his own nightmares, were all intertwined, all seared into his flesh in the coal bin. Ka-Tzetnik—with his very being, his madness, his delusions of grandeur, his genius, the disgust he provokes—renders Auschwitz present in other times and spaces. This is both his power of attraction and his power of repulsion.

Notes

1. De-Nur's pretrial deposition was published by Szeintuch in English (2007; trans. Friedman-Cohen) and in Hebrew (2009, 28–30). All excerpts quoted here are from Friedman-Cohen's translation.
2. The story of Chief Inspector Michael Goldman-Gilad is told in Bergman, Ehrlich, and Gouri's (1974) film, *The 81st Blow.*
3. After the publication of the first edition of *Salamandra* in 1946, Ka-Tzetnik began to omit personal information (dropping more identifying details with each successive edition), so that his story might be that of 'any one' of the survivors.
4. This may be explained in two ways: (*a*) the primary experience was not worked through, for cognitive reasons; (*b*) although processed, the experience (memory) was not accessible (due to repression or other factors). At this stage, I will not go into the considerable difference between these two explanations.
5. Bricha ('flight' or 'escape', in Hebrew) was a post-war movement that sought to bring 250,000 Jewish survivors of the Holocaust from eastern and central Europe to Palestine.
6. De-Nur claims that he helped her escape the ghetto (Szeintuch 2003).
7. Readers may not find this convincing in and of itself, but the description of the deportation in *Sunrise over Hell* was written before any possible meeting between Ka-Tzetnik and Prof. Sinai in Israel.

8. Jehoshua Eibeshitz (1916–2019) was a Holocaust survivor, writer, and Holocaust researcher who gathered thousands of testimonies from survivors and established the H. Eibeshitz Institute for Holocaust Studies in Haifa.
9. Nevertheless, Szeintuch does not completely rule out the possibility that Ka-Tzetnik may have had some brief experience of life at the crematoria.
10. *Phoenix over the Galilee* appears to be an autobiographical work about the author Ka-Tzetnik and his development in the Land of Israel, rather than an integral part of the Salamandra series. The book sets out to constitute the myth of Ka-Tzetnik and should be read, not as part of the series, but as a reflective work, detached from the author's original experiences. It is also significant, for reasons that I will explain below, that this book was written after the Eichmann trial.
11. In so doing, I realize that I am, in a sense, adopting Ka-Tzetnik's own characterization of himself.
12. According to Szeintuch, the word 'sister', in the case of Daniella, does not denote a blood relationship. Indeed, very few scholars are of the opinion that Feiner had a sister named Daniella, although it is worth noting, in this context, the testimony of De-Nur's daughter Daniella, who claims that she was named after her father's sister—a twin sister, no less. In an interview with Daniella De-Nur published in the *Ha'aretz* daily on 24 June 2003, Yossi Klein wrote: 'To his mind, Yehiel De-Nur is not a writer but a chronicler, a documenter. Yet, even his biography is filled with uncertainty. According to one version, he was born in 1909, and according to another (erroneously), in 1917. In his "Curriculum Vitae", he wrote: "Ka-Tzetnik was born in 1943, in Auschwitz." *He named his daughter Daniella after his twin sister*, who perished in the camps, and *he gave Daniella a ring that had belonged to her aunt*, which she swore never to take off.'
13. At this point, it seems that De-Nur was already engaged in constituting the myth of Ka-Tzetnik.
14. Probably the manuscript written by his friend Shmuel Nadler, who died while crossing a river.
15. This is well explained by the theory of structural dissociation. As a response to extreme trauma, two distinct personas are created—one that remains frozen 'there and then', and another that continues to function (at least ostensibly). As I have shown in previous studies (Ataria 2017, 2018), the figures are often unable to coexist, giving rise to a struggle between them, to the point of destruction.
16. Added in square brackets in this and other quotations from Ka-Tzetnik's works are elements of the Hebrew text not reflected in the published English translations.

17. It is interesting to note, in this context, that Szeintuch (2003, 21) remarked, in a conversation that took place on 14 July 1994, that the diary must have gotten wet (while crossing the river) and must be in terrible condition. De-Nur simply responded, 'True', without further elaboration.
18. At the same time that Daniella was sent to work as a prostitute in the camps, Feiner may have been imprisoned at one of the Auschwitz subcamps, where, by some miracle, they may have met. Feiner himself, like Harry in *House of Dolls*, was a medic at one of these camps. In light of what we know of Feiner's imprisonment at Auschwitz and its subcamps (see appendix), however, it is hard to see how such a thing could have happened.
19. In *Shivitti*, in the transcript of the first session, Ka-Tzetnik (1989, 12) relates to this event as follows: 'Then, inside the coalbin in the now evacuated truck, I didn't know where I was. I knew nothing then.'
20. One might say that, before he could begin to write, Ka-Tzetnik required further distance: a third-order split. Feiner 'died' on the day of his arrival at Auschwitz, occasioning the birth of Ka-Tzetnik, who, in turn, created Harry. When he reached Palestine, a further circle was created: {(De-Nur)➔(Ka-Tzetnik)➔(Harry)}. Although it is no more than a play on words, it is hard to ignore the fact that Harry's name, as written in Hebrew, may be read *ha-ari*, that is 'the Aryan'.
21. One of the problems with passages such as this is that they give the impression that the 'scribe' (who may have been—indeed almost certainly was—a Jew himself) took some sort of sadistic pleasure in the act, when, in reality, the process was more like an assembly line, carried out with complete indifference.
22. Translated from Yiddish and Hebrew by Kathryn Hellerstein and Lisa Katz.
23. The image of a yellow fog also appears in connection to Daniella in *Sunrise over Hell* (see above), and would seem to be particularly significant in the Salamandra series, as it evokes a point in time and space in which reality cannot yet be distinguished from dream.

References

Ataria, Yochai. 2017. *The structural trauma of western culture: Toward the end of humanity*. New York: Palgrave Macmillan.

———. 2018. *Body disownership in complex posttraumatic stress disorder*. New York: Palgrave Macmillan.

Bos, Pascal. 2018. Sexual violence in Ka-Tzetnik's house of dolls. In *Holocaust history and the readings of Ka-Tzetnik*, ed. Annette F. Timm, 105–138. London: Bloomsbury Publishing.

Ka-Tzetnik. 1955. *Dos hoyz fun di lyalkes*. Buenos Aires: Unión Central Israelita Polaca en la Argentina.

———. 1961. *Piepel.* Trans. Moshe M. Kohn. London: Anthony Blond.
———. 1977. *Phoenix over the Galilee.* Trans. Nina De-Nur. New York: Pyramid.
———. 1978. *Sunrise over hell.* Trans. Nina De-Nur. London: Corgi.
———. 1989. *Shivitti: A vision.* Trans. Eliyah Nike De-Nur and Lisa Herman. New York: Harper & Row.
———. 1993. Curriculum Vitae (Hebrew). In *Guide for teachers, moderators, and students on the Holocaust and the rebirth of Israel in the books of Ka-Tzetnik* [Madrikh lamoreh, lamanḥeh, latalmid benose hasho'ah utekumat yisra'el bekitvei k. tzetnik], ed. Eran Litvin and Dorit Sharir. Tel Aviv: Ministry of Education and Hakibbutz Hameuchad.
Libsker, Ari, dir. 2008. *Stalags: Holocaust and pornography in Israel* (Hebrew). Heymann Brothers Films.
Ronen, Avihu. 1989. Jews of Zaglembie during the Holocaust, 1939–1943 (Hebrew). PhD diss. Tel Aviv University.
Szeintuch, Yechiel. 2003. *Katzetnik 135633: A series of dialogues with Yechiel De-Nur* [Kemesiaḥ lefi tumo: Siḥot im yeḥiel di-nur], ed. Carrie Friedman-Cohen. Jerusalem: Ghetto Fighters' House and Dov Sadan Institute.
———. 2007. On Katzetnik's unknown testimony at the Eichmann trial. *The Mendele Review* 11 (12), November 11. http://yiddish.haifa.ac.il/tmr/tmr11/tmr11012.htm
———. 2009. *Salamandra: Myth and history in Katzetnik's Writings* [Salamandrah: Mitos vehistoryah bekhitvei k. tsetnik: Yetsirato hadu-leshonit beyidish uve'ivrit shel k. tsetnik al reka habiografyah shelo], ed. Carrie Friedman-Cohen. Jerusalem: Dov Sadan Project, Hebrew University and Carmel.

CHAPTER 3

Losing the Source of Memory

We know that memory can be deceptive; nevertheless we continue to trust it. Traumatic memory can be particularly deceptive, to the point that survivors of extreme trauma may lose confidence in their own memories, uncertain whether the event they remember happened as they remember it. They may even doubt whether the event happened at all, or whether it happened to them. In this chapter, I will explore the different ways in which Levi and Ka-Tzetnik contend with this issue.

3.1 The Nature of Traumatic Memory

Primo Levi addresses the issue of memory in the preface and first chapter of *The Drowned and the Saved*. The particular complexity of the issue in relation to the Holocaust is readily apparent. Even as the events themselves were still unfolding, the perpetrators knew that they must destroy evidence at all costs, and the victims felt compelled to document the crimes against them—in diaries from the very 'heart of hell' (Gradowski 2017), for example. The Germans thus destroyed evidence, both in the literal sense and in the deceptive terminology they employed, while the Jews engaged in historical documentation—almost obsessively in some cases (Goldberg 2017).

With the passing years, victims' raw memories may deteriorate and are 'often influenced unconsciously by things learned later, by readings, or by the accounts of other people' (Levi 2015, 2417–8). It is clear to Levi that

Y. Ataria, *Primo Levi and Ka-Tzetnik*,
https://doi.org/10.1007/978-3-030-76743-3_3

memory can be fallible: 'The memories residing within us are not engraved in stone not only do they tend to fade over the years; they often change or even grow to incorporate extraneous features' (2420).

One of the main problems with the testimonies of trauma survivors is that, with time, reliable stories become eroded. The need to tell a story that can be heard by those who were not there forces survivors to shape their raw memories into structured narratives, which eventually become automatic stories, that is, formulaic accounts that grow stronger with each retelling, at the expense of original memory. Under such circumstances, there is a gradual process of leakage of memories and their replacement with formulaic, virtually automatic descriptions—as Levi put it: 'A memory that is recollected too often, and expressed in the form of a story, tends to harden into a stereotype, a tried-and-true formula, crystallized, perfected, adorned, that installs itself in the place of the raw memory and grows at its expense' (2420–1).

Levi's concern is that partial truth will be preferred over original memory. One of the reasons that survivors will prefer to base their stories on partial, more comfortable truths, is that one must be able to live with one's own past. The purpose of the story is not to describe what really happened, but to allow survivors to live their lives. Indeed, it is typical of survivors of extreme trauma that 'the person who remembers wanted to become the person who forgets and has succeeded' (2426). While perpetrators wish to deny what they have done (or what they know to have been done), victims seek to 'skip the more painful episodes'.[1] Consequently, 'such moments … tend to become dim with time and lose their contours' (2427). Despite these reservations, Levi believes, with regard to his own memories, that 'time has discolored them slightly, but they concur by and large with this background, and to me they seem untainted by the drifting I have described' (2429).[2]

Years after his liberation, Levi found it hard to reconstruct his original experience as a prisoner. In an interview he gave to Marco Vigevani in 1984, he explained: 'Now, after so many years, it is hard even for me to return to the state of mind of the prisoner of that time, of myself back then,' adding, 'writing the book [*If This Is a Man*] has worked for me as a sort of "prosthesis", an external memory set up like a barrier between my life today and my life then.' In order to recall the experience of being a prisoner at Auschwitz, Levi would then turn to his book as if it were the source of the experience itself: 'Today I relive those events through what

I have written' (Levi 2001, 251). In another interview, conducted by Milvia Spadi for West German radio in September 1986, Levi stressed:

> My story is entirely anomalous, because between that experience and me stand a certain number of books that function as artificial memory. Had I not written *If This Is a Man*, I would probably have forgotten many things. ... I have given a large number of interviews, and all of this interposes itself between the authentic experience and the present. (Spadi 2003, 29)

Levi is aware of the fact that his story takes over and, in some ways, imprisons him. To use the metaphor of the map and the territory: in telling his story, Levi drew a particular map, which, over time, became somewhat disconnected from the territory it was meant to represent, so that, at a certain point, he was left only with the map, without the territory—a story detached from the original experience. In cognitive terms, it may be explained as follows: every time a certain memory is accessed, it is recoded in connection with the current situation. When the same story is told over and over again, it is constantly recoded in new contexts, thereby becoming detached from the original event. As a result, we become imprisoned in our own overbaked stories. De-Nur too appears to have lost his connection to the original experience. In order to gain a better understanding of this phenomenon, let us return to the Eichmann trial.

3.2 The Consequences of the Eichmann Trial for Ka-Tzetnik

Yehiel De-Nur's invitation to testify at the Eichmann trial was related, inter alia, to a chance encounter he had with Eichmann at the office of Alfred Dreier, commandant of the Gestapo in Katowice, and again in Sosnowiec, a short time later. It is important to note that De-Nur was one of the few witnesses at the trial who had not merely seen Eichmann, but had had some sort of interaction with him. It was, in fact, Eichmann himself who tore up Feiner's exit permit, thereby sealing his fate.

> Dreier and some local Gestapo men whom the ghetto people knew by name left the building together with Eichmann. A few days later, Bohm, among other things told me that the Gestapo officer who visited the Centrale together with Dreier was Adolf Eichmann. It is worth mentioning that when I was with Dreier what was etched in my memory was his gaze, a

> penetrating hypnotic and fearful gaze. I looked at this face and saw only the eyes. I will never be able to forget that gaze. It appeared to me as if the man was looking at me through the holes of the death skull's eyes on his hat. It was clear that by tearing up my papers that day the Gestapo man sealed my fate and sentenced me to death. It is difficult to say that I will be able to identify the man, because I actually saw, as I explained; only his eyes, and they were etched in my memory and blurred the rest of his face.[3] (Szeintuch 2007)

De-Nur did everything he could to appear at the Eichmann trial under his literary name, Ka-Tzetnik, but was informed by the prosecutor Gideon Hausner, only a few minutes before he was supposed to take the stand, that the judges had refused to allow him to testify under his nom de plume, insisting that he must use his *real* name, Yehiel De-Nur (Yablonka 2004).

As we have seen, Ka-Tzetnik's books contain a wealth of precise historical information. We may also assume that they include many of Feiner-Ka-Tzetnik-De-Nur's own experiences, recounted with some accuracy even when ascribed to other characters—a method he adopted, inter alia, to insulate himself, to make the events further removed. Indeed, it is no coincidence that in all of his books, with the exception of *Shivitti*, he uses the third person ('he').

At Eichmann's trial, Ka-Tzetnik was forced to speak as De-Nur, or, perhaps more accurately, De-Nur was forced to speak as Ka-Tzetnik. In this process, he (De-Nur) must have said to himself, *I am the one who went through all of this. I am the one in all of these stories. The experiences are mine. The memories are mine. The pain is mine. I am Harry. I am Feiner. I am the salamander. I. I. I.* Emotionally speaking, it was too much to process, especially in court, with Eichmann's gaze boring into him; all the more so since we know, from his books, how sensitive Ka-Tzetnik was to being gazed at.

During his testimony, under Eichmann's gaze—the same Eichmann who had torn up his papers, effectively sending him to Auschwitz—he (indeed, it is very hard to determine who 'he' is here) accepted something he had previously denied. The experience had been his; the stories he (or, more accurately, Ka-Tzetnik) had written were his (namely, De-Nur's) own. This was the moment of trauma in all its fury. Trauma is the moment at which victims realize what has happened and that it is they themselves who experienced it.[4] He was at Auschwitz, and any attempt to dissociate

Feiner, Harry, and Ka-Tzetnik from De-Nur was artificial and ultimately impossible—a defence mechanism that could only last so long. It was all the same person (hence the difficulty in using the word 'he' in this case). It was this realization that penetrated De-Nur/Ka-Tzetnik's world on the witness stand. It was at this point that De-Nur finally understood that the experiences he had lived through had been his own. This was the moment of his trauma—the moment at which De-Nur froze. De-Nur collapsed, but in order to survive, he created an even more aggressive defence mechanism, detaching himself entirely from his past, losing contact with his memories. Put another way, De-Nur's collapse at the Eichmann trial marked the symbolic suicide of Ka-Tzetnik.

Although Ka-Tzetnik wished to write in the name of those who had died, this was merely a defence. What he wrote in fact was his own experience. This is also the reason that Ka-Tzetnik was effectively unable to write after the Eichmann trial.[5] After the trial, he could no longer deny the fact that the story was his own. He could no longer renounce the idea of 'I': I experienced Auschwitz. I and no other; I and not him; I and not them:

> The number on the top of this page of manuscript has just jumped out at me. I can't believe my eyes: I've filled dozens of folio pages with my tiny letters without even realizing the newness of what I'm doing: I am writing in the first person! Until now, all of my books have used the third person, even though I've had to go through contortions doing so. All I've ever written is in essence a personal journal, a testimonial on paper of I, I, I. (Ka-Tzetnik 1989, 70–1)

Speaking and writing in the name of the victims was thus not merely an oath that had saved him, but a tool that ostensibly allowed him (De-Nur) to return to normal life after the camps. Employing the third person allowed him to tell his story while erecting the necessary defences. After the Eichmann trial and the trauma he experienced on the stand, this defence mechanism collapsed and a new, far more aggressive one arose in its place: complete detachment from his personal experiences in the camps. Under these circumstances, his books became the only source he had left for these experiences, yet, as we have seen, the books were based on a variety of different stories. Ka-Tzetnik may have possessed the ability to distinguish between his experiences and those of other survivors, before the Eichmann trial. From the moment of the collapse, however, when Ka-Tzetnik and De-Nur were divorced from one another, De-Nur lost direct contact with his original experiences—an avenue blocked by the new and aggressive detachment. Thus, even if his pre-trial deposition does show a certain capacity to tap into the original experience, this capacity was lost after the collapse at the trial.

In studying the figure of Ka-Tzetnik, we gain a deeper understanding of the experience of survivors as they attempt to get on with their lives. Survivors turned witnesses are unable to forget that which they want more than anything not to remember. They long not to recall that which their bodies refuse to consign to oblivion. The survivor is a victim of present-absent memory. As Semprún (1997, 160–1), who was imprisoned at Buchenwald for fifteen months, from January 1944, wrote: 'I want only to forget, nothing else.... Only forgetting could save me.' In order to live or, more accurately, to make living possible, the survivor must forget: 'I came back to life. In other words, to oblivion: that was the price of life. A deliberate, systematic forgetting of the experience of the camp. ... I had to choose between literature and life; I chose life. I chose a long cure of aphasia, of voluntary amnesia, in order to survive' (195–6). True oblivion, however, is a chimera. One may try to build more and more lines of defence, and, on a high cognitive level, the event may even be erased (or repressed), yet the body remembers the trauma all too well.[6] The survivor wishes to forget, but is haunted by memory. It is not an orderly narrative memory, yet it is from chaos that it seems to draw its strength. It is its very absence that makes it so viciously powerful.

The force of traumatic memory is the result of an inherent conflict, since it is, at once, both present and absent: present on the level of physical experience, and absent on the cognitive, autobiographical level. This conflict is further exacerbated by the survivors' anxiety at the fact that they do know something after all. The source of this knowledge, however, is unknown. Essentially, they are unable to rule out the possibility that their nightmares may derive from real events. The root of the problem, so it seems, lies in the nature of the original experience, that is, at the time of the traumatic event.

Traumatic memory is the result, inter alia, of a dissociative climate that produces two personas at the time of the event itself, thereby fragmenting the experience and creating lacunae on the one hand, and razor-sharp memories on the other—both impervious to language. Furthermore, while the lacunae drag survivors into the absence and the silence, the bodily memories (equally silent and painful) hound and haunt them.

Indeed, at the heart of non-conceptualized traumatic memory lies an annihilating void.

From De-Nur's perspective, memory was a threat to be blocked at all costs. In order to endure, survivors must learn to forget, to detach themselves from their experiences. De-Nur, however, tried to have it both ways: to detach himself from his traumatic memories while maintaining a secret path to them. His solution was Ka-Tzetnik, in the sense that De-Nur and Ka-Tzetnik were indeed detached from one another, and only Ka-Tzetnik had access to the traumatic memories. The result was two personas: De-Nur, who continued to live and function in the world; and Ka-Tzetnik, who remained stuck in the black hole, there and then. At the Eichmann trial, De-Nur and Ka-Tzetnik were merged, so that De-Nur was forced to connect to his memories—the black hole of trauma—causing him to collapse. In order to allow him to function again, he had to resort to new, more aggressive mechanisms, losing the connection to his memories through the persona of Ka-Tzetnik in the process. All that De-Nur had left at this point were his books, which, as we have seen, combined reality and nightmare.

Notes

1. For further discussion, see Ataria (2014a, b).
2. According to Rosenfeld (2011), Levi, towards the end of his life, felt that his memory was beginning to fade, and it was a source of no little anxiety to him. Since totalitarian regimes seek to control the personal memories and past experiences of their victims—as illustrated by the case of Winston Smith in Orwell's (1977) novel, *1984*, for example—the fear of losing one's memory in such circumstances is very real, and holding onto one's memories is one of the central struggles of prisoners under such regimes (Applebaum 2004; Arendt 1973; Solzhenitsyn 1975).
3. It is amazing to see, especially in light of the above observations, how Ka-Tzetnik was suddenly able to be extremely clear about what he knew and what he did not know. This is precisely what makes Ka-Tzetnik such an enigma.
4. I write this with all due caution. It is not my contention that the traumatic event itself is not important, but rather that in very specific cases, when the traumatic event occurs when the victim lacks awareness, then bearing witness—as the moment of realization—harbours explosive traumatic potential. For an extensive discussion, see Caruth (1996) and Felman and Laub (1992).

5. As noted earlier, Ka-Tzetnik continued to write, but his books were not the same, and Ka-Tzetnik himself, it seems, was no longer the same Ka-Tzetnik.
6. For further discussion, see Ataria (2016a, b, 2018, 2019a, b).

References

Applebaum, Ann. 2004. *Gulag: A history*. New York: Anchor Books.

Ataria, Yochai. 2014a. Traumatic memories as black holes: A qualitative-phenomenological approach. *Qualitative Psychology* 1 (2): 123–140.

———. 2014b. Acute peritraumatic dissociation: In favor of a phenomenological inquiry. *Journal of Trauma & Dissociation* 15 (3): 332–347.

———. 2016a. I am not my body, this is not my body. *Human Studies* 39 (2): 217–229.

———. 2016b. Post-traumatic stress disorder: A theory of perception. *Body, Movement and Dance in Psychotherapy* 11 (1): 19–30.

———. 2018. *Body disownership in complex posttraumatic stress disorder*. New York: Palgrave Macmillan.

———. 2019a. Total destruction. In *Jean Améry: Beyond the minds limits*, ed. Yochai Ataria, Amit Kravitz, and Eli Pitcovski, 141–158. New York: Palgrave Macmillan.

———. 2019b. When the body stands in the way: Complex posttraumatic stress disorder, depersonalization and schizophrenia. *Philosophy, Psychiatry, & Psychology* 26 (1): 19–31.

Caruth, Cathy. 1996. *Unclaimed experience: Trauma, narrative, and history*. Baltimore: Johns Hopkins University Press.

Felman, Shoshana, and Dori Laub. 1992. *Testimony: Crises of witnessing in literature, psychoanalysis, and history*. Florence: Routledge.

Goldberg, Amos. 2017. *Trauma in the first person*. Trans. Shmuel Sermoneta-Gertel and Avner Greenberg. Bloomington: Indiana University Press.

Gradowski, Zalmen. 2017. *From the heart of hell: Manuscripts of a Sonderkommando prisoner, found in Auschwitz*. Trans. Barry Smerin and Janina Wurbs. Oświęcim: Auschwitz-Birkenau State Museum.

Ka-Tzetnik. 1989. *Shivitti: A vision*. Trans. Eliyah Nike De-Nur and Lisa Herman. New York: Harper & Row.

Levi, Primo. 2001. *The voice of memory: Interviews 1961–1987*. Ed. Marco Belpoliti and Robert Gordon. Trans. Robert Gordon. New York: New Press.

———. 2015. *The complete works of Primo Levi*. Ed. Ann Goldstein. Various translators. 3 vols. New York: Liveright.

Orwell, George. (1949) 1977. *1984*. New York: New American Library.

Rosenfeld, Alvin H. 2011. *The end of the Holocaust*. Bloomington: Indiana University Press.

Semprún, Jorge. 1997. *Literature or life*. Trans. Linda Coverdale. New York: Viking.
Spadi, Milvia. 2003. *Le parole di un uomo: Incontro con Primo Levi*. Rome: Di Renzo.
Szeintuch, Yechiel. 2007. On Katzetnik's unknown testimony at the Eichmann trial. *The Mendele Review* 11 (12), November 11. http://yiddish.haifa.ac.il/tmr/tmr11/tmr11012.htm
Yablonka, Hanna. 2004. *The State of Israel vs. Adolf Eichmann*. Trans. Ora Cummings and David Herman. New York: Schocken Books.

CHAPTER 4

The Voiceless Voice of the Muselmann

In *Sunrise over Hell*, Ka-Tzetnik (1978, 205–6) offers the following description of the Muselmann:

> 'Mussulman': the flower of the twentieth century, the crown of its creation. By nature and substance the Mussulman was as follows: the camplings, for weeks on end tightly packed against each other in their hutch, would be lying in the self-same rags, handed out to them on arrival, which they never, day or night, took off; not before their moment of departure, that is. While the swarms of indigenous lice in the hutches kept up their proliferating best, with a distinct predilection for setting up house and multiplying in human bodies. The lice made the skin erupt in sores. Fingernails tearing at their flesh, the camplings' mouths fairly gaped with the luxuriant pleasure of their self-laceration, panting with the pleasurable relish of picking at their own rash-crusted bodies, they pulled the scabs from their sores for the lice to creep in under the skin, and in the comfort of the gashes contentedly nibble away at the tissues.Next to come into the open were the Mussulmen: human beings, no heavier than their bones, with cobwebs for intestines. What distinguished the Mussulman was his incapacity to feel hunger, or, for that matter, to eat. Hence, any *arriviste* detected lugging about with him two portions of bread, gained immediate recognition as the Mussulman he had become; not by virtue of the sudden inheritance he had come into. As much as for the imminent bequest of it to his fellows.
>
> It was sufficient for a Mussulman to allow anything into his guts for it to come running out the other end. The Mussulmen therefore took to the latrine for a habitat, their trousers a slime of excrement, their one hand

Y. Ataria, *Primo Levi and Ka-Tzetnik*,
https://doi.org/10.1007/978-3-030-76743-3_4

> fiercely clawing at their bread, their other engaged in wiping off the diarrhoea; the eyes, the nose, the mouth, every orifice of the body, all oozing with mucus. For speech to register with his brain, the Mussulman had to be addressed repeatedly. Yet no one guarded his bread more closely. To keep vigil over the bread, with the uniquely-Auschwitz instinct of survival, was so deeply rooted in the pre-Mussulman phase of his subconscious mind, that any attempt to steal it immediately alerted him, even though it might be yesterday's bread ration, never to be eaten by himself.

Primo Levi, in *If This Is a Man* (2015, 85), describes the Muselmann as the epitome of evil:

> They crowd my memory with their faceless presence, and if I could encompass all the evil of our time in one image, I would choose this image, which is familiar to me: an emaciated man, head bowed and shoulders bent, on whose face and in whose eyes no trace of thought can be seen.

Both authors agree that the Muselmann is not merely an accident or a byproduct of the totalitarian state and progress, but proof of the successful implementation of the principle of 'progress through technology',[1] taken to the extreme in the context of totalitarianism. That said, it is clear why they believe that the Muselmann is key to understanding the concentration and extermination camps. This chapter will address the respective ways in which Levi and Ka-Tzetnik try to describe the Muselmann's inner world.

4.1 The Muselmann: A Profile

4.1.1 Origin of the Term

Surprisingly, many writers and scholars do not hesitate to use the term 'Muselmann' without exploring or attempting to explain its origin. Indeed, to this day, we do not know the etymology of the term 'Muselmann' or even whether it originated among the victims or the perpetrators (Ryn and Klodzinski 1987). Within the overall framework of Nazi code language, without which it is hard to understand the nature of the regime and the process of extermination (e.g., concepts such as 'Lager' or 'Final Solution'), the term Muselmann played a particularly important role in the world of the camps.

While the *Encyclopedia of the Holocaust* (Gutman 1990) explains that the term derives from the image of a Muslim prostrated in prayer, the *Lexicon of the Holocaust* (Levin 2005) suggests that it originated in the swaying walk of these prisoners, reminiscent of the movements of a Muslim dervish.

According to Giorgio Agamben (1999, 45), 'The most likely explanation of the term can be found in the literal meaning of the Arabic word Muslim: one who submits unconditionally to the will of God'. At the same time, Agamben stresses the gap between the resignation of the Muselmann and the submission of the Muslim believer: 'While the Muslim's resignation consists in the conviction that the will of Allah is at work every moment and in even the smallest events, the Muselmann of Auschwitz is instead defined by a loss of all will and consciousness.'[2]

4.1.2 *Physiological Characteristics*

The Muselmann suffers from extreme malnutrition. The transformation from ordinary prisoner to Muselmann occurs when an individual has lost a third of her or his body weight. Their muscles were atrophied, their legs affected by severe oedema, and they could hardly move. They suffered from diarrhoea and incontinence. Their eyes were sunken and glassy, their expression mechanical and sad, their skin ashen, thin, and hardened. They breathed slowly and with great difficulty, were always cold, and shivered constantly (Ryn 1990a, b). That said, Sofsky (1996) stresses that the Muselmann cannot be reduced to physical features.

The Muselmann, many survivors suggest, is neither alive nor dead, no longer human, completely apathetic, having regressed to an autistic state—numb and unable to grasp reality (Bettelheim 1960, 152–3). It would be inaccurate, however, to say that the Muselmänner simply lost their will; it was shattered and crushed—utterly exhausted and annihilated.

4.1.3 *Being-at-Home in Auschwitz*

No one in the camps felt pity for the Muselmann, who was hated by all the prisoners: 'According to the law that what man despises is also what he fears resembles him, the *Muselmann* is universally avoided because everyone in the camp recognizes himself in his disfigured face' (Agamben 1999, 52). The threat posed by the Muselmänner to the ordinary prisoner stemmed from the unpredictability of their behaviour and, more importantly, from the fact that they were a constant reminder of the overarching aim of the concentration camp:

> The *Muselmann* embodies the anthropological meaning of absolute power in an especially radical form. ... Like the pile of corpses, the *Muselmänner* document the total triumph of power over the human being. Although still nominally alive, they are nameless hulks. In the configuration of their infirmity, as in organized mass murder, the regime realizes its quintessential self. (47–8)

The Muselmann represents the predictable end of each and every prisoner who had not become a functionary. The Muselmann dwelled within them and had to be concealed: 'The prisoner's most pressing concern was ... to constantly cover over the *Muselmann* who at every moment was emerging in him' (52). All in all, it seems that the Muselmann felt at home in Auschwitz and, in a certain sense, was the reason why the camp was built—an idea that is all the more horrifying because Auschwitz was not in fact established for the sake of sadism.

4.1.4 A Muselmann Even in Death

The Muselmann has undergone a transformation from human to inhuman, from living body to lifeless object:[3] 'There is thus a point at which human beings, while apparently remaining human beings, cease to be human. This point is the *Muselmann*' (Agamben 1999, 55). The Muselmann passes through the gate of death although not entirely dead, but not entirely alive either: 'One hesitates to call them living; one hesitates to call their death death' (Levi 2015, 85). Thus, in their very essence, the Muselmänner negate not only life but death as well. They represent a new state, in which death loses its meaning. Not even the passage from animate to inanimate organism can be called death when it is not only life that has lost its dignity, but death itself: 'precisely this degradation of death constitutes the specific offense of Auschwitz' (Agamben 1999, 72). In the concentration and extermination camps, 'Men do not die, but are instead produced as corpses',[4] and 'Death, at this point, is a simple epiphenomenon' (75, 86). The Muselmänner are thus denied even the possibility of dying and, unable to pass into the world of the dead, simply remain Muselmänner.

4.2 The Muselmann as a Lacuna

From Levi's perspective (2015, 2415), 'The most substantial material for reconstructing the truth about the camps is the survivors' memories'. At the same time, however, he stresses that his books are not history books (179–80). This raises a fundamental question regarding the very institution of testimony: the victims themselves, the drowned, the murdered, are no longer alive, and are thus unable to testify. That leaves only the living—listed here in reverse order of their importance as witnesses: (*a*) the executioners; (*b*) prisoners who acted in the 'grey zone'; (*c*) 'ordinary' prisoners (without privileges), who were the majority of concentration and extermination camp inmates, and few of whom survived. Thus, the closer witnesses were to the executioners (without judging the ways in which prisoners strove to survive), the greater their ability to testify to events in the camps, both in terms of the quantity of information to which they had access and in terms of their mental capacity (due to better physical conditions) to process that information. Their reliability as witnesses, however, decreases in inverse proportion to that proximity, as it would certainly be in their interest to hide significant portions of the story (this may be expressed by the formula ability/reliability). As Levi himself put it, such people 'distance themselves from genuine memories, temporarily or permanently, and fabricate a convenient reality. For them the past is a burden; they feel revulsion at what they did or what was done to them, and tend to replace it with something different' (2423). It thus comes as no surprise that 'the largest category of privileged persons par excellence—namely, the ones who earned privileges through subservience to the camp authority—did not bear witness at all, for obvious reasons, or their testimony was erratic, distorted, or completely false' (2416). Prisoners without privileges, on the other hand, often found it hard to testify to events outside the realm of their personal experience. At the far end of the spectrum, some prisoners lost their cognitive capacity, hence their ability to perceive reality had been damaged, undermining their ability to bear witness. This would appear to be the reason that Levi repeatedly underscored the fact that he had testified only to things that he himself had endured.

When we refer to 'ordinary' prisoners, those who did not perform any particular function, we are, in effect, speaking about the Muselmänner. The Muselmänner are the lacuna that shapes the survivors' testimony, whether directly or indirectly. To better understand this point, it is worth noting a number of possible meanings of the concept 'lacuna': a space; a gap; a situation in which there is no legal precedent; a word that lacks an equivalent in another language; square brackets—a situation in which we lack information regarding missing portions of a text (e.g., 'He was [ ] and [ ]'); a situation in which a given body of knowledge lacks essential information in that field; an area of scientific knowledge that has not been sufficiently studied.[5]

The Muselmann is not merely a space, a gap, or an absence, but an unexplained phenomenon—cognitively, psychologically, philosophically, and even legally. In order to understand the Nazi regime and the concentration camps, we must first understand the Muselmann, but since the Muselmann is a lacuna, any attempt to understand the nature of the regime and the reality of the camps will necessarily encounter fundamental difficulties. Consequently, there will be square brackets [ ] at the heart of every explanation of the concentration camps. This is the enormous excess that study of the camps engenders.

The figure of the Muselmann symbolizes the excess that lies beyond the boundaries of representation.[6] The survivor's challenge is to tell the story of the Muselmann from the Muselmänner's perspective, as they alone are 'the submerged, the complete witnesses' (Levi 1988, 70).[7] Scholars and survivors agree that such a task is impossible, almost by definition. Indeed, we have numerous descriptions of what the Muselmänner looked like from the outside (walking dead, swaying corpses, etc.), but one would be hard-pressed to find any scientific, literary, or phenomenological study that manages to convey what it actually felt like to be a Muselmann.[8] In fact, it is hard to find testimonies that describe this experience at all—even from the perspective of witnesses who do not claim to have been Muselmänner themselves. Indeed, according to Agamben (1999, 41), Muselmann is synonymous with 'untestifiable'.

Levi constantly reiterates the idea that the Muselmann, as the ultimate victim, is also the ultimate witness—the 'complete witness', so that 'we will not understand what Auschwitz is if we do not first understand who or what the *Muselmann* is' (Agamben 1999, 52). The paradox is thus that there are two distinct (even opposing) subjects within the witness: the survivor and the victim. Essentially, it is unclear how (if at all) the survivor (who seeks to become a witness) in the here-and-now is able to give voice to the inhuman left behind in the there-and-then.[9] We must therefore remember that when we encounter the survivor it is not at all clear that we are encountering the victim. There is a significant, perhaps unbridgeable gap between survivor and victim, that is despite the fact that they both reside within the same individual:

> the first, the survivor, who can speak but who has nothing interesting to say; and the second, who "has seen the Gorgon," who "has touched bottom," and therefore has much to say but cannot speak. Which of the two bears witness? *Who is the subject of testimony?* (120).

Levi, according to Agamben, is 'the only one who consciously sets out to bear witness in place of the *Muselmann*' (59) and that is because, in Levi's writing, 'Muselmann and witness, the inhuman and the human are coextensive' (151). I find this characterization inaccurate. In fact, Levi, as I will show, has an inherent block that prevents him from representing the Muselmann. Careful study reveals that Levi's real motivation was the anxiety of becoming Hurbinek—the child who was trapped in 'the tomb of his muteness' (Levi 2015, 225), prisoner of his inability to express himself in human language.[10] Thus, despite Agamben's claim to the contrary, Levi is incapable of giving voice to the Muselmänner or, at least of establishing a perimeter around the structural lacuna they represent. Indeed, to the extent that testifying on behalf of the Muselmänner signifies replacing the square brackets [ ] with some sort of text, Levi stands helpless before that menacing void. He may write about the square brackets [ ], but is nevertheless unable to fill the vacuum between them [ ] with content, unable to write from within the [ ]. The reason for this inability is, in my opinion, Levi's obsessive insistence on making the story of Auschwitz accessible to readers. In this sense, his skill as a writer allows him to convey his unique experience but also to avoid facing the ever-present Hurbinek, who represents his deepest anxiety.

Hurbinek was a child of around three, paralysed from the lower back down, who had never learned to speak. Levi (2015, 225) describes him as 'a nothing, a child of death, a child of Auschwitz'. Even the name Hurbinek was given to him by the prisoners in the camp. Despite his condition, 'his eyes, lost in his pinched, triangular face, flashed, terribly alive, full of demand, of insistence, of the will to be unchained, *to shatter the tomb of his muteness*' (ibid.). I would be saying nothing new—as Levi wrote as much himself—were I to suggest that, to Levi, the boy represented the anxiety that many survivors experienced in their dreams, that no one would listen to them: 'Why is the pain of every day so constantly translated, in our dreams, into the ever repeated scene of the story told and not listened to?' (57). The anxiety of failing to get people to listen to his story appears to have accompanied Levi throughout his life. To Levi's mind, living was not merely about telling a story, but about telling it to people who would listen and understand. Levi knows that even if he were to find a way to write from the very depths of the square brackets, he could not be sure that readers would be able to hear it, and it is this anxiety that led him, consciously or unconsciously, to avoid those brackets.

Agamben (1999) claims that Levi manages to give voice to Hurbinek's silence precisely because he gives voice to the remnant of the human in the inhuman, which is the voice of the victim. This is not entirely correct, since (as we have seen) Levi's writing is guided by the fear of dying 'free but not redeemed', like the child Hurbinek. Levi is prepared to pay a heavy price not to be forced to remain silent and misunderstood, and, for that reason, ultimately finds it hard to give voice to the drowned. It is worth noting Levi's (2015, 1137) own words here: 'Yes, probably we were wrong. We sinned by omission and by commission. In keeping silent we committed the sin of laziness and of lack of faith in the power of the word; and when we did speak we sinned, often, by adopting and accepting a language that was not ours.' Levi's decision to make Auschwitz an accessible story came at a high cost: abandoning the Muselmann, abandoning the square brackets [ ]. In his writing, Levi explains a great deal, but, in a certain sense, fails to address the lacuna. Thus, although we, as readers, may feel that Levi has taken us into the camps and helped us to understand them, this is not the case from Levi's own perspective. Hurbinek remains silent. Levi fails to bring him back to life, even in a story.

Agamben (1999, 150) claims that 'the survivor and the *Muselmann*, like the tutor and the incapable person and the creator and his material, are inseparable'. In some ways, the voice that Agamben seeks resembles the 'affirmative middle voice' sought by LaCapra (2014), prompted by processes of working through, during the course of which the survivor does not deny what happened but is fully aware of being in the here and now, recounting (now) something that occurred there and then. When survivors describe the events of the past, they oscillate between here-now and there-then, human and inhuman, survivor and victim. There is a certain disjunction—a crack—and it is through this crack that testimony emerges. In this state, 'the witness has greater authority than the witnessed thing' (Agamben 1999, 150). Although the fracture that Agamben describes is an apt characterization of the state of the survivor, it offers little insight into the Muselmänner from their own perspective—and it is precisely in this light that Ka-Tzetnik's motivation to write should be understood. This was the task that Ka-Tzetnik took upon himself: to give voice to the voiceless Muselmann. Before exploring Ka-Tzetnik's attempt to describe the inner world of the Muselmann, however, we need to take a step back and address the subject of Ka-Tzetnik as a witness.

4.3 The Liminal No Man's Land of Testimony

A victim can only be a witness after the event: 'Then, inside the coalbin in the now evacuated truck, I didn't know where I was. I knew nothing then… Perhaps someone within my skeleton did see it all, but I saw nothing, knew nothing' (Ka-Tzetnik 1989, 12–13). The victim may see what is going on, but is unable to process the experience. The events have somehow been 'filmed' by the eye, but it is unclear whether they have been codified, and, if so, in what manner. Survivors must then try to locate the fragments of memory while *knowing that they do not know* what actually happened and, at the same time, *knowing what they would rather not know*. Before his second LSD treatment, Ka-Tzetnik writes: 'And in my heart I murmured a silent prayer that once I was under the influence of LSD I would again manage *to avoid the sight of that which I had come here to see*' (29). The reference would seem to be to the author's uncertain encounter with Daniella, Harry's sister in the Salamandra series, as a prostitute in the service of the Nazis. In the fifth and final session with Prof. Bastiaans, Ka-Tzetnik returns to the experience of having been forced to see an orgy at the Nazi officers' quarters and Daniella taking part in it. Ka-Tzetnik avoids seeing what he knows and wishes he did not know. This knowledge (latent) haunts him, and he, in return, avoids knowing that which he cannot help but know. (Yet, he does not know.)

In the process of locating, deciphering, and denying memory, the survivor is neither fully here nor fully there: 'Now I am both here and there.' The survivor oscillates between two perspectives, the present and the past. In order to encounter the there-and-then, the survivor must turn to the skeleton, to the inhuman within: 'Not only does my body now carry within it the bony skeleton from then', but that skeleton itself is the 'last flickering spark, which did not quite die out in my mind then' (13). It is the skeleton within him that enables Ka-Tzetnik to testify about Auschwitz, the inhuman within the 'successful' witness that tells the victims' story. Seen from this perspective, Ka-Tzetnik's question regarding *Salamandra* (*Sunrise over Hell*)—'But was it really I who wrote it all?' (15)—makes perfect sense.

As we have seen, Agamben (1999) argues that the crack between the human and the inhuman, between the survivor and the murdered victim, is necessary for the emergence of testimony. With this in mind we may attempt to answer Ka-Tzetnik's question, 'Was it really I who wrote it all?' His books were written neither by the human nor by the inhuman, but by a third entity that is neither here nor there but in the liminal space between the human and the inhuman. This is borne out by his reaction to the ostensibly routine question posed by the prosecutor Gideon Hausner at the Eichmann trial: 'Why do you hide behind another name in your books?'[11] In *Shivitti*, Ka-Tzetnik describes what he felt when asked that question:

> The moment it flashed into my brain all hell broke loose. Not only did they want me to melt the two identities into one, but they wanted a public confession, an open declaration that this was so. Escaping to no-man's land was my only solution—becoming a vegetable in a hospital ward. (70)

At this point, Ka-Tzetnik adopts the doctor's diagnosis: 'How did Prof. Bastiaans put it? "At that moment your soul proceeded to split."' At the very heart of the experience is a split, and this split is the one and only chance the survivor has to continue living: 'I look at my unconscious self, and I look at the self staring at my self; I look and see the key to the split. It stands behind the curtain of the swoon: the secret of the split deciphered' (100). Up to this point, the process that Ka-Tzetnik underwent is consistent with various theories that seek to explain what a victim experiences at the time of trauma, and, to some extent, is even consistent with Agamben's theory. From this point forward, however, Ka-Tzetnik demands that we revise our theories regarding the process of testimony and what Agamben calls authentic testimony, from the perspective of the victim who remained there. Indeed, at the end of his treatment, Ka-Tzetnik writes: 'From now on survival duty was to be a bearer of testimony in the trial of God vs. Satan—the trial that is being conducted in the heart of man' (106). The survivor-witness is no longer fractured between the human and the inhuman or between God and Satan, but is a witness in the trial between them.

I would suggest another possible interpretation. When Ka-Tzetnik explains that his body carries within it 'the bony skeleton from then', he appears to be referring not only to the inhuman that was always within him, but to something deeper as well: '*They* and the others are buried within me, and each continues living his own life within me. Over their ashes I vowed to be a voice to *them*, and when I left Auschwitz *they* walked with me' (18). Between the human and the inhuman, there is no single liminal figure, but rather many figures—fused in the coal bin. Ka-Tzetnik, the anonymous prisoner, is thus able to choose the voice of any Ka-Tzet: 'Those who went to the crematorium wrote this book! ... The nameless ones! It's them! Them! All those anonymous ones! Write their name: K. Tzetnik!' (15–16).

One of the characteristics of extreme trauma is the loss of a subjective perspective on reality,[12] expressed in a sense of splitting. When victims lose their own perspective, they may unconsciously experience the trauma from the perspective of another. Thus, when Ka-Tzetnik walks around the city of Leiden between sessions, he is reminded of his Dutch friend, Baby: 'My tears were Baby's tears as he lay by my side on the hutch-planks. And they were my own, as I was moved to tears by the streets of Holland, taken along in an Auschwitz labor crew' (50–1). The survivor who lost the perspective from within his own body at the time of the event and therefore lacks a figure to which he can return is only able to experience Auschwitz through the gaze of another, and when that happens he oscillates uncontrollably between here-now and there-then, between his body in the present and the body of the other in the past. Consequently, he cannot testify from a subjective perspective in the first person but only from the perspective of the other, because the experience *there* was in the third, not the first, person. I will illustrate this point by means of Ka-Tzetnik's description of the murder of Harry's mother.

Ka-Tzetnik writes, 'My mother. I see her naked and marching in line, one among Them, her face turned toward the gas chambers. "Mama! Mama! Mama!"' (100). A few lines later, however, he switches perspective, experiencing his mother's incineration from within: 'It is my own self I see. My own face. Coiled in my mama's skull I was burned' (103). The split enables (perhaps even compels) Ka-Tzetnik to be in two places at the same time. In Ka-Tzetnik's case, however, the split is far more complex, since he not only experienced the event from his own perspective as a passive observer or from his mother's perspective, but from another perspective as well—that of the cremator. Immediately after describing the experience from his mother's perspective, he writes the following: 'and there, joined to the flesh of my family, I was fodder for Auschwitz' (ibid.). Ka-Tzetnik's initial experience would thus seem to include the perspectives of the victim and the passive observer (perhaps an ordinary camp inmate, without any particular function), as well as the prisoner who actively participated in the extermination programme—in this case, a

Sonderkommando. Ka-Tzetnik's complete detachment at the time of the event allowed him—in his case, one might even say left him no alternative, since, as we have seen, the figures were fused together in the coal bin—to experience a particular occurrence from various perspectives.

I would argue that this detachment from the experience at the time of its occurrence underlies all of Ka-Tzetnik's work. As we have seen, his books are often set in remarkably precise historical contexts—because detachment allows him to be a kind of documenting machine. He did not experience the concentration camp from his own perspective and is therefore able to describe it 'from nowhere'—known in scientific discourse as the objective-scientific perspective. Detachment allows him (and perhaps leaves him no alternative) to adopt the experiences of others in the camp. In this sense, and only in this sense (and I will come back to this topic later in the book), it is entirely irrelevant whether he actually had a sister named Daniella and a brother named Moni, and the real life experiences of Yehiel Feiner, Yehiel De-Nur, or any other figure, are of no importance whatsoever. Ka-Tzetnik writes in the name of a prisoner who could have been, and this prisoner could have had a sister and a brother. Ka-Tzetnik describes their experience—that of the prisoner, his sister, and his brother—and is able to do so because he himself did not *experience* the events at the time, in the first person. More precisely, he may in fact have experienced these events in the first person, but they were forgotten, repressed, or undocumented.

In order to better understand this point, it is worth noting the way in which Ka-Tzetnik describes his own experience in relation to that of the Jew in Fig. 4.1: 'I couldn't tear my eyes away from the Jew [in the photograph] on the wall. So many times had I been in his situation, but never had I attained such a state of transcendence. For in moments like this I panicked' (xiii). In other words, panic prevented him from codifying the event, and he almost certainly detached himself specifically in cases such as these: 'This time I don't fall into a faint, because [I've separated from myself,] I've split myself in two' (100). And indeed, when he describes his encounter with Daniella, his sense of shock and the consequences—immediate splitting:

> I behold *Feld hure* branded between my sister's breasts. And I see myself instantly splitting in two. I see how I leave my body, separating into two selves.... I stare at myself, dragged by the feet back to the block and see the key to my nightmares. It's hidden beneath the brand between my sister's breasts' (99–100).

Fig. 4.1 A Jew Humiliated and Desecrated Phylacteries. This is the photograph that Ka-Tzetnik refers to. It was taken in Olkusz, Poland, on 'Bloody Wednesday' (31 July 1940), probably by a German. The figure at the centre of the picture is Rabbi Mosze Hagerman, who was forced to don his desecrated prayer shawl and phylacteries, stand barefoot, and pray near Jews lying face down on the ground. (Source: https://www.yadvashem.org/holocaust/this-month/july/1940-2.html)

Where there should have been a personal memory, there is a lacuna, which fills up with the experiences of others. Whenever Ka-Tzetnik writes 'I', it is a prisoner he has adopted in the deepest sense, to whom he gives voice. The following incident will serve to illustrate this point.

In one of his sessions with Prof. Bastiaans, while describing a range of events, Ka-Tzetnik returns to what appears to be a kind of origin story. Two days after the outbreak of the war, he is taken to dig trenches, and encounters Hitler's soldiers for the first time, in a Polish city. A Jew digging next to him was too slow, and a German took the shovel from him and beat him to death with it. During the trance, under the effect of the hallucinogenic, while passing from one horrifying event to the next, Ka-Tzetnik returns to that first encounter and says, 'Would God I had died for thee! I got to my feet. And I am he' (83–4). This is an accurate description (or at least that is my contention) of the process that Ka-Tzetnik undergoes: it is at that very moment that Yehiel Feiner dies, and, from that point on, he begins to live the lives of the dead. Yehiel Feiner is no more; there is only Ka-Tzetnik—a man who has become the Jews who have died and continue to live through him. Ka-Tzetnik has no memories that are his own and has no memories that are not his own. He experiences the camps through the dead and can only recount their deaths. It is worth examining Ka-Tzetnik's attempt to testify in the name of the Muselmann in this light, as it is his ability to bear witness from the perspective of another that ostensibly allows him to experience Auschwitz through the eyes of the Muselmann.

4.4 The Null Set: The Voice of the Muselmann

Like Primo Levi, Ka-Tzetnik prepared himself for the day after. While Levi set out to provide the most accurate testimony possible, Ka-Tzetnik set out to tell the story of the Muselmänner. To that end, he entered their world while still in the camp. Ka-Tzetnik felt duty-bound to tell their story:

> All are here now—in this mound of ash… He flung himself upon them. Took them in his arms Held them tight. He was lying on the mound, his arms deep, deep in the ash… He picked himself up from the ash. His eyes swept over everything in sight: only he, of all in this place, has a voice to command an echo. He knew: locked in the pupils of his eyes was the planet Auschwitz before he had turned to stone. And only he, of all in this place, can take these pupils out with him… He was walking and with him the soundless blocks of Auschwitz and the piles of musselmen within them… I vow on your ash embraced in my arms, to be a voice unto you, and unto the Ka-Tzet now voiceless and consumed; I will not cease to tell of you even unto the last whisper of my breath. So help me God, amen. (Ka-Tzetnik 1971, 112–13)

In order to understand Auschwitz a certain code (*tsofen*) must be deciphered. This code appears to be the Muselmann. The premise is that the Muselmänner, who lacked a function—or perhaps performed the only function that was truly important in Auschwitz—were the only ones who fully understood the Nazi system, on their own flesh. According to Ka-Tzetnik, it was only when a prisoner became a Muselmann that he or she arrived at Auschwitz:

> He tagged after them. All at once he felt superfluous, cast out to the camp, dumped into the stream of Mussulman refuse sloshing by him. With a shock the reality of the camp hit him. As though he had only just arrived; as though a moment ago he had not been here at all. All those milling around him became a vortex sucking him in like a drop in a raging current. Soon, together with them, he will be swept along to wherever they stream... Only now he felt the people's being there yesterday and their overnight disappearance. He now felt his own body and skin in their disappearance. (Ka-Tzetnik 1961, 62)

Beyond his well-known oath to all of the victims, Ka-Tzetnik felt a particular obligation towards the Muselmänner. It seems that in some cases, the Muselmänner actually protected him:

> Moni dug himself in under their skeleton. They lay on his body, covering him. He could feel them upon him, and he could feel them deep within him. The agony of their Mussulmanity filled his being to suffocation. He felt he was going to be one of them... Moni hid among the Mussulmen. Once more he felt that an invisible hand was safeguarding him in Auschwitz. (91–3)

Moni hides among the Muselmänner, and they protect him with their bodies, in a real, physical sense that, in the distorted reality of the concentration camps might even be called maternal ('They lay on his body, covering him... Moni hid among the Mussulmen. Once more he felt that an invisible hand was safeguarding him in Auschwitz'). As they protect him, they penetrate the very depths of his being and reconstitute him as a Muselmann.

As we have seen, there seems to be a consensus among the survivors, that prisoners who became Muselmänner lost the ability to understand the Muselmann (that is, their own) experience. Although the Muselmänner may have had the ability to comprehend their present experiences, if only to some extent, their existence was completely detached from everything that had happened to them before they became Muselmänner or might happen to them after they emerged from that state. Thus, even if the Muselmänner did have some understanding of their situation (doubtful in and of itself), the survivors had no access to these insights, which were beyond their reach, as if on another planet:

> 'Often', Bergson said, 'I sit here trying to remember how we ever got here, but I just can't remember a thing. I only know that the night of the theater, I was already a Mussulman. Besides that I can't remember a thing. If we get out of here alive, we won't even be able to tell what happened to us. We

> won't remember a thing. That is the real tragedy. The world won't even know what happened to us here'. (191)

We see that even someone who was once a Muselmann and managed to emerge from that state is unable to reconstruct the experience, as a result of the structural lacuna—a void that cannot be represented, as it intrinsically rejects the very notion of representation. In the case of Moni, I would suggest that his intimate encounter with the Muselmänner allowed him to absorb the Muselmann experience without having become a Muselmann himself, and it was this narrow crack that enabled Ka-Tzetnik to begin writing about the Muselmänner from within their own world.

Ka-Tzetnik frequently returns to the topic of the Muselmann in all of his writings. In *Piepel* (1961), however, he seems to have made a particular effort to describe the Muselmann's inner world. First, we must understand that an ordinary prisoner in the camp, if not yet a Muselmann, could easily become one in less than a day: 'There's just six hours between a full belly and a hungry one in camp. And once you lose your *funktion*, inside of six hours you're just as hungry as the rest of them there in the hutches' (38). In this sense, the Muselmann poses the greatest threat of all to any prisoner.

Ka-Tzetnik focuses on two main aspects of the Muselmänner: their physical appearance and their cognitive state. Cognitively, they know nothing and understand nothing, and have lost both their memories and the ability to orient themselves:

> Thousands of human shadows drag by Moni, this way and that. Their blank stares collide with him as they seek something, not remembering what. They crawled down from their hutches, went out of their blocks to go to the latrine, but they no longer know the way. They cannot tell the front of the camp from the rear, where the latrine is located. Everywhere, the same appearance. All blocks look alike. Everywhere range the same rows of barbed wire, the same block gates. They no longer know the way, just as they no longer know that, before even they felt the need to go to the latrine, the slimy excreta had already run out of them; there it is dripping from their trouser hems on to their bare feet, without them even feeling it. Thousands upon thousands. Merchants with breads inside their trousers cut a path through them. With contraband it is best to go amidst Mussulmen. No one pays them any attention. To all appearances, they are the purpose of it all here. It is for them the Auschwitz was created. (50–1)

Physically, the Muselmann is nothing but a skeleton:

> The latrine block is packed from wall to wall. Especially around the rear gate. Near the water taps, all along the walls, stand Mussulmen holding their trousers in their hands, wiping from their nude legs the feces which had oozed out of them on the way to the latrine. In their armpits they hug yesterday's bread ration which they are no longer capable of eating and never will eat. Their trunks are swathed in a motley of tatters and strings—all the wealth they had managed to amass in the course of their Auschwitz life. The spindle-legs jutting nakedly down from the tatterbatch trunks give them the appearance of toy ostriches with tall steel filaments for legs... Their limp mouths display gumless teeth, fleshless and long as piano keys. (111–17)

This description is no different from many other literary descriptions of Muselmänner. It is a graphic, physical description that makes no attempt to enter their inner world (keeping in mind that the question is not only whether it is possible to enter the inner world of the Muselmann, but whether such a world even exists). In the following passage, however, Ka-Tzetnik tries to go a step further, to enter the Muselmann's inner world:

> In the third tier, opposite the stash, lie only out-and-out Mussulmen. It is Zygmunt that put them there, as a charm against the evil eye and as the guardians of the treasure opposite. For this purpose, Zygmunt always chooses Mussulmen in whom the nasty urge to eat has atrophied, who no longer even eat their own rations. He orders them to keep a sharp eye out for anyone who thinks he's going to steal into the stash at night. He is as sure of them as one can be sure of eunuchs in a harem. Zygmunt pays them off by promising not to ship them to the crematorium. And guard they do. Not in order not to be sent to the crematorium—that no longer registers with them. They guard because they have been told to guard. Everything in their brains has dried out. (54–5)

We learn that Muselmänner, in their extreme state, do not understand their own condition, and simply do as they are told, without will or consciousness experience. Yet, even this description fails to enter the Muselmann experience or reality. We do find such an attempt, however, in the passage below.

> He did not know whether a moment ago he had been dozing or awake. He did not know whether it was the beginning of the night, or the end. Hunger now pounced on him again with renewed ferocity, like a beast which had been stalking its quarry for fully a year for just this moment. Moni was terrified. His eyes tore open. He felt: this is the final hunger! Gripping the

> sideboard of the hutch with both hands, he sank his teeth into the wood. Quickly to swallow something, quickly! His mouth tore to bite into the dark air. It's the final hunger! After this he will never again be hungry. He knew it. Everybody in Auschwitz know that; every Mussulman feels it just once in his Auschwitz life. *He felt he was now crossing a border.* Every campling's last border. The last border of hunger. He was turning Mussulman. (225)

From this description we learn that there is a certain critical moment that Ka-Tzetnik calls the final or last hunger, after which the prisoner becomes a Muselmann. Ka-Tzetnik continues:

> The last hunger! He wept, but no tears came. Every bit of moisture had long since dried up in him. Fear only pries his eyelids apart. His fingers convulsively pinch at the vacant darkness. He felt blades of hunger scraping the parched walls of his entrails. He shoves a fist in between his teeth: to swallow something fast; to rush something to his entrails—anything: a bite of hutch wood! His foot! His sleeve! Hunger flickered madly inside his brain like the wick of an evaporated oil lamp. (225–6)

This would indeed appear to be an attempt to describe the inner world of the Muselmann—a world completely dominated by hunger. If accurate, we must conclude that the Muselmann is capable of feeling, that is, experiencing—even feeling hunger is a kind of experience. The question is thus whether this description indeed captures the inner world of the Muselmann or of someone on the verge of becoming a Muselmann. The next passage underscores this point:

> The horror of the oncoming Mussulmanity seized him. All at once he saw his own image as in a slide projection. He was afraid to look. He shut his eyes tight, but the *vision* would not leave—clinging to his sealed eyelids, or hovering in the dark when he opened them, as *on a projection screen.* He saw: Moni, the old campbird, drags his feet across the assembly area from block to block—a Mussulman. Somebody snatches the bread ration from under his arm without his knowing or even feeling what is being done to him. This Moni turns, stares blankly, and drags on. He goes, not knowing he is going. A kapo lets him have the truncheon across his skull. The blow feels as if it had landed on a head not his. He lets out a squeal, freezing there, not running away. A Mussulman never runs away. Nobody recognizes him. Nobody knows who he is. And Moni doesn't remember anybody either. He dissolves among thousands of Mussulmen. He is a drop in a skeleton river flowing to the sea of ash. He shuffles across the camp, back and

> forth, back and forth. He does not know where he has come from or where he is going. He does not know who he is. (226–7)

Ostensibly, this is a description of the world of the Muselmann from within. Upon careful reading, however, it becomes clear that this is not the case. The description is in fact of the moment before becoming a Muselmann, when Moni imagines himself ('vision ... on a projection screen') a Muselmann—an eventuality that fills him with horror. In other words Moni faces the spectre of 'Muselmannity', but has not yet succumbed to it. And indeed, Ka-Tzetnik continues:

> Moni! Why this is he himself—Moni! He sees his trousers, and below—the red sock band around his ankles. That one there on the screen opposite his eyes doesn't know that one is—Moni. That one doesn't know anything any more. But he himself knows that one to be Moni! Now they are still two apart. *Now he is still capable of seeing that one and knowing that it's himself.* But tomorrow, or the day after, they will merge into each other and this Moni will no longer will able to see the other Moni. And just as that one doesn't know, he will no longer know that he himself is—Moni. He will no longer even be able to feel sorry for the other, console him, protect him, hang on him. (227)

Careful reading reveals, once again, that the description is in fact written from the perspective of one who is on the verge of Muselmannity, since he is able to distinguish between himself and the Muselmann ('now they are still two apart'). He has not yet been reduced exclusively to his body, and, in turn, to an object. When that happens, 'this Moni' will no longer be able to see 'that Moni'. This Moni, however, *does* see that Moni—that is to say he still possesses the ability to reflect and to act, and is thus not yet a Muselmann (by Ka-Tzetnik's own definition, cited above). He stands on the threshold, but has not yet crossed over, has not yet experienced the last hunger, still wants to be saved: 'He isn't a Mussulman yet! Why, he still realizes with everything in him that he must save himself immediately. It's after the last hunger that you become a Mussulman, this doesn't seem to have been the last hunger' (229). We also learn from this passage that even if there is a critical moment at which one becomes a Muselmann, it comes at the end of a gradual and protracted process.

As Moni lay among the other prisoners, who, at this point, might have been alive or dead, 'He felt he was helpless. ... His own brother might be lying next to him without his even knowing. ... A year—and now he, too, is in this unending stream' (230). It is clear that he has not yet become a Muselmann (and if he has, Ka-Tzetnik is unable to describe his experience from within), since he has not yet lost the will to save himself, and still has the capacity to devise a plan to steal food from the stash in block 16. Whether the plan actually succeeds is irrelevant. The point is that Moni still retains some cognitive function and has not yet become a complete Muselmann (alternatively, we might argue that the Muselmann does not lose all cognitive function).

We thus see that even at the very edge, Ka-Tzetnik's descriptions of the Muselmann remain external, from the perspective of a prisoner on the verge of becoming a Muselmann. That is because the Muselmänner are a 'null set', wholly devoid of perspective—and therefore Ka-Tzetnik too, even when he renounces himself completely, lacks perspective. This may be the key to understanding the difficulty that survivors have in testifying to their experiences: at Auschwitz, first-person perspective disappears, the subjective structure is disarticulated, hence there is no longer a person to testify.

Ka-Tzetnik is able to renounce his perspective and identify completely with other prisoners. Moreover, Ka-Tzetnik attests to the fact that he himself was a Muselmann. Nevertheless, he is unable to write about life at the camp *from the perspective of the Muselmann*. As we have seen, there is agreement among survivors (Agamben 1999; Levi 2015) that even Muselmänner who managed to emerge from that state (I intentionally do not use the word 'recover') are unable to testify to their experience. This is an unbearable failure for Ka-Tzetnik, who swore not only to recount the lives of those who were murdered, but especially the deaths of the Muselmänner.

4.5 The Map and the Territory: Levi and Ka-Tzetnik

According to Bartov (1997, 52), 'Ka-Tzetnik does what Levi ultimately reproaches himself for having been unable to accomplish, namely, he writes from the point of view of the drowned, the Mussulman, the living skeleton who no longer has a consciousness'. As we have seen, however, it would be hard to say that Ka-Tzetnik manages to describe the Muselmann's inner experience. It would be more accurate to say that his attempt not only to understand the inner world of the Muselmänner, but to find the words to describe it to the reader, crashed against the immense lacuna of the Muselmann. Looking back, with more than fifty years of hindsight, the attempt appears to have been doomed to failure from the start. What is of interest here, however, is the process itself.

The difference between Levi and Ka-Tzetnik may thus be described as follows: while Levi defines the limits within which testimony is still possible, without attempting to penetrate the lacuna, Ka-Tzetnik crashes against the Muselmann's doors. Although doomed to failure—or perhaps for that very reason—Ka-Tzetnik manages to get as close to the lacuna as humanly possible, and in so doing gives the reader a better understanding of the Muselmann's existence, or, at the very least, some notion of the territory in which the Muselmann emerged.

If we are to begin to understand the Muselmann, the lacuna of Auschwitz, I believe that both Levi and Ka-Tzetnik are necessary. While Levi draws the map and defines the boundaries, providing an objective picture of the situation, it is a bird's-eye view, an accurate description, but always from the outside. Ka-Tzetnik, on the other hand, may fail to describe the Muselmann from within, but his repeated and inevitable failures, in and of themselves, afford some measure of understanding. Ka-Tzetnik's tormented efforts to come as close to the limit as he can, recreate the territory of the crushed soul in the concentration camp. The map alone does not give us the necessary proximity, while the territory engulfs us and does not allow us to get our bearings. The combination of the two affords us greater, albeit imperfect, understanding of the Muselmann.

Notes

1. This is, in fact, the slogan (*Vorsprung durch Technik*) of the automaker Audi—a company that exploited some 16,500 slave labourers during World War II, while part of its parent company, Auto Union (est. 1932). According to an internal probe launched by Audi, 4500 Auto Union labourers perished at the Flossenbürg concentration camp in Bavaria, where they were interned.
2. For further debate, see Anidjar (2003).
3. Without going into details, I would like to point out the important distinction between the lived body (body-as-subject: *Leib*) and the dead body (body-as-object: *Körper*). For further discussion, see Ataria (2016, 2018, 2019a, c, Forthcoming).

4. Although beyond the scope of the present discussion, it is worth noting that this phrase directly echoes Heidegger.
5. Based on various dictionaries.
6. In this sense, the Muselmann is a lacuna at the heart of western culture, since 'All Western faith and good faith became engaged in this wager on representation' (Baudrillard 2006, 5).
7. I have followed Rosenthal's translation here, as it is closer to the original Italian.
8. For a preliminary phenomenological analysis, see Ataria and Gallagher (2015) and Ataria (2020).
9. To be precise, at least in some cases, the survivor seeks (is compelled) to become a witness in order to survive.
10. This is probably why many consider the poet Paul Celan the only one to have successfully given voice to the voiceless.
11. The very manner in which the question was asked shows just how judgemental the attitude towards Holocaust survivors was even at this stage. Note also the question repeated over and over again by the prosecutor Gideon Hausner, 'Why didn't you resist?' The question was rhetorical, of course.
12. This may also be termed a loss of grip (Ataria Forthcoming; Arieli and Ataria 2018; Ataria and Horovitz 2020).

References

Agamben, Giorgio. 1999. *Remnants of Auschwitz: The witness and the archive.* Trans. Daniel Heller-Roazen. New York: Zone Books.

Anidjar, G. (2003). *The Jew, the Arab: A history of the enemy.* Stanford, CA: Stanford University Press.

Arieli, Amos, and Yochai Ataria. 2018. Helplessness: The inability to know-that you don't know-how. *Philosophical Psychology* 31 (6): 948–968.

Ataria, Yochai. 2016. I am not my body, this is not my body. *Human Studies* 39 (2): 217–229.

———. 2018. *Body disownership in complex posttraumatic stress disorder.* New York: Palgrave Macmillan.

———. 2019a. When the body stands in the way: Complex posttraumatic stress disorder, depersonalization and schizophrenia. *Philosophy, Psychiatry, & Psychology* 26 (1): 19–31.

———. 2019b. Becoming nonhuman: The case study of the GULAG. *Genealogy* 3 (2): 1–27.

———. 2020. Investigating the origins of body-disownership: The case study of the Gulag. *Journal of Phenomenological Psychology* 51 (1): 44–82.

———. Forthcoming. *Consciousness in flesh.* New York: Palgrave Macmillan.

Ataria, Yochai, and Shaun Gallagher. 2015. Somatic apathy: Body disownership in the context of torture. *Journal of Phenomenological Psychology* 46 (1): 105–122.

Ataria, Yochai, and Omer Horovitz. 2020. The destructive nature of severe and ongoing trauma: Impairments in the minimal-self. *Philosophical Psychology* 34 (2): 254–276.

Bartov, Omer. 1997. Kitsch and sadism in Ka-Tzetnik's other planet: Israeli youth imagine the Holocaust. *Jewish Social Studies* 3 (2): 42–76.

Baudrillard, Jean. 2006. *Simulacra and simulation*. Trans. Sheila Faria Glaser. Ann Arbor: University of Michigan Press.

Bettelheim, Bruno. 1960. *The informed heart: Autonomy in a mass age*. Glencoe: The Free Press.

Gutman, Israel, ed. 1990. *The encyclopedia of the Holocaust*. 4 vols. New York: Macmillan.

Ka-Tzetnik. 1961. *Piepel*. Trans. Moshe M. Kohn. London: Anthony Blond.

———. 1971. *Star eternal*. Trans. Nina De-Nur. New York: Arbor House.

———. 1978. *Sunrise over hell*. Trans. Nina De-Nur. London: Corgi.

———. 1989. *Shivitti: A vision*. Trans. Eliyah Nike De-Nur and Lisa Herman. New York: Harper & Row.

LaCapra, Dominick. 2014. *Writing history, writing trauma*. Baltimore: Johns Hopkins University Press.

Levi, Primo. 1988. *The drowned and the saved*. Trans. Raymond Rosenthal. New York. Simon and Schuster.

———. 2015. *The complete works of Primo Levi*. Ed. Ann Goldstein. Various translators. 3 vols. New York: Liveright.

Levin, Itamar, ed. 2005. *Lexicon of the Holocaust* [Lexikon hasho'ah]. Tel Aviv: Yediot Aharonot, Sifre Hemed.

Ryn, Zdziław. 1990a. Between life and death: Experiences of concentration camp mussulmen during the Holocaust. *Genetic, Social, and General Psychology Monographs* 116 (1): 5–19.

———. 1990b. The evolution of mental disturbances in the concentration camp syndrome (KZ-Syndrom). *Genetic, Social, and General Psychology Monographs* 116 (1): 21–36.

Ryn, Zdziław, and Stanisław Klodzinski. 1987. An der Grenze zwischen Leben und Tod. *Eine Studie über die Erscheinung des "Muselmanns" im Konzentrationslager'*. In *Die Auschwitz-Hefte: Texte der polnischen Zeitschrift 'Przegląd lekarski' über historische, psychische und medizinische Aspekte des Lebens und Sterbens in Auschwitz*, ed. the Hamburger Institut für Sozialforschung, vol. 1, 89–154. Weinheim/Basel: Beltz.

Sofsky, Wolfgang. 1996. *The order of terror: The concentration camp*. Trans. William Templer. Princeton: Princeton University Press.

CHAPTER 5

'Writing or Life': Ka-Tzetnik Through the Prism of Semprún

The attempt to write about 'what happened there' can be a process of working through and recovery. At times, however, the process of writing not only about the death camps but from within them as well may result in a process whereby the survivor repeatedly re-enacts (acts out) death. A well-known and generally accepted point of view in the field of trauma studies is that silence comes with a heavy price (Felman and Laub 1992). That is not to say, of course, that writing necessarily offers a path to working through trauma. This chapter explores the emotional cost paid by survivors who attempt to describe the experience of prisoners in the concentration and extermination camps.

* * *

How does one write Auschwitz? This is one of the most difficult issues faced by survivors who have attempted to write about and from within Auschwitz. In view of the horror, many survivors found the task difficult, if not impossible. In the case of the concentration and extermination camps, Semprún (1997) wrote: 'It would take hours, entire seasons, an eternity of telling to come close to accounting for them all.'[1] Nevertheless, Semprún argues, the real impediment to describing the subjective experience is neither time nor scope, but the density of the experience itself. The facts, it seems, are not that hard to describe. The inner experience of the

Y. Ataria, *Primo Levi and Ka-Tzetnik*,
https://doi.org/10.1007/978-3-030-76743-3_5

concentration and extermination camp prisoner, on the other hand, is indescribable.

Immediately at the time of his liberation from the concentration camp Semprún understood that ordinary writing techniques would not suffice to recount this reality: 'All you have to do is begin. The reality is there, waiting. And the words as well. Yet I start to doubt the possibility of telling the story. Not that what we lived through is indescribable. … Only the artifice of a masterly narrative will prove capable of conveying some of the truth of such testimony' (13). This is an important assertion, the implication of which is that factual truth must be abandoned, at least to some extent, if anything essential is to be said about what happened 'there'.

The survivor's story is rooted in death and recounted from within death itself: 'Telling the story of that death right through to the end would be an endless task' (35). It seems that from a subjective perspective, no one actually survived the concentration and extermination camps, where subjective perspective itself collapsed—or, in the words of Semprún, 'I have not really survived death' (15). In the camp, death is 'the sole conceivable reality, the only true experience. Everything since then had been simply a dream' (16). Elsewhere he writes, 'It was only a dream. Life, the trees in the night, the music at Le Petit Schubert: only a dream. It had all been a dream ever since I left Buchenwald' (154), adding that 'nothing was real outside the camp, that's all. The rest was only a brief pause, an illusion of the senses, an uncertain dream. And that's all there is to say' (251). If so, Semprún wonders whether he himself is not merely the dream of one of his characters: '[I would have the impression] of being a dream myself' (16).

This oneiric quality pertains, first and foremost, to the survivor's very existence. As Kertész, who was fifteen years old when he was deported—first to Auschwitz-Birkenau and then to Buchenwald—wrote in *Fiasco* (Kertész 2011, 28): 'I suppose I never truly believed in my own existence.' In this sense, the purpose of writing is, above all, to prove to the survivor, the very fact of her or his own existence. Although Kertész asserts, 'Having got that off my chest, I can discern only one possible explanation for my stubborn passion: maybe I had started writing in order to gain my revenge on the world. To gain revenge and regain from it what it had robbed me of' (93), he is not satisfied with this explanation and offers another:

> Lacking in certainty to the degree that I was, I somehow had to convince myself that I existed after all. I responded to the preserved murder attempts—both real and symbolic—now with neurasthenic apathy, now with aggression. However, I recognized fairly quickly (I am a rational creature, after all) that I was more vulnerable than the outside world. In the end, out of weakness and impotence, as well as out of a certain desperation and a sort of vague hope, I began to write. That's it, it's done: here is the answer to my question. (94)

The feeling that life after the camp is a dream and the camp itself is the only possible reality permeates the survivor's writing and personality: 'Nothing is true except the camp, all the rest is but a dream, now and forever. Nothing is real but the smoke from the crematory of Buchenwald, the smell of burned flesh, the hunger, the roll calls in the snow, the beatings' (Semprún 1997, 236). In a similar vein, Primo Levi (2015, 397–8)—to whom Semprún constantly returns in *Literature or Life*—writes:

> It's a dream within another dream, varying in its details, unique in its substance. I am at the table with my family, or friends, or at work, or in a verdant countryside—in a serene, relaxed setting, in other words, apparently without tension and pain—and yet I feel a subtle, profound anguish, the definite sensation of a looming threat. And in fact, as the dream proceeds, little by little or brutally, each time in a different way, everything collapses and is destroyed around me, the scene, the walls, the people, and the anguish becomes more intense and more precise. Everything has now turned into chaos; I am alone at the center of a gray and murky void, and, yes, I *know* what this means, and I also know that I have always known it. I am again in the Lager, and nothing outside the Lager was true. The rest was a brief holiday, or a trick of the senses, a dream: the family, nature in flower, the house. Now this internal dream, the dream of peace, is over, and in the external dream, which continues coldly, I hear the sound of a well-known voice: a single word, not imperious, but brief and subdued. It is the dawn command of Auschwitz, a foreign word, feared and expected: get up, '*Wstawać*'.

The survivor is charged with the task of recounting death, not life. According to Semprún (1997, 52), this requires 'shedding light on reality through fiction', that is to say that one must have 'both an oeuvre and a biography'. It goes without saying that, in so doing, a survivor ceases to be a 'good witness'. Indeed, when Semprún combines fact and fiction in response to enquiries by a French soldier and two British soldiers regarding the fate of Henri Frager (leader of a French Resistance network), the French soldier has trouble understanding him: 'I could tell him that Frager was dead. He had been shot by the Germans.... On that day, I was the one who erased the name of Henri Frager from the camp's central card index.' Rather than simply relating the fact of Frager's death, however, Semprún chooses the path of fiction, which, by his own admission, undermines his credibility as a witness: 'I probably wasn't a good witness, the right kind of witness.' We cannot ignore the fact that this was a conscious decision on Semprún's part, because he believed that 'anyone could have told him about the crematory, the deaths from exhaustion, the public hangings, the torment of the Jews in the little camp' (71–2).

The prisoners knew they had a story to tell, but that doing so would be no simple task. Ultimately, in order to be listened to, a story must be well told. Semprún reports a conversation that took place in the camp a few days after liberation: 'What does that mean, "well told"?' asked one of the inmates. 'You have to tell things the way they are, with no fancy stuff!' replied another, and most of the others agreed. At this point, Semprún himself interjected: 'Telling a story well, that means: so as to be understood,' stressing that 'you can't manage it without a bit of artifice. Enough artifice to make it art!' (123). Without artifice, the simple facts are inaccessible and therefore unbelievable. Another inmate agreed with Semprún and affirmed, 'It is so unbelievable that I myself plan to stop believing it, as soon as possible!' (124), while a further participant in the discussion, a former professor at the University of Strasbourg, added:

> I imagine there'll be a flood of accounts. [...] Their value will depend on the worth of the witness, his insight, his judgment.... And then there will be documents.... Later, historians will collect, classify, analyze this material, drawing on it for scholarly works.... Everything will be said, put on record.... Everything in these books will be true ... except that they won't contain the essential truth, which no historical reconstruction will ever be able to grasp, no matter how thorough and all-inclusive it may be. [...] The other kind of understanding, the essential truth of the experience, cannot be imparted.... Or should I say, it can be imparted only through literary writing. [...] Through the artifice of a work of art, of course! [...] In any case, the documentary has its limitations, insuperable ones.... A work of fiction, then, but who would dare? [...] Perhaps there would be a literature of the camps. (124–7)

When testifying to the inconceivable, the realistic approach stumbles, because 'realism betrays this reality, which is fundamentally hostile to it' (181). The role of fiction is crucial, since through it and only through it can one reach the truth: 'Fiction that would be as illuminating as the truth, of course. That would help reality to seem true-to-life, truth to seem convincing' (165).

In December 1945, in a cinema in Locarno, Semprún unwittingly saw a newsreel with footage filmed by the Allied armies as they entered the concentration camps: 'Skeletal deportees at the end of their strength lay collapsed in bunks.... The camera's eye watched the American army's bulldozers pushing hundreds of wasted corpses into common graves.' Some of the scenes he saw had been filmed at Buchenwald, and Semprún was shocked—less by the images themselves than by 'the difference between the seen and the experienced'. Although the footage confirmed the reality of Buchenwald and was proof that it had not been a dream ('My life, therefore, was more than just a dream'), the real, factual, true images were so difficult for Semprún to watch, because he understood that the task of conveying the experience of a camp inmate was nearly impossible: 'Although the newsreel footage confirmed the truth of the actual experience (which was sometimes difficult for me to grasp and situate among my memories), at the same time these images underlined the exasperating difficulty of transmitting this truth, of making it, if not absolutely clear, at least communicable.' One of the problems, to Semprún's mind, was that the newsreel images were silent. It seems that the experience of the walking dead of the camps cannot be conveyed without the commentary of 'the Lazaruses of that long death'. Yet, as we have seen, even the survivors cannot live up to this task. Therefore, in order to communicate the experience of the camp prisoner, Semprún argues, 'one would have had to treat the documentary reality ... like the material of fiction' (198–201).

Survivors who insist on telling their stories, who refuse to offer 'simple eyewitness accounts' (127), pay a heavy price: life itself. Semprún stresses that the experience of a survivor who seeks to write about death from within the silence, or, alternatively, about life from within death, is not one of relief. On the contrary, as Semprún explains, the reason he did not write immediately after liberation in December 1945 lay not in his inability to write, but in his inability to survive writing. The cost of writing from within death was life itself:

> I possess nothing more than my death, my experience of death, to recount my life, to express it, to carry it on. I must make life with all that death. And the best way to do this is through writing. Yet that brings me back to death, to the suffocating embrace of death. That's where I am: I can live only by assuming that death through writing, but writing literally prohibits me from living. (163)

Semprún is aware of the stark contrast between himself and Levi on this point: 'While writing may have torn Primo Levi from the past, assuaging the pain of memory … it thrust me back into death, drowning me in it' (250). Kertész appears to agree with Semprún, as he writes in *Kaddish for an Unborn Child* (2004, 83–4): 'It turned out that the material oozing from my ballpoint pen, as from an infective pustule, into the entire tissue of the plan, each and every cell of it, was such, I would say, as to pathologically alter that tissue, each and every cell of it.' The reason for this contrast between Levi on the one hand and Semprún and Kertész on the other is clear: Levi does not write from within the nothingness; he does not write the world of Hurbinek—although he understands it well. Levi deals with the map and avoids the territory.

Semprún continues his line of thought and stresses how hard it is to write about the concentration camp from the perspective of the present, that is, from his own perspective, as one who, in the act of writing, is cast back into in the concentration camp:

> My stumbling block—but it's not a technical problem, it's a moral one—is that I can't manage, through writing, to get into the present, to talk about the camp in the present … so all my drafts begin before, or after, or around, but never *in* the camp … And when I finally get inside, I'm blocked, and cannot write. Overwhelmed with anguish, I fall back into nothingness: I give up … only to begin again elsewhere, some other way … And the same thing repeats itself. (Semprún 1997, 166)

On 1 May 1964, in Salzburg, when Semprún was awarded the Formentor Prize, for *The Long Voyage*, he was also given a copy of his book translated from the original French (which was not his mother tongue) into Spanish (his mother tongue). Beyond the title, however, the book was blank, because the censors of the Franco regime had not approved it. The message, to Semprún's mind, was crystal clear:

> The sign was easy to interpret, the lesson easy to draw: I had not yet accomplished anything. This book it had taken me almost twenty years to be able to write was vanishing once more, practically as soon as it had been finished. I would have to begin it again: an endless task, most likely, transcribing the experience of death. (273)

There is another message here, however. Spanish was Semprún's mother tongue, but like Jean Améry, for example, he lost the language upon which one's sense of home in the world is founded. His decision to write in French was a conscious attempt to make 'exile into a homeland' (275), since he felt that he had lost the ability to feel at home anywhere in the world: 'In short, I no longer had a native language' (ibid.). Semprún even considered rewriting the book himself, 'in Spanish, disregarding the existing translation', creating a 'different book, which you could have turned into a new French version, a whole new book!', and concluding that the book must be constantly written and rewritten, as 'the task is infinite' (275–6).

For Semprún the process of writing was one of re-enacting (acting out) the extermination, of 'refusing to live' (226). So too Ka-Tzetnik, who burnt his writings and rewrote them again and again. In 1949 or 1950, De-Nur wrote to his wife, Nina:

> It seems that I must pass through hell a second time. Apparently, I did not succeed [the first time], because I had not [yet] been sufficiently refined and purified to be worthy of touching this holy subject. Now I feel, in burning myself and immersing myself [as if in a ritual bath], after seven clean [days; a reference to the purification process of a menstruant] of sorrow and sadness, mine and yours, I am worthier of touching this subject again, and purer, having been cleansed of the dross of every earthly desire—of publicity, for example.[2] (Szeintuch 2003, 30)

There are a number of reasons that may have brought Ka-Tzetnik to burn his writings, some conscious and others unconscious.[3] In any event, the content of his books, his mode of expression, his comportment while writing, and his testimony at the Eichmann trial all support the idea that Ka-Tzetnik repeatedly re-enacted the extermination ('It seems that I must pass through hell a second time').

Ka-Tzetnik claims, ad nauseam, that the motivation behind his writing is a sacred covenant of brotherhood, forged in a gaze: 'God Give me this day the silent word, like the one Their eyes gave on Their way to the crematorium' (Ka-Tzetnik 1989, 108). The attempt to find the exact word destroys Ka-Tzetnik. He 'confesses' to Prof. Bastiaans that he is unable to find the words to tell what happened at Auschwitz[4]:

> But what can I do when I'm struck mute? I have neither word nor name for it all.... For Auschwitz there is no name other than Auschwitz. My heart will be ripped to pieces if I say, 'In Auschwitz they burned people alive!' or 'In Auschwitz people have died from starvation.' But that is not Auschwitz. People have died from starvation before, and people did burn alive before. But that is not Auschwitz. What, then, is Auschwitz? I don't have the word to express it; I don't have the name for it. Auschwitz is a primal phenomenon. I have no key to unlock it. But don't the tears of the mute speak his anguish? And don't his screams cry his distress? Don't his bulging eyes reveal the horror? I am that mute. ... How could I communicate to them the way I myself burn, searching for the word to name the look in the eyes of those who would talk through me to the crematorium, with eyes that fused with mine? (31–2)

Note the expressions that Ka-Tzetnik uses here, assuming that these are not merely empty words (by no means a trivial matter in Ka-Tzetnik's case): the word burns Ka-Tzetnik, or, alternatively, Ka-Tzetnik and the word burn together. Writing re-enacts the process of extermination. This is how Kertész (2004, 29–31), for example, describes the writing process:

> Not everyone who writes has to write, but in my case there was no getting away from the fact that I had to ... and that night had to ensue for me to see at last in the darkness, to see among other things the nature of my work, which in its essence was nothing more than digging, the continued digging of the grave that others had begun to dig for me in the air and then, simply because they did not have time to finish, hastily and without so much as a hint of diabolical mockery (far from it: just like that, casually, without so much as a look around), they thrust the tool in my hand and left me standing there to finish, as best I could, the work that they had begun. ... For my ballpoint pen is my spade, and if I look ahead, it is solely to look backwards.

At the same time, however, we must bear in mind that the process of writing is not only a process of re-enacting death. It entails an inherent paradox: deliverance from one kind of death only to suffer another. Writing is a process whereby survivors save themselves from suicide by killing themselves slowly: 'The fact that I have always sturdily, one might say radically, guarded the chattel I regard as most important (myself) … against any form of effective self-destruction that is not a decision of my own free will … of course, I am merely guarding it for another form of destruction' (58–9).

For the survivor, testimony and writing are a process of immolation and death, and not necessarily a process of healing, as Levi affirms. Indeed, echoing the famous words of the poet Paul Celan, Levi (2018, 81) writes: 'It seems too good to be true, but it is so; the widespread devaluation of the word, written and spoken, is not definitive, is not universal; something has been salvaged. Strange as it may seem, even today someone who speaks the truth will be listened to and believed.' The word, however, has the potential not only to revive, but also to destroy, and the writer must develop defence mechanisms against this tendency of the written word to become a dagger thrust deep into the flesh. This would appear to be the reason behind Ka-Tzetnik's decision to write in the third, rather than the first, person.

Notes

1. Jorge Semprún (b. Madrid, 1923—d. Paris, 2011) was a member of the Spanish Communist Party and the French Resistance. In 1943, he was arrested and tortured by the Gestapo and sent to the Buchenwald concentration camp. His experiences during this period are recounted in two books: *The Long Voyage* (*Le grand voyage*, 1963) and *What a Beautiful Sunday* (*Quel beau dimanche!*, 1980). In a further book, *Literature or Life* (*L'Écriture ou la vie*, 1994), Semprún explores various issues pertaining to deportation and traumatic memory. The title of this chapter 'Writing or Life' is a translation of the original French title of this book.
2. This passage should not necessarily be taken at face value, in light of De-Nur's own remarks about how important he is and how he is 'revealing' deep insights into himself as a writer. In general, the interviews with De-Nur—especially those published in Szeintuch's (2003) book—should be treated as expressions of a conscious intention on the author's part to create a certain mythology around himself.
3. Much of the criticism of Ka-Tzetnik appears to be based on the premise that he acted consciously. Personally, I find that it is Ka-Tzetnik's lack of self-awareness that makes him so interesting. This is, however, open to debate.
4. As noted earlier, such descriptions must be approached critically.

References

Felman, Shoshana, and Dori Laub. 1992. *Testimony: Crises of witnessing in literature, psychoanalysis, and history*. Florence: Routledge.

Ka-Tzetnik. 1989. *Shivitti: A vision*. Trans. Eliyah Nike De-Nur and Lisa Herman. New York: Harper & Row.

Kertész, Imre. 2004. *Kaddish for an unborn child*. Trans. Tim Wilkinson. New York: Vintage Books.

———. 2011. *Fiasco*. Trans. Tim Wilkinson. New York: Melville House.

Levi, Primo. 2015. *The complete works of Primo Levi*. Ed. Ann Goldstein. Various translators. 3 vols. New York: Liveright.

Levi, Primo, with Leonardo De Benedetti. 2018. *Auschwitz testimonies, 1945–1986*. Ed. Fabio Levi and Domenico Scarpa. Trans. Judith Woolf. Cambridge: Polity Press.

Semprún, Jorge. 1997. *Literature or life*. Trans. Linda Coverdale. New York: Viking.

Szeintuch, Yechiel. 2003. *Katzetnik 135633: A series of dialogues with Yechiel De-Nur* [Kemesiaḥ lefi tumo: Siḥot im yeḥiel di-nur], ed. Carrie Friedman-Cohen. Jerusalem: Ghetto Fighters' House and Dov Sadan Institute.

CHAPTER 6

Hitler, Ka-Tzetnik, and Kitsch

Ka-Tzetnik's stories are often dismissed as kitsch designed to cater to the most superficial of needs:

> In the belief that Auschwitz was a terra incognita, another planet, known to exist but unimaginable and inconceivable, Ka-Tzetnik chose[1] to render it by means of kitsch, as if relying on the commonplace and the trite could protect him and enable him to represent its hidden, unknown reality. In a certain sense, Ka-Tzetnik's adoption of kitsch was a kind of repetition compulsion—a shield against the unknown, a form of escapism, to a world of familiar, predigested language. As a rhetorical style, kitsch provides the protective cover (the aesthetic lie) that allows one to exclaim the horror of facing the negative sublime: trauma and death. Kitsch contains the cry, envelops it and enables it to exist in that form. (Dudai 2005, 138)

Similarly, Miron (1994, 200) characterizes Ka-Tzetnik as being addicted to 'kitsch and death'. According to Miron, the same addiction fuelled both his writing and his public persona—culminating in his appearance at the Eichmann trial. This is a grave accusation. Miron and those who share his criticism effectively argue that because (a) Ka-Tzetnik lacked talent as a writer, (b) his only recourse was to kitsch, resulting in (c) his portrayal of the Holocaust as pornography. In this chapter, I will try to show that Ka-Tzetnik's use of kitsch,[2] whether consciously or unconsciously, reflects his profound understanding of the Nazi extermination machine: Hitler himself, as we shall see, is a figure that exudes kitsch.

Y. Ataria, *Primo Levi and Ka-Tzetnik*,
https://doi.org/10.1007/978-3-030-76743-3_6

6.1 Hitler as a Manufacturer of Kitsch

Friedländer (1984, 14) asserts that 'Nazism's attraction lay less in any explicit ideology than in the power of emotions, images, and phantasms'. Hitler was an expert at creating kitsch on a previously (and probably subsequently) unprecedented scale. Hans-Jürgen Syberberg, director of *Hitler: A Film from Germany* (US title: *Our Hitler*), argues that 'Hitler was the greatest film maker of all times. He made the Second World War' (in Friedländer 1984, 21). Indeed, even we who know the horrors cannot resist the magnetic attraction of Nazi kitsch. It is hard to deny that Nazism possesses a kind of force, a 'voluptuous anguish and ravishing images, images one would like to see going on forever' (ibid.).

Hitlerian kitsch, claims Friedländer, is not the familiar kitsch of 'artificial flowers' (25) or strawberry-filled chocolates, but a unique kind of kitsch, rooted in death: 'This kitsch of death, of destruction, of apocalypse is a special kitsch, a representation of reality that does not integrate into the vision of ordinary kitsch' (26). As Friedländer stresses, it is kitsch predicated on an inner paradox: 'Faced with a kitsch representation of death, everyone knows that two contradictory elements are amalgamated: on the one hand, an appeal to harmony, to emotional communion at the simplest and most immediate level; on the other, solitude and terror' (27). Furthermore, Friedländer argues, this impossible juxtaposition exerts a powerful hold on all of us: 'All of us live among kitsch; we are plunged into it up to our necks. Hence the importance and the hold this type of imagery and sentiment has on us, a hold that is formed into frisson thanks to the counterpoint of death and destruction' (39). Hitler, explains Friedländer, understood both the power of kitsch and the power of death. More importantly, however, he understood the power entailed in the juxtaposition of these two opposing forces. In fact, Hitler's genius lay precisely in his ability to combine these two vectors: 'Again and again, new associations form around this juxtaposition of kitsch and death' (35).

Kitsch has the power to bring myth to life, albeit in a shallow and sentimental fashion: 'Kitsch is a debased form of myth' that 'nevertheless draws from the mythic substance—a part of its emotional impact—the death of the hero; the eternal march, the twilight of the gods' (49). Heroic death lies at the heart of Nazi ideology, as Friedländer points out: 'One couldn't insist too much on the primordial aspect of the theme of death in Nazism itself' (41). Hitler was enchanted by death, which he promoted and glorified by means of the lowest kind of kitsch. Thus, for example,

Joachim Fest recounts that Hitler 'had a distinct preference for nocturnal backdrops. Torches, pyres, or flaming wheels were continually being kindled' (42). Kitsch allowed propaganda to transform the image of death—from banal to sublime:

> The important thing is the constant identification of Nazism and death; not real death in its everyday horror and tragic banality, but a ritualized, stylized, and aestheticized death, a death that wills itself the carrier of horror, decrepitude, and monstrosity, but which ultimately and definitely appears as a poisonous apotheosis. (43)

Beyond Nazi propaganda, there is also Hitler himself, as both a mythical figure and an ordinary man:

> Everyone knows of the Führer's taste for sweets and cream cakes, for sentimental films, adventure stories and operettas. … In the eyes of the masses, Hitler appeared neither a solemn monarch nor a mysterious tyrant, neither as representative of an elite habituated to the burden of power nor as toiling servant of the state risen from the ranks. Hitler, as has been said so often, is the projection of tastes and desires most broadly accepted in his times. (67)

Hitler might be said to have been, at once, both manufacturer and consumer of kitsch. As Hitler's friend and favourite architect, Albert Speer, noted in his prison journal: 'I recall his ordering showing in the Chancellery of the films of burning London, of the sea of flames over Warsaw, of exploding convoys, and the rapture with which he watched those films' (70).[3] In light of Hitler's fondness for kitsch, it is particularly interesting to examine Ka-Tzetnik's kitsch-laden writing.

6.2 Kitsch: Approaching Truth

There is no doubt that Ka-Tzetnik employed kitsch in his books, or that the element of death is clearly present. Unlike the Nazis, however, it is generally a banal, dull, or meaningless death. Although Daniella, for example, may be a sainted figure, Ka-Tzetnik does not depict heroic or mystical death or express a hidden desire for absolute nothingness. Although certain sentences may be interpreted as conveying a sense of pleasure in death, it is almost never death for the sake of some higher purpose.

In effect, when it comes to kitsch, Ka-Tzetnik presents a picture that is almost the opposite of the one depicted by Hitler. The man who loved cream cakes used kitsch as a means to promote death as the Nazi ideal, while Ka-Tzetnik used kitsch to show just how twisted and wretched death is. Ka-Tzetnik's use of kitsch—whether consciously or unconsciously, as a matter of choice or lack of choice—attests to his profound understanding of the Nazi method.[4] The Nazi machine knew how to get the most out of kitsch, as did Ka-Tzetnik. The Nazis presented death as something sacred and messianic, while in Ka-Tzetnik's books, although the dead themselves are sainted, there is nothing holy about the manner in which they died, which is utterly wretched.

Pursuing this line of thought, in kitsch literature *justice must prevail, truth must come to light, evil must be punished, and honesty and generosity must be rewarded.* None of this happens in Ka-Tzetnik's books, on the contrary. Furthermore, a kitsch atmosphere gives us the feeling that a happy ending is imminent. In that sense, Ka-Tzetnik's writing includes an element of surprise, for if we expect any last-minute change in the plot, that would, for example, allow Moni (in the novel *Piepel*) to be saved, we will be disappointed. Moni is beaten forcefully, so that he will not suffer too long. That is his reward. His happy ending is to die outside the fence.

According to Bartov (1997, 52–3), it is Ka-Tzetnik's kitsch style of writing that allowed him to describe things that many others could not:

> Nor is his writing on horror in any way contrived (in stark contrast to his attempts to describe 'normality'), and precisely because of its wholly uninhibited, raw nature, his representation of evil is not only disturbing but in many ways annihilating of the manner in which we all desire to see and understand the interaction between humanity and the Holocaust. … Conversely, Ka-Tzetnik's anguished, at times almost insane, obsession with depravity, his wild fantasies, and his anarchic refusal to conform to any rules of the genre have barred him from gaining attention in cultures that prefer a well-told story, insist on close attention to matters aesthetic, require some moral lesson, and instinctively reject such baffling, messy, and often repelling accounts. At his best, his kitsch is of such an extraordinary nature that it penetrates the most hidden, darkest, and most repulsive recesses of the human psyche.

Ka-Tzetnik thus appears to have succeeded—not despite his style, but precisely because of it—where so many had failed. His writing, although often imbued with kitsch, manages to bring the reader to feel the territory itself. That is why I am convinced, despite the various problems posed by Ka-Tzetnik's writings and persona, of the importance of his books for our understanding of the primal experience of the prisoner—while at the camps and later.

Notes

1. Is 'chose' the right word here? I believe this is yet another example of a paper that sets out to say something about Ka-Tzetnik and is prepared to use a variety of methods to prove its original thesis while ignoring possible nuances.
2. A careful reading will show that Ka-Tzetnik's writing defies definition as kitsch. His descriptions of Jewish prostitutes, for example, are inconsistent with the idea of kitsch as 'art adapted to life' (Friedländer 1984, 25), for if 'kitsch is adapted to the tastes of the majority' (ibid.), how could Ka-Tzetnik have known in 1946 (or even late 1945) that there would be a demand among Israeli readers for such stories—as witnessed by the later commercial success of the Stalag genre of fiction? Was he so astute as to anticipate, by some thirty years, Foucault's insight that 'A whole sleazy erotic imaginary is now placed under the sign of Nazism' (Foucault 2000 [1974], 165)? In light of the above, it would be fair to say that Ka-Tzetnik has been read with systematic superficiality.
3. We also know how impressed (and enchanted) Hitler was by Lang's film, *Metropolis* (1927).
4. In this context, it is very interesting to read the following passage from Kundera's *The Unbearable Lightness of Being* (1984, 251–4): 'Those of us who live in a society where various political tendencies exist side by side and competing influences cancel or limit one another can manage more or less to escape the kitsch inquisition: the individual can preserve his individuality; the artist can create unusual works. But whenever a single political movement corners power, we find ourselves in the realm of totalitarian kitsch. When I say totalitarian, what I mean is that everything that infringes on kitsch must be banished for life: every display of individualism (because a deviation from the collective is a spit in the eye of the smiling brotherhood); every doubt (because anyone who starts doubting details will end by doubting life itself); all irony (because in the realm of kitsch everything must be taken quite seriously); and the mother who abandons her family or the man who prefers men to women, thereby calling into question the holy decree Be fruitful and multiply. In this light, we can regard the gulag as a septic tank used by totalitarian kitsch to dispose of its refuse. ... In the realm of totalitarian kitsch, all answers are given in advance and preclude any questions. It

follows, then, that the true opponent of totalitarian kitsch is the person who asks questions. A question is like a knife that slices through the stage backdrop and gives us a look at what lies hidden behind it. In fact, that was exactly how Sabina had explained the meaning of her paintings to Tereza: on the surface, an intelligible lie; underneath, the unintelligible truth showing through.'

References

Bartov, Omer. 1997. Kitsch and sadism in Ka-Tzetnik's other planet: Israeli youth imagine the Holocaust. *Jewish Social Studies* 3 (2): 42–76.

Dudai, Rina. 2005. Kitsch and trauma—A case study: *The house of dolls* by Ka-Tzetnik (Hebrew). *Mikan* 6: 125–142.

Foucault, Michel. 2000. 'Anti-retro', an interview with Pascal Bonitzer and Serge Toubiana [originally published as 'anti-retro: Entretien avec Michel Foucault', *Cahiers du Cinema* 251–2 (July–August, 1974)]. In *Cahiers du Cinema, vol. 4, 1973–1978: History, ideology, cultural struggle*, ed. David Wilson, 159–172. London: Routledge.

Friedländer, Saul. 1984. *Reflections of Nazism: An essay on kitsch and death.* Trans. Thomas Weyr. New York: Harper & Row.

Kundera, Milan. 1984. *The unbearable lightness of being.* Trans. Michael H. Heim. New York: Harper & Row.

Lang, Fritz, dir. 1927. *Metropolis.* Written by Thea von Harbou and Fritz Lang. Universum Film (UFA).

Miron, Dan. 1994. Between books and ashes (Hebrew). *Alpayim* 10: 196–224.

PART II

Primo Levi

CHAPTER 7

Levi's Suicide as a Scandal

Primo Levi died on 11 April 1987 at 10:05 in Torino, in the house where he was born and lived nearly his entire life. Although there is no absolute proof that it was suicide, few scholars doubt that Levi indeed killed himself. We should therefore say that Primo Levi *committed suicide* on 11 April 1987 at 10:05 in Torino, in the house where he was born and lived his entire life—except for 'that time'.[1] Most Levi scholars have contemplated the link between Levi's suicide and his time as a prisoner at Auschwitz. This chapter explores some of the ways in which they have sought to establish such a link (or a lack thereof).

7.1 A Travel Warning

How is it possible that Levi, the restrained and collected writer, committed suicide? Levi's suicide has led scholars from various disciplines to question their previous understanding of the man and his oeuvre, and to suggest a new approach—one that views Levi's entire life after the liberation from Auschwitz as a precursor to his suicide, and his suicide as a defining moment of his life. Indeed, for many researchers (and ordinary readers), Levi's suicide forced a paradigmatic shift. Rosenfeld (2011, 188) stresses that the 'sense of Levi as stalwart survivor was badly shaken by the news of his death', while Lang (2013, 12–13) presents the view that 'to accept the verdict of Levi's suicide projects backward a shadow on his writing as well as on his life—that it *does* alter his texts' (an approach that Lang

Y. Ataria, *Primo Levi and Ka-Tzetnik*,
https://doi.org/10.1007/978-3-030-76743-3_7

himself rejects). There are many such examples. Zertal (2002, 137), for instance, writes: 'Later, in a *delayed* act of self-destruction, Levi took his own life, making his words all too tangible.'[2] This characterization (and others like it) essentially entails two assertions, one general and the other specific: first, as Levi has 'proven', Auschwitz necessarily leads to self-destruction, and second, that Levi's own writings should be revisited in the wake of his suicide, in search of passages evincing such self-destruction. It is hard to see how such a broad generalization, regarding all survivors, could have been made had it not been for Levi's suicide, which dramatically influenced Holocaust scholarship—due to Levi's standing as one of the mythical witnesses of Auschwitz. In essence, because of the way in which Levi is perceived, a particular change (his suicide) resulted in a general change of perception: self-destruction is almost inevitable; Levi is the proof. Indeed, even if we try to avoid or deny it, Levi's suicide—or, more precisely, the nature of the connection (if any) between Auschwitz and suicide—is, in a certain sense, the point of departure for any analysis of his life and the nature of his writing.[3] This is especially true of studies that take the existence of an inherent link between mode of writing and the possibility of being 'cured' of Auschwitz (as if Auschwitz were a disease) for granted. What lies behind the anxiety and even anger engendered by Levi's suicide is the premise that Levi's writing represents a process of working through trauma, making it inconceivable that such a mode of writing would not lead to recovery but to suicide. It goes without saying that this is a rather simplistic point of departure, yet it is often the basis of current discussion. In order to understand this point, it is worth taking a step back.

Scholars who espouse the view that there are (in principle) two types of writing trauma—one that enables working through and hence processes of recovery, and one that compulsively repeats or acts out the trauma—often claim that there is an inherent link between the mode of writing and the way in which survivors live their lives. While according to the prevailing theory (henceforth, the Theory), writing rooted in working through allows the survivor to undergo processes of recovery, writing driven by a compulsion to act out the traumatic event prevents the survivor from experiencing such processes. For those who espouse the Theory, the fact that Levi's writing is a paragon of working through and recovery means that his suicide is not merely a mystery; it is a veritable disaster. If the Theory is unable to explain a writer such as Levi, then perhaps it is entirely without merit. The Theory is equally challenged, however, at the opposite end of the spectrum: Ka-Tzetnik, who was tormented and whose writing compulsively acts out the process of extermination (as detailed in the first part of this book), should have committed suicide. In this sense, the suicide of Tadeusz Borowski in 1951, at the age of twenty-eight, only three days after the birth of his daughter, is practically welcomed (from a theoretical perspective), in light of the strong link between the compulsive repetition of his writing and the way in which he ended his life—inhaling gas from a stove.[4] Ezrahi (1995, 124–5) expresses this idea a little differently, comparing the ways in which the deaths of the two writers are approached: 'The chasm between these two models … constitutes a double paradigm…. Levi is allowed to have taken his life because of his wife's nagging or his mother's illness or a love affair or experimental antidepressants or even a slip on the stairs.' On the other hand, Ezrahi stresses, 'Borowski … must fulfill the script by remaining forever trapped within the electrified barbed wire, his stories a form of "repetition compulsion" and his head in the oven a final enactment of his incompleted fate in the gas chambers of Auschwitz.' In this sense, and only in this sense, Ka-Tzetnik's natural death is at odds with the Theory.

In light of the above, I have chosen Levi's suicide as the point of departure for this part of the book, although fully aware of the problems this raises. As Ezrahi (125) writes:

> Those who view even Levi's suicide under the sign of Auschwitz have returned to his writings to show that a kind of self-deception prevailed in the strategies of distancing that characterize much of his creative work. In taking issue with such an interpretation I do not mean, of course, to submit the reductionist claim that suicide was a stranger to Levi. I am, rather, insisting on the ambiguities of his treatment of it in his writings as well as warning against reading his last moments back into a lifetime of writing such that it would abolish the distances he built, a bridge as well as a barrier of words, between the survivors and the death-world.

The attempt to link Levi's suicide unequivocally to Auschwitz is also problematic on another level, unrelated to Levi himself. Suicide cannot be reduced to a narrow deduction, whereby A led to B. Suicide is always a complex event that cannot be reduced to a single cause: 'Many are the thoughts in a person's heart' (Prov. 19:21).

Having said that, one of the reasons I have allowed myself to use such a problematic and provocative point of departure is that Levi himself does so—for example, in his analysis of Jean Améry. Levi describes an incident in which Améry chose to strike back at someone who had humiliated him—an incident to which Levi ascribes considerable significance:

> A man who gets into fistfights with the whole world regains his dignity but pays a very high price because he is certain of his own defeat. Like every suicide, Améry's, in Salzburg in 1978, admits a nebula of explanations but, in retrospect, the episode of his taking on the Pole provides one interpretation (Levi 2015, 2510).

If Levi takes the liberty of offering an explanation for Améry's suicide, we too may try to suggest an explanation for Levi's suicide—in the knowledge that any explanation will necessarily be partial and that the process is more important than the conclusion.

7.2 An Attempt to Dissociate Levi's Suicide from Auschwitz

Lang (2013) seeks to dissociate Levi's suicide from his experiences at Auschwitz. His motivation is clear: to preserve Levi's message as a human being who survived Auschwitz *as* a human being—first and foremost in his own eyes (in the coming chapters we will see how Levi himself wavered in this position). Many believe that Levi's suicide undermined his entire oeuvre, for obvious reasons: Levi exemplifies the therapeutic writing process rooted in working through. If in fact he did take his own life, then the sterile Theory would no longer apply to one of its most prominent subjects. Indeed, we cannot ignore the fact that Levi's writing is often cited as the epitome of therapeutic writing, devoid of pathos or unconscious repetition of the extermination process. Rosenfeld (2011, 187–8) explains this point as follows:

> Among all those who had survived the death camps and gone on to write about them, Levi seemed to be one of the few who had achieved some permanent measure of artistic control over his experience. His writings never shrank from a direct confrontation with the horrors of Nazism, but at the same time they were conspicuously free of outrage or self-pity, of overt expressions of bitterness, emotional fury, or uncontained rage… Although he had plenty to be angry about, Levi had reached an unusual level of intellectual and moral poise in his books. It seemed indeed that he had come through his ordeal and, in his person as well as in his writings, showed that

it was possible for the civilized values of intelligence and humane feeling to survive the Nazi assault against them. This sense of Levi as stalwart survivor was badly shaken by the news of his death.

Another possible explanation of Levi's suicide, consistent with the dichotomy of writing that works through versus writing that acts out the trauma (the Theory), is that we had misread him, and his writing was never in fact part of a process of working through, but more of a compulsion, like that of Ka-Tzetnik. His suicide would thus have been 'inevitable'.

Lang (2013) examines a number of factors that may have contributed to Levi's suicide. The constant attention and care required by his mother and his mother-in-law weighed on him and limited the control he was able to exercise over his life—and this at the height of his acclaim as an author. He himself suffered from a number of physical ailments—foot ulcers (vestiges from Auschwitz), shingles, a bladder blockage that required surgery—as well as anxiety that his memory might fail. Levi was also plagued by severe depression that proved resistant to medication (more on this in Chap. 11). It is in this context that he remarked to Ruth Feldman, the American translator of his poetry: 'In certain respects, it's even worse than Auschwitz' (Lang 2013, 4). Lang further contends that 'individual issues among them might have sufficed as causes or reasons for suicide.... And surely, if explanations by means of sufficient cause *ever* explain suicide, the aggregate of factors cited would suffice even without the additional reference to Auschwitz' (3–4). Lang thus dismisses Elie Wiesel's famous, superficial but possibly accurate remark, which reflected the thoughts of many: 'Levi died at Auschwitz forty years later.'[5] If this is true, then the process that Levi himself describes in *The Drowned and the Saved*, the passage from survivor to witness, collapses. Writing was not a liberation for Levi and may even have been a prison.

Lang argues that scholars who refuse to accept Levi's suicide are not motivated by rational considerations, but by a desire to preserve Levi's image as an exemplary survivor, a human being who refused to sink into victimhood, and as the ultimate witness. They argue, inter alia, that a chemist like Levi could have found an easier (and less brutal) way to kill himself—indicating that his death was not suicide, but an accidental fall. According to Lang, this argument was occasioned by the idea that 'for Levi to commit suicide would diminish or contradict too much else in his life and work, what he had lived through and for. An implication of this view is a contention that he *should not* have done it or, more strongly, that he *could not* have done it' (5, emphasis in the original); and 'to accept the verdict of Levi's suicide projects backward a shadow on his writing as well as on his life—that it *does* alter his texts' (12–13, emphasis in the original). Lang thus tries to uphold Levi's message and 'philosophy' (as he terms Levi's thinking) without denying the apparent fact of his suicide. Lang reasons that Levi was five feet five and the banister on the landing was three feet high, making it hard to understand how he could have fallen. The approach that Lang takes is in keeping with Levi's own scientific mindset: if the facts show that Levi could not have fallen, one can only infer that he took his own life.

Lang's struggle to accept the conclusion that Levi committed suicide while dissociating his suicide from Auschwitz is more complex: 'Obviously, Auschwitz *together* with the factors mentioned would have been sufficient reason; but the assembly of factors *without* Auschwitz would also by such common standards as apply have sufficed' (10). Lang appears unable to accept Levi's death as a delayed result of Auschwitz. The interesting and important question is *why*? Paradoxically, the most likely explanation of Lang's need to dissociate Levi's suicide from his experiences at Auschwitz is rooted in the same rationale that led others to reject the idea that Levi killed himself, out of fear that it would alter his philosophy, with far-reaching implications. Lang too, it seems, feared that Levi's suicide would cast a dark shadow on the entirety of his philosophy, perhaps even undermining his central messages. It is worth noting that some of Levi's biographers (Angier 2002; Thomson 2003)—those who do not dissociate his suicide from Auschwitz—suggest (in fact are almost tempted to assert) another possibility: Levi's writing about Auschwitz merely postponed his suicide. In other words, had it not been for his writing, Levi would have taken his own life much sooner, perhaps immediately after liberation. Writing allowed him to put off his suicide to a later date. Put more simply and bluntly, Levi survived to testify and when he completed that task he killed himself. I find this a somewhat romantic (and dangerous) idea that some of us might want to believe. At the same time, however, it is very difficult to prove. This explanation appears to stem, once again, from our inability to accept the fact that Levi's life was complex. He was not merely a paragon of working through. There were a variety of forces at work within his soul, and some were destructive.

As we have seen in the context of the Theory, the link between writing and life, or between writing and death, is practically taken for granted, without employing any real critical thinking. In order to dissociate Levi's suicide from Auschwitz, Lang goes a step further, attempting to show that Levi did not necessarily become a writer as a result of his experiences at Auschwitz. In asking whether Levi would in fact have become a writer had he not been deported to Auschwitz, Lang conjures up his pre-war attempts at writing: 'The back-story of Levi as a writer is more substantial than the impression he conveys. At least some of what he wrote as a student proved to be more than diversionary or casual jottings. … He wrote versions in these pre-war years of two of the "elements" ("Lead" and "Mercury") that later appeared in *The Periodic Table*' (56). Lang even expresses doubts regarding Levi's assertion that his first book *If This Is a Man* 'lacked any literary intention'.[6] Lang thus seeks to portray Levi's philosophy as independent of Auschwitz. The result is a nuanced approach that asserts the influence of Levi's experiences as a prisoner in the Lager on his philosophy and writing while maintaining that his work cannot be reduced to those experiences—no easy task, especially in light of Levi's last book, *The Drowned and the Saved*, published about a year before his death.

7.3 Rereading Levi in Light of His Suicide

Cynthia Ozick (1989) argues that, contrary to Levi's previous works, *The Drowned and the Saved* is full of fury and rage—rage that is, like that of Améry, almost uncontrollable. What is more, Ozick suggests, this rage ultimately became self-destructive, that is, directed at Levi himself. It is possible that Levi, in his final volume, surrendered to his instincts, abandoning his restrained and ironic style, unleashing a frontal attack (like Améry, many would be tempted to add). In a sense, Ozick believes that Levi's suicide was a product of his outburst in this book. If we accept this line of thought, it is hard to avoid the conclusion that, at least in some senses, Levi's suicide and his final work, in conjunction with one another, symbolize the victory of the Nazi system even over someone we had believed to be resistant.

Few agree with Ozick's approach, but her voice is important, as it offers a precise expression of the Theory or the link between writing and life. Indeed, prior to *The Drowned and the Saved*, Levi may be said to have written in order to live, while in this final work, it is writing that leads to his death. Levi's correspondence with Heinz Riedt, the German translator of *If This Is a Man* further supports the theory that his last book, *The Drowned and the Saved*, was also the coda of his life. In a letter to Riedt from May 1960, Levi states that, in a sense, the purpose of his writing was 'to "talk back" to the Kapo who wiped his hand on my shoulder' (Levi 2015, 2541).

The letters that Levi received from Germans and chose to publish in *The Drowned and the Saved* show a refusal on the part of his correspondents to truly listen. If the purpose of the German translation of *If This Is a Man* was to point a loaded gun at the Germans, the indifference with which it was received ultimately led to Levi's pointing that very same gun at himself. That indifference also led to the change reflected in *The Drowned and the Saved*. The result, according to Ozick's disturbing argument, was Levi's suicide.

Rosenfeld (2011, 192), on the other hand, is not of the opinion that *The Drowned and the Saved* is all fury and rage: '*The Drowned and the Saved* is a more forceful book than any Levi had published previously, but in my reading of it, it does not, in fact, show us the author enraged.' Nevertheless, Rosenfeld appears to agree with Ozick more than he would care to admit: 'There is an emphatic note of grievance that runs through the essays in this collection, *but* there is also *more than a little self-criticism*. Levi is hard on himself in this book, indeed, much too hard.' The word 'but' in the above sentence conceals more than it reveals. What Rosenfeld seems to be saying is as follows: 'There is an emphatic note of grievance that runs through the essays in this collection, ~~but~~ *and* there is also more than a little self-criticism.' Rosenfeld thus, perhaps unintentionally, goes even further than Ozick. He suggests that Levi interprets Améry's suicide (which will be discussed at length in the next chapter) as the result of self-accusation and rage directed inwards rather than at the murderers. In other words, according to Rosenfeld, Levi's gun, like that of Améry, was not aimed at the Germans, but, a priori, at himself, due to self-accusation.

Rosenfeld argues that we cannot rule out the possibility that Levi himself died of 'the survivor's disease',[7] beset with 'guilt, shame, self-accusation, futility and failure' (202). To this we must add Levi's feeling of having been thwarted by his own waning strength and the indifference of his target readership (i.e., the German public), ultimately leaving him with the sense—despite all he had written—of having been silenced.

* * *

We will probably never be able to say with certainty how Primo Levi died. Was it suicide? And if it was suicide, was it brought on by depression unrelated to Auschwitz, as Lang claims, or did he die in Auschwitz and only completed the process forty years later (as Wiesel suggests)?

Should his suicide affect our understanding of his writing and his personality? Did he kill himself out of a sense of guilt? Was Levi's suicide an act of courage by a man who wished to die liberated? Did Levi commit suicide in order to send us a message?

There are no answers to these questions. Levi appears to have taken his own life, and it is not at all certain that it was not as a result of the depression from which he had suffered over the course of the preceding months—not necessarily because of his experiences at Auschwitz. That being said it is hard not to rethink Levi's writings in light of his suicide.

These topics will be explored in greater depth in the coming chapters. Despite the impossibility of drawing clear conclusions, I believe (or at least hope) that the process itself can teach us a great deal, not only about Levi's life, death, and writing but also about the tremendous difficulty faced by victims of extreme trauma who attempt to testify to their experiences, to speak about that which may not be spoken and to give it voice.

Notes

1. As it is termed by Lyotard, in *Heidegger and "the Jews"* (1990).
2. This sentence does not appear in the English edition of Zertal's *Death and the Nation* (English title: *Israel's Holocaust and the Politics of Nationhood*).
3. Thus, for example, Thomson's (2003) biography of Levi begins with his suicide, as does Lang's *Primo Levi: The Matter of a Life* (2013). The decision to begin a book about Levi with his suicide is undeniably significant, even if the author's intention is to object to the reduction of Levi to his suicide—a position clearly taken by Lang.
4. Borowski was a non-Jewish Polish prisoner at Auschwitz, member of the Kanada Kommando, whose best-known story, 'This Way for the Gas, Ladies and Gentlemen' (1976) was first published in 1946, soon after his liberation.
5. A conference on Levi at the Israel Academy of Sciences opened with this superficial statement.
6. A careful reading of Levi's interviews offers numerous indications that Levi himself recognized this.
7. What an odd use of the word 'disease', as if it were some sort of angina. In this context, it is worth recalling an ironic remark made by Levi in 1961: 'And for critical diseases, and also for those that are not critical but incurable—such as hunger oedema, which is universal—there is a single but radical medicine, and everyone knows it. This is "the chimney", as it is simply called: it is the oven at Birkenau' (Levi 2018, 98).

References

Angier, Carole. 2002. *The double bond: Primo Levi, a biography*. New York: Farrar, Straus and Giroux.

Borowski, Tadeusz. 1976. *This way for the gas, ladies and gentlemen*. Trans. Barbara Vedder. New York: Penguin.

DeKoven Ezrahi, Sidra. 1995. Representing Auschwitz. *History and Memory* 7 (2): 121–154.

Lang, Berel. 2013. *Primo Levi: A matter of a life*. New Haven: Yale University Press.

Levi, Primo. 2015. *The complete works of Primo Levi*. Ed. Ann Goldstein. Various translators. 3 vols. New York: Liveright.

Levi, Primo, with Leonardo De Benedetti. 2018. *Auschwitz testimonies, 1945–1986*. Ed. Fabio Levi and Domenico Scarpa. Trans. Judith Woolf. Cambridge: Polity Press.

Lyotard, Jean François. 1990. *Heidegger and "the Jews"*. Trans. Andreas Michel and Mark S. Roberts. Minneapolis: University of Minnesota Press.

Ozick, Cynthia. 1989. Primo Levi's suicide note. In *Metaphor and memory*, 34–48. New York: Knopf.

Rosenfeld, Alvin H. 2011. *The end of the Holocaust*. Bloomington: Indiana University Press.

Thomson, Ian. 2003. *Primo Levi: A life*. New York: Henry Holt and Company.

Zertal, Idith. 2002. *Death and the nation: History memory politics* [Ha'umah vehamavet: Historiyah zikaron politikah]. Or Yehuda: Dvir.

CHAPTER 8

Améry and Levi: Hostility Disguised as Admiration

While Levi's suicide was a scandal, Améry's suicide was reasonable, almost necessary (that is, if we accept the Theory—that writing generated by acting out can lead to loss of self). Indeed, Améry would have been the first to sign a declaration that *no one wants survivors of his kind*. The difference between Levi and Améry is clear. For example, it is hard to imagine Levi writing a sentence such as 'I speak as a victim and examine my resentments' (Améry 1980, 63). Moreover, it seems that Améry (1999) believed that, sometimes, suicide—perhaps only suicide—can make us human. It is hard to see Levi agreeing with such a statement (although, as we shall see, he may have fully embraced the idea in the end). In any event, the open dialogue between Levi and Améry demands a closer examination of the link between their suicides.

* * *

The original German title of Améry's *At the Mind's Limits* (1980)—*Jenseits von Schuld und Sühne. Bewältigungsversuche eines Überwältigten* (Beyond Guilt and Atonement: Attempts to Overcome by One Who Was Overcome)—is symbolic of his eventual absolute defeat:

> In almost all situations in life where there is bodily injury there is also the expectation of help; the former is compensated by the latter. But with the first blow from a policeman's fist, against which there can be no defense and

Y. Ataria, *Primo Levi and Ka-Tzetnik*,
https://doi.org/10.1007/978-3-030-76743-3_8

> which no helping hand will ward off, a part of our life ends and it can never again be revived. (29)

Améry believes, 'Whoever was tortured, stays tortured. Torture is ineradicably burned into him' (34). To Améry's mind, torture never really ends: 'It was over for a while. It still is not over. Twenty-two years later I am still dangling over the ground by dislocated arms, panting, and accusing myself. In such an instance there is no "repression"' (36). And since torture is ongoing, one can never recover.[1] In fact, the more time passes, the more the wound becomes infected: 'He … has had to learn that it was not a wound that was inflicted upon him, one that will scar over with the ticking of time, but rather that he is suffering from an insidious disease that is growing worse with the years' (57). Indeed, when one reads Améry, his suicide seems like the natural continuation of his existential state, as a 'dead man on leave' (86) or a terminal patient. In the words of Imre Kertész (2004, 77), 'The disease my wife's mother had suffered from was, in reality, Auschwitz itself, and there is no cure for Auschwitz.'

Améry and Levi were both Auschwitz survivors, and although Levi did not remember Améry, it seems that they were housed in the very same barracks. Améry accuses Levi of having 'forgiven'. Levi, for his part, tries to explain not only that the accusation itself is false, but that it could not be otherwise, as he himself categorically rejects the possibility of forgiveness: 'I do not know of any human actions that can undo a wrong' (Levi 2015, 2511). The very fact that Levi felt the need to defend himself against the accusation, however, shows just how grave it was. The disagreement between Levi and Améry was not limited to the subject of forgiveness, atonement, and understanding. Careful reading reveals a deep-seated (albeit well concealed) hostility between the two.

Améry and Levi were both educated professionals, but that did not mean that they suffered a similar fate: 'Certainly, there were also differences. In the camp chosen here as an example, chemists, for instance, were employed in their profession, as was my barracks mate Primo Levi from Turin, who wrote the Auschwitz book *If That Be a Man*' (Améry 1980, 3). This sentence is filled with tension. The fact that Améry notes that there were differences is not incidental. There are always differences, and those differences, in the context of the camp were, presumably, a matter of life and death (and Levi would be the first to admit that). After nine months in the camp,[2] Levi began to work in his profession, in a laboratory indoors, while Améry worked as an unskilled labourer, 'who had to do his job in the open—which meant in most cases that the sentence was already passed on him' (ibid.). Améry thus distinguishes himself from Levi: although both were professionals and both understood German (with the significant difference that it was the former's mother tongue), Améry was at the bottom or very close to the bottom of the food chain (i.e., just above the Mussulman), unlike Levi—at least by Améry's account. This sentence also reveals the rage directed, within the totalitarian framework of the concentration camp, not against the oppressor but against one's fellow prisoners. In this sense, the dialogue between Améry and Levi is steeped in the laws of the camp. Améry seems to be saying to Levi: *yes, we were both there, but we did not share the same experience; I survived, but I was still one of the 'drowned'.*[3]

Thus, according to Améry, although Levi was *there*, in Auschwitz, he did not sink low enough; he was not one of the drowned. It is, in fact, a kind of inverse hierarchy of holiness: the lower one sank, the holier, more perceptive, enlightened, and insightful they became—with regard to the camp in particular, and society and humanity in general. Levi was, of course, a prisoner at Auschwitz and could write about his experiences there, but he never reached rock-bottom and was therefore insufficiently enlightened and incapable of comprehending the Nazi system. Only the drowned can write Auschwitz. As we have seen, Levi himself accepts this principle, which he repeats numerous times throughout his works, beginning with his first book, *If This Is a Man*.

Améry claims that, as an intellectual, he suffered more than others in the camp: 'After a certain time there inevitably appeared something that was more than mere resignation and that we may designate as an acceptance not only of the SS logic but also of the SS system of values' (11). The reference appears to be to 'a tragic dialectic of self-destruction' (10), as a result of which the tortured developed a sense of admiration for the torturer:

> With heart and soul they went about their business, and the name of it was power, dominion over spirit and flesh, orgy of unchecked self-expansion. I also have not forgotten that there were moments when I felt a kind of wretched admiration for the agonizing sovereignty they exercised over me. For is not the one who can reduce a person so entirely to a body and a whimpering prey of death a god or, at least, a demigod?

In Améry's resentment-filled world, he is little more than an occupational accident, or as Kertész describes Köves in *Fiasco* (2011, 125–6):

> He had lived a certain kind of life, stumbled into certain situations, ditched his choices; and finally the colours of failure had emerged out of it all, it had been impossible to deny it any more. It may have begun at birth—or no, rather with his death, or to be more accurate, his rebirth. For Köves had survived his own death [in Auschwitz]; at a certain moment in time when he ought to have died, he did not die, although everything had been made ready for that, it was an organized, socially approved, done deal, but Köves had simply been unwilling to satisfy the circumstances, was unable to withstand the natural instinct for life which was working inside him, not to speak of the good luck on offer, so therefore—defying all rationality—he had stayed alive. Because of that he had been subsequently dogged constantly by a painful sense of provisionality, like someone who is only waiting in a temporary hiding place to be called to account for his negligence.

Améry (1980) demands that history be written without forgetting the victims and without ignoring rage and resentment. Améry's demands are radical (and it remains to be seen whether he lived up to his own standards). For example, he calls upon young people who were born or came of age after the war to repudiate the previous generation:

> You don't want to listen? Listen anyhow. You don't want to know to where your indifference can again lead you and me at any time? I'll tell you. What happened is no concern of yours because you didn't know, or were too young, or not even born yet? You should have seen, and your youth gives you no special privilege, and break with your father. (96)

Améry is up to his neck in resentment, 'But no one wants to relieve me of it, except the organs of public opinion-making, which buy it. What dehumanized me has become a commodity, which I offer for sale' (80). He thus presents the pitiful state of the survivor, forever trapped in his victimhood: ignored and silenced at first, and then, when he is finally heard, he feels like a prostitute selling her own flesh—that is, still a victim.

Améry is a survivor who has lost everything: identity, homeland, language, and body. Even in his own eyes (some would say *especially* in his own eyes), he is nothing more than a stain—someone for whom everyone is waiting to disappear. Because he is also an intellectual, however, Améry ultimately accepts this dialectic, thereby becoming an absolute victim—which is precisely what makes the suffering of the intellectual at Auschwitz unique (from Améry's perspective). Moreover, the moment the dialectic is accepted, in a totalitarian world in which one is compelled to follow every thought down to its final consequence (Koestler 1952), his suicide is inevitable. In a similar vein, Kertész (2011, 217) writes:

> In the room where they run through the list of names, from time to time, and they reach my name, which is quite soon, given that my initial is B, someone will cry out: "What! Is he still around?! Let's get rid of him." His colleague will just wave that aside, saying, "Why bother?! He'll snuff it of his own accord anyway!"

This seems to describe Améry's situation perfectly: one who was, at least to his own mind, living on borrowed time: 'To be a Jew, that meant for me, from this moment on, to be a dead man on leave, someone to be murdered, who only by chance was not yet where he properly belonged; and so it has remained, in many variations, in various degrees of intensity, until today' (Améry 1980, 86). Améry's identity as a Jew is wholly negative, having thoroughly internalized the other's gaze: 'The antisemite forced the Jew into a situation in which he permitted his enemy to stamp him with a self-image…[4] All of Germany—but what am I saying!—the whole world nodded its head in approval of the undertaking, even if here and there with a certain superficial regret' (86–7). Thus, according to Améry, to be a Jew is to walk the earth 'like a sick man with one of those ailments that cause no great hardships but are certain to end fatally' (95). As a Jew, he asserts, 'Every day anew I lose my trust in the world' (94).

Améry insists that it is not the sanity of the victims that should be questioned. Rather, it is the world that has gone mad and they alone have maintained their sanity. At the same time, however, the victims cannot escape the consequences of the world's insanity. Améry is the absolute victim, sacrificed every day on the altar—with a certain passion, it must be said. Despite this fact, or precisely because of it, he is able to see the world with lucid clarity.

To return to the dialogue between Levi and Améry, Levi (2015, 2503) refers to Améry as 'a potential friend and a privileged interlocutor'. He describes Améry's life as one that 'knew neither peace nor the quest for peace' (ibid.) and attributes his suicide to a problem of identity: 'For the young Hans, a returning Jew, to be Jewish is simultaneously impossible and obligatory. This is where the rupture begins that pursues him until death and ultimately provokes it' (2504).[5]

A sensitive point is the time they spent in the same barracks. Améry had already been there a number of months at the time of Levi's arrival. Levi writes as follows:

> Our memories of the lower depths are very similar in physical details, but they diverge on a curious particular. While I have always maintained that I preserve a complete and indelible memory of Auschwitz, I have forgotten him. He says he remembers me, although he had me confused with Carlo Levi.... He even claims that we spent a few weeks in the same barrack, and that he hasn't forgotten me because there were so few Italians, which made us a rarity; and also because during my last two months in the Lager I was largely able to practice my profession as a chemist, an even greater rarity. (2505)

Although Levi's attitude to Améry is generally positive, there is tension in his every sentence—even in the way he introduces Améry as 'young Hans ... a Jew'. Levi stresses that despite his excellent memory, he does not remember Améry, while Améry remembers him. Levi leaves this as a cold fact, merely informing the reader that Améry had actually confused him, as others had (something he addresses in *Lilith and Other Stories* [1360]), with another Levi—the writer Carlo Levi. Levi, here, seems to offer an explanation (or alibi, if you will) of the fact that Améry remembered him but he did not remember Améry.

The tension increases when Levi wryly observes: 'Unlike Améry and others, however, I felt only moderately humiliated by manual labor,' adding upon reflection: 'Obviously I was not yet "intellectual" enough. What was wrong with it, anyway?' (2508). In this passage, which is pure, surgical irony, Levi appears to accuse Améry/Mayer, as he calls him (disparagingly?), of having created unnecessary drama around the question of the intellectual in Auschwitz. In a sense, beneath the surface, Levi wonders whether Améry's life as an intellectual was in fact so exceptional and whether his approach was not in fact an attempt to create a distinct elite—a German elite, once again.

Levi stresses that Améry, as a German intellectual, had an important advantage: understanding the German language. Although it is true, as Améry himself points out, that he was pained by the degradation of his mother tongue, in the context of the camp, he had a tremendous advantage that cannot be ignored: 'We realized that knowledge of German was a dividing line. Those of us who understood them, and responded articulately, were able to establish the semblance of a human relationship' (2474). Therefore, 'His [Améry's] suffering was different from that of us speakers of other languages, who were reduced to the condition of deaf-mutes. His suffering, if I may, was more spiritual than physical' (2509).

Levi argues that his suffering was worse than Améry's, due to his complete foreignness: 'The way we experienced incommunicability was much more radical. I am referring in particular to the Italian, Yugoslav, and Greek deportees.... For us Italians, the impact with the language barrier began even before deportation, dramatically, and while we were still in Italy' (2474). Levi further distinguishes the Italians from the other groups:

> As Italian Jews we felt especially defenceless. Along with the Greeks we were the lowest of the low, and in some ways we were worse off than the Greeks because they were at least used to discrimination, there was a long history of anti-Semitism in Salonika and many of them were old hands, had developed hardened shells, through their contacts with other Greeks. But the Italians, so used to being treated as equals of all other Italians, had no shield, we were as naked as eggs without shells. (Levi 2001, 229)

Levi's criticism is delicate. He generally expresses understanding for Améry's linguistic loss, yet, within the material world, in the camp, it was an incontrovertible fact that knowing German conferred an enormous advantage. Indeed, Améry's very survival may have been due to his knowledge of German. Levi goes on, however, to deliver a scathing message, well hidden within parentheses:

> By nature, the intellectual (the German intellectual, allow me to add to his formulation) tends to become complicit with Power and therefore to sanction it. He tends to follow in the footsteps of Hegel and deify the State, any State: the mere fact of existing justifies its existence. (Levi 2015, 2517)

It is hard to imagine a more serious accusation. Levi claims, albeit indirectly, that Améry/Mayer's suffering is not the suffering of any intellectual, but the unique suffering of a *German* intellectual—with far-reaching implications. Améry describes how he learned to hit back, but this was by no means a radical transformation. His world had been and remained that of the dialectic of Hegel—one of the intellectual forebears of modern

Germany—entailing the worship of power for its own sake. The obvious (and disturbing) conclusion is that Améry's suffering stemmed not only from the actions of the Germans, but from his own inability to change his inner world, imbued as it was with German culture. Améry committed suicide because he 'traded blows' with Germany, but since he himself was Germany he was, in effect, trading blows with himself. Indeed, Améry recounts that any homesickness he felt was tainted by self-hatred. Améry never managed to dissociate from the German constellation of values and failed to do what he demanded of all Germans—dissociate from the father—which is why he killed himself.

To return to Ozick's claim that Levi, in *The Drowned and the Saved* trades blows with the German people, despite his famous assertion: 'I ask for justice, but I am personally incapable of throwing punches or answering a blow with a blow' (2511), it must be said that Levi was not German but Italian. Therefore, when it comes to trading blows with the German people, there can be no comparison between Levi's experiences and those of Améry. Ozick's argument thus loses its force.

From Levi's perspective, Améry was and remained a German, which is why he refers to him as 'Hans Mayer, alias Jean Améry' or 'Améry/Mayer'. When Améry, as a German, trades blows with the German people, it is himself he cannot forgive and with whom he trades blows. In effect, Améry and Mayer struggle with one other. As in the short story 'Description of a Struggle', by Kafka, the struggle is internal. Levi and Améry thus differ significantly: the process that Améry undergoes stems, inter alia, from his strong identification with the Germans—a fact over which he has no control, as he himself is an integral part of German culture (in contrast to his complete lack of identification with his Jewish roots—which were, in fact, practically non-existent).[6] Levi was not raised a German, and to the extent that he felt anything at all towards the 'German people', it was as an external entity rather than as part of an inner struggle or a struggle against the father. Améry's experience—not only as someone raised within German culture, but as someone who was tortured by the Gestapo, in addition to being imprisoned in Auschwitz—thus diverges from that of Levi. Although the end result may have been the same, the causes were different.

In conclusion, although attempts to compare the suicides of Améry and Levi may be interesting, even enlightening, they do not reveal the reason for Levi's suicide. In the next chapter, I will try to go a step further in unravelling this mystery, by examining the way in which Levi chose to end his life: a jump that is a fall that is a jump.

Notes

1. For further debate, see Ataria (2020, 2018, 2019), Ataria and Neria (2013), and Ataria and Horovitz (2020).
2. All too often, Améry seems to forget the period in which Levi did not work indoors.
3. Améry aims a similar barb at Hannah Arendt, arguing that it is not evil that is banal, but Arendt's characterization of it as such:

   > And the enormous perception at a later stage, one that destroys all abstractive imagination, makes clear to us how the plain, ordinary faces finally become Gestapo faces after all, and how evil overlays and exceeds banality. For there is no 'banality of evil,' and Hannah Arendt, who wrote about it in her Eichmann book, knew the enemy of mankind only from hearsay, saw him only through the glass cage... For the tortured, the torturer is solely the other... As a start, one can take the view that they were merely brutalized petty bourgeois and subordinate bureaucrats of torture. But it is necessary to abandon this point of view immediately if one wishes to arrive at an insight into evil that is more than just banal... My boys at Breendonk contented themselves with the cigarette and, as soon as they were tired of torturing, doubtlessly let old Schopenhauer be. But this still does not mean that the evil they inflicted on me was banal. (25, 34–5)

   Améry thus establishes a hierarchy of suffering: some suffered less than others and some suffered more. Although Arendt was interned in a camp in France, her experience, albeit as a Jew without a home in the world, clearly did not resemble that of survivors of Auschwitz.
4. This statement reveals the profound influence of Sartre on Améry.
5. For an extensive discussion of this subject, see Ataria (2017).
6. At least according to the myth that Améry seeks to construct. We know today that this characterization is not entirely accurate. See Heidelberger-Leonard (2010).

References

Améry, Jean. 1980. *At the mind's limits: Contemplations by a survivor on Auschwitz and its realities.* Trans. Sidney Rosenfeld and Stella P. Rosenfeld. Bloomington: Indiana University Press.

———. 1999. *On suicide: A discourse on voluntary death*. Trans. John D. Barlow. Bloomington: Indiana University Press.

Ataria, Yochai. 2017. *The structural trauma of western culture: Toward the end of humanity*. New York: Palgrave Macmillan.

———. 2018. *Body disownership in complex posttraumatic stress disorder*. New York: Palgrave Macmillan.

———. 2019. Total destruction. In *Jean Améry: Beyond the minds limits*, ed. Yochai Ataria, Amit Kravitz, and Eli Pitcovski, 141–158. New York: Palgrave Macmillan.

———. 2020. Investigating the origins of body-disownership: The case study of the Gulag. *Journal of Phenomenological Psychology* 51 (1): 44–82.

Ataria, Yochai, and Omer Horovitz. 2020. The destructive nature of severe and ongoing trauma: Impairments in the minimal-self. *Philosophical Psychology*.

Ataria, Yochai, and Yuval Neria. 2013. Consciousness-body-time: How do people think lacking their body? *Human Studies* 36 (2): 159–178.

Heidelberger-Leonard, Irène. 2010. *The philosopher of Auschwitz: Jean Améry and living with the Holocaust*. London: Tauris.

Kertész, Imre. 2004. *Kaddish for an unborn child*. Trans. Tim Wilkinson. New York: Vintage Books.

———. 2011. *Fiasco*. Trans. Tim Wilkinson. New York: Melville House.

Koestler, Arthur. 1952. *Darkness at noon*. Trans. Daphne Hardy. New York: Signet Books.

Levi, Primo. 2001. *The voice of memory: Interviews 1961–1987*. Ed. Marco Belpoliti and Robert Gordon. Trans. Robert Gordon. New York: New Press.

———. 2015. *The complete works of Primo Levi*. Ed. Ann Goldstein. Various translators. 3 vols. New York: Liveright.

CHAPTER 9

Levi's Suicide: Between Leaping and Falling

As we have seen in Chap. 7, even if Levi did commit suicide, his philosophy need not automatically be associated with the manner of his death. For those who do see a connection between Levi's writing and his suicide, however, the specific method by which he chose to end his life becomes significant. As a chemist, it would surely have been easier for Levi to take poison, for example, yet he chose to leap to his death—a fact that brings to mind Camus's novel *The Fall*. It is from the perspective of this novel, as well as Camus's essay 'The Myth of Sisyphus' that I will examine Levi's death in this chapter. I will also suggest that Levi's suicide lies somewhere between leaping and falling. As Semprún expresses a similar idea, the second part of the chapter will take a closer look at his own attempted suicide/fall.

9.1 Levi Through the Prism of Camus

In 'The Myth of Sisyphus', Camus (1955) argues that 'there is but one truly serious philosophical problem, and that is suicide'. Camus addresses 'the relationship between individual thought and suicide', stressing that he had 'never seen anyone die for the ontological argument'. On the other hand, he have seen 'many people die because they judge that life is not worth living'. Camus believes that 'killing yourself amounts to confessing. It is confessing that life is too much for you or that you do not understand it' (3–5). He goes on to claim that in order to understand the world we

Y. Ataria, *Primo Levi and Ka-Tzetnik*,
https://doi.org/10.1007/978-3-030-76743-3_9

are thrown into, 'A single certainty is enough for the seeker', who then 'simply has to derive all the consequences from it' (23). It is by no means clear, however, that even a single certainty exists in life—not after Auschwitz. Conversely, one might argue that, after Auschwitz, the *only* certainty in life is Auschwitz itself.

At the heart of Camus's writing lies the notion of the absurd, which may also be expressed (albeit somewhat superficially) as 'sin without God'. The absurd arises in light of the gap between the meaninglessness of the world and our own existence on the one hand, and our artificial attempts to ascribe meaning to them on the other. Camus stresses that there are many ways of leaping from a meaningless world to one laden with meaning, all of which he defines as 'philosophical suicide'. 'There are many ways of leaping,' he writes, 'the essential being to leap' (31). Religion and philosophy are classic examples of leaps that afford meaning to life or at least attempt to do so. Ultimately, however, such leaps are suicide. In other words, Camus believes that movements such as Nazism and socialism seek to provide an overarching response to the 'human crisis', but are ultimately leaps and philosophical suicide, as membership in these movements (motivated by a desire for the end) does not create true meaning. Camus does not just mean suicide; he means leaping. One may leap from a bridge to one's death and it is one kind of suicide, and one may leap from a meaningless world to one laden with meaning and it is another kind of suicide altogether. The matter of leaping and suicide, or, more precisely, leaping as suicide as opposed to suicide as leaping, is crucial to our understanding of Levi's leap-fall in the stairwell of Corso Re Umberto 75.

In 'The Myth of Sisyphus', the absurd leads to one of two possible results: suicide or recovery. It is almost too easy to say that since Levi, despite everything, did not recover, the only remaining option was suicide. This is precisely the kind of binary thinking that the present volume seeks to uproot. Since Levi was not a man of all or nothing, it is hard to see how the dichotomy of recovery/suicide might be applied to his case. Levi is in fact known for his observations regarding states of ambiguity such as the grey zone. As one who thoroughly understood the grey zone, it seems highly unlikely that a leaping solution would even have been within the realm of possibility for him. On the other hand, if Levi indeed committed suicide in the way that he did, then there is certainly something of the leap in his death. I will therefore argue that Levi's was not a pure leap, but rather a leap-fall.

In light of the above, I will attempt to explain Levi's suicide through the prism of the later Camus of *The Fall*, as opposed to the earlier Camus of *The Stranger*. The key is the difference between suicide by falling and suicide by all other methods. In his suicide by falling, Levi evokes the fall of European man. If, as Felman (2002) has suggested, Ka-Tzetnik's collapse at the Eichmann trial represents a new way of bringing traumatic testimony to the courtroom, then, by analogy, Levi's suicide may be seen as a way of projecting traumatic testimony to the entire European sphere—not, however, because he lacked standing as a writer and a witness. On the contrary, his suicide only had the effect that it did because of his phenomenal success at that time. Levi's suicide calls upon us to really listen to the voice of the victim.

One can leap to one's death or fall. The young woman in *The Fall* leapt to her death from the Pont Royal, yet it is Clamence (namely, we the readers) who is the book's protagonist—Clamence who, like Europe's 'civilized man', endlessly continues to fall. The following is the well-known scene in *The Fall*, in which Clamence witnesses the young woman's suicide:

> Look, the rain has stopped! Be kind enough to walk home with me. I am strangely tired, not from having talked so much but at the mere thought of what I still have to say. Oh, well, a few words will suffice to relate my essential discovery. What's the use of saying more, anyway? For the statue to stand bare, the fine speeches must take flight like pigeons. So here goes. That particular night in November, two or three years before the evening when I thought I heard laughter behind me, I was returning to the Left Bank and my home by way of the Pont Royal. It was an hour past midnight [...]. On closer view, I made out a slim young woman dressed in black. The back of her neck, cool and damp between her dark hair and coat collar, stirred me. But I went on after a moment's hesitation. [...] At the end of the bridge I followed the quays toward Saint-Michel, where I lived. I had already gone some fifty yards when I heard the sound—which, despite the distance, seemed dreadfully loud in the midnight silence—of a body striking the water. I stopped short, but without turning around. Almost at once I heard a cry, repeated several times, which was going downstream; then it suddenly ceased. The silence that followed, as the night suddenly stood still, seemed interminable. I wanted to run and yet didn't stir. I was trembling, I believe from cold and shock. I told myself that I had to be quick and I felt an irresistible weakness steal over me. I have forgotten what I thought then. 'Too late, too far ...' or something of the sort. I was still listening as I stood

> motionless. Then, slowly under the rain, I went away. I informed no one. (Camus 1958, 69–70)

From the moment he crossed the bridge and heard the drowning woman's cry and did nothing, simply walking on without turning around, Clamence begins to hear laughter—laughter that exposes his hypocrisy, his duplicity, the fact that he ultimately acted only in his own self-interest.

Abel Herzberg (2016, 27), a survivor of Bergen-Belsen, writes: 'The Kapo is the person who at all times seeks to follow his own interests.' That describes Clamence, who represents complacent bourgeois Europe, perfectly. And indeed, Clamence was interned at a Nazi concentration camp in North Africa—not an extermination camp, but not exactly a sanatorium (in the manner of Mann's *The Magic Mountain*) either.[1] At the camp, Clamence (by chance or not) was appointed 'pope', that is to say a Kapo: 'Of what did it [my pontificate] consist? Well, I was something like a group leader or the secretary of a cell. The others ... got into the habit of obeying me' (Camus 1958, 126).[2] Clamence showed personal preferences: 'Even among us, I could not maintain complete equality. According to my comrades' condition, or the work they had to do, I gave an advantage to this or that one. Such distinctions are far-reaching, you can take my word for it' (ibid.). And far-reaching they were for Clamence: 'Let's just say that I closed the circle the day I drank the water of a dying comrade.' It goes without saying that he had perfectly good reasons for what he did (there are always good reasons): 'I drank the water, that's certain, while *convincing myself* that the others needed me more than this fellow who was going to die anyway and that *I had a duty to keep myself alive for them*' (126–7). The 'pope' is thus a Kapo and a successful lawyer, who, after having left Paris, made his home in the Mexico City bar in Amsterdam, Holland—a country that saw 75–80 per cent of its Jewish population deported.

Clamence lives 'on the site of one of the greatest crimes in history', 'in the Jewish quarter or what was called so until our Hitlerian brethren made room ... real vacuum-cleaning' (11). Clamence compares the city of Amsterdam to hell: 'For we are at the heart of things here. Have you noticed that Amsterdam's concentric canals resemble the circles of hell. The middle-class hell' (14). The reference is, of course, to Dante's circles of hell in the *Divine Comedy*. Dante's *Inferno* is also a central element in *If This Is a Man*. In 'The Canto of Ulysses', Levi describes how he tried to teach the clever and good-hearted Pikolo (assistant to the Kapo), Jean, Italian, by means of verses from the *Divine Comedy*: 'The canto of Ulysses.

Who knows how or why it comes into my mind. … If Jean is intelligent he will understand. He *will* understand—today I feel capable of so much' (Levi 2015, 106; emphasis in the original). Levi struggles to remember Dante's words, but knows that he must explain them to Pikolo, 'before it's too late; tomorrow he or I might be dead', perhaps because, as he affirms, it is only at this moment that he himself truly understands them. Levi feels a sense of mission that, with the help of Dante, he might convey to Pikolo, 'the reason for our fate, for our being here today' (109). The *Divine Comedy* allows Levi, so he believes, to understand Auschwitz (and 'a single certainty is enough for the seeker'), or at least the reason for the fate of the prisoners there. For Camus, the *Divine Comedy*, explains the meaning of European man's existence—at once pope and Kapo—and this is the true meaning of the term 'judge-penitent', that Clamence uses to describe himself.

The Fall outlines the process a person goes through from the moment they refuse to heed the call of the Other—a process that resembles a prolonged suicide. Clamence clearly identifies the root of his problems, yet knows that were he given the opportunity to rectify his sin, he would still not jump from the bridge to save the young woman from the icy waters. He is aware of what makes his life a Dantean inferno, yet continues not only to choose it but to derive enjoyment from it as well. It is a spiritual suicide that results in multisystem collapse; indeed, Clamence's physical health also deteriorates. He chooses a slow death—torn between enjoyment and guilt, or, more precisely, taking sadistic enjoyment in his guilt and constantly seeking to re-enact it—a situation that Camus (1956, 9) describes as follows: 'The wound that is scratched with such solicitude ends by giving pleasure.' It is this process that Camus attempts to understand and describe. *The Fall* thus becomes the coherent and convincing suicide note of European man, who has consistently failed to do the right thing at the right time.

The main reasons for suicide, according to Levi, are shame and guilt. In *The Drowned and the Saved*, he writes, 'Many people (and I myself) felt "shame"—that is, a sense of guilt—both during and after imprisonment, as numerous witnesses have verified and confirmed.' What is more, 'Upon emerging from the darkness, we suffered from the renewed awareness that we had been maimed'. Yet, those who resisted were 'protected from "shame"', which reawakened when survivors turned their thoughts to their abasement in the camps. In this context, Levi remarks: 'I believe that this very turning back to gaze at the dangerous waters, *acqua perigliosa*, was the cause of many cases of suicide after (sometimes immediately after) liberation' (2459–61). It is hard not to see the link between Levi's thoughts on this subject and the story of Clamence in *The Fall*:

> I don't know how to name the odd feeling that comes over me. Isn't it shame, perhaps? Tell me, *mon cher compatriote*, doesn't shame sting a little? It does? Well, it's probably shame, then, or one of those silly emotions that have to do with honor. It seems to me in any case that that feeling has never left me since the adventure I found at the heart of my memory,[3] which I cannot any longer put off relating, despite my digressions and the inventive efforts for which, I hope, you give me credit. (Camus 1958, 68–9)

Clamence refuses to turn around when he hears the woman jump and is thus haunted by his memories, unable to forget:

> Till tomorrow, then, *monsieur et cher compatriote*. No, you will easily find your way now: I'll leave you near this bridge. I never cross a bridge at night. It's the result of a vow. Suppose, after all, that someone should jump in the water. One of two things—either you do likewise to fish him out and, in cold weather, you run a great risk! Or you forsake him there and suppressed dives sometimes leave one strangely aching. (15)

Levi describes survivor's guilt, but why should a victim feel guilty? One reason would appear to be that 'in totalitarianism … executioners and victims alike perform a total service in a single cause … though naturally … that service is by no means an identical service' (Kertész 2004, 72). Put another way, 'No one was left without a role in this game' (Kertész 2008, 26). The concentration camp perfected the process of rendering the victim guilty: 'In order to intimidate us, or in other words, through the very ceremony itself they turned us into the ultimately perverted accomplices of an ultimately perverted act' (2004, 106). All sides are thus tainted: '"Or that you can sail through the whole thing without being tarnished by it. You'd be wrong, very wrong!" I exclaim.... "No one who is tortured," I yell, "No one can remain untarnished.... Afterwards you won't be able to speak of innocence any longer, at best of survival"' (Kertész 2011, 345–6). It is therefore nearly impossible to emerge from the camp without a sense of guilt and shame, thus, even when one could not have acted otherwise. This does not prevent the victim from experiencing feelings of shame, despite (and perhaps because of) their irrationality.

The guilt that gnaws at Levi ('like a worm') is the same guilt that gnaws at European culture, as exposed in *The Fall*, through the character of Clamence—lawyer, pope, and Kapo. We have seen Clamence drink the water of a dying comrade, and Levi asks in *The Drowned and the Saved* (2015, 2467), 'Maybe I was alive in someone else's place, at someone else's expense. I might have supplanted him, in effect killed him.' One is consumed from within, dragged down by impossible guilt.

As we have seen, Clamence is riddled with guilt, but also filled with enjoyment. He passes from the first person singular—*I am guilty*—to the first person plural—*we are guilty*; and it is this act of 'pluralization' that saves him and allows him to find enjoyment in his guilt. Clamence thus transforms his sense of guilt into a tool that allows him to continue to behave in exactly the same fashion. Ultimately, by fully embracing guilt, Clamence claims a kind of innocence—at least in bourgeois terms. Clamence's terminology resembles that of Levi in another matter as well. Levi writes: 'I felt innocent, to be sure, but herded among the saved and thus in permanent search of a justification, in my own eyes and in the eyes of others. Those who survived were the worst, that is to say, the fittest. The best all died' (ibid.). When Clamence tries to remember the name of his dying comrade, we also discover that the best did not survive: 'No, no, it wasn't Du Guesclin; he was already dead, I believe, for he stinted himself too much' (Camus 1958, 126–7).

Indeed, *one of the hardships the victims faced was the fact that their oppressors—as well as those who were deep in the dark grey zones—used the same words, the same logic, the same rhetoric.* Both oppressor and victim may use the word 'guilt', but does it have the same or even a similar meaning? If only there were separate languages, in which the same words might mean completely different things. It seems that Levi himself was deeply conflicted in the matter of guilt and shame, and, although it would have been clear to him, at least on a rational level, that his guilt was not the same as that of Clamence, it may not have been so in his inner world. In other words, Levi was not necessarily convinced by his own analytical reasoning. Indeed Levi was consumed with guilt and shame. For example, he tells how, how he would feel judged by people, especially young people:

> Consciously or not, he [the survivor] feels accused and judged, compelled to justify and defend himself. ... It is more realistic to accuse oneself or be accused by others of having failed in terms of human solidarity. ... Almost everyone feels guilty for not coming to the aid of another person. The

> presence beside you of a fellow prisoner who is weaker, more unprepared, older, or too young, pestering you by asking for help... But I also remember, with discomfort, that much more often I shrugged my shoulders impatiently at other requests, and this was after I had been in the Lager for almost a year and had thus accumulated a hefty dose of experience. But I had also assimilated to the core the primary rule of the camps: to look out for oneself first of all. (Levi 2015, 2463–4)

At this point, Levi tells the story of what was, for him, a remarkably disturbing experience:

> In August 1944, it was very hot at Auschwitz. A torrid, tropical wind kicked up clouds of dust from the bombed-out buildings, dried the sweat off our backs, and thickened the blood in our veins... How much water can a two-inch pipe one or two meters in length contain? One liter, if that. I could drink it all immediately, it would have been the safest thing. Or leave a little for the next day. Or split it evenly with Alberto. Or reveal the secret to the whole work squad. I chose the third option: egotism expanded to the nearest person, which an old friend of mine has rightly called '*nosismo*'—we-ism. We drank all the water, in short greedy sips, taking turns under the faucet, just the two of us. Secretly. But on the march back to camp I found myself next to Daniele, who was covered with gray cement dust, his lips cracked and his eyes glazed over, and I felt guilty. I traded glances with Alberto, we understood each other immediately and hoped no one had seen us. But Daniele had noticed us in that strange position, on our backs next to the wall amid the rubble. He had suspected something was up and then guessed what it was. Many months later, in Belorussia, after the liberation, he had harsh words for me: *why the two of you and not me?* The 'civilian' moral code was resurgent, the same code by which I, a free man today, am appalled by the death sentence meted out to the Kapo... I could not figure this out then, nor can I today, but the shame existed and it is still there, concrete, heavy, perpetual. Today Daniele is dead, but in our affectionate, fraternal get-togethers as survivors, the veil of that failure to act, that unshared glass of water, stood between us, transparent, unexpressed, but tangible and 'costly.' (2464–6)

Levi insists that what went on at the concentration camp cannot be approached with here-and-now eyes, which is why he finds it hard to judge even the Kapo from the perspective of the world *outside the camp* (which will be discussed at length below). Nevertheless, the sense of guilt remains—painful and costly:

> Do you feel shame because you are alive in the place of someone else? ... You find no obvious transgressions. You did not take anyone's place, you did not beat anyone (but would you have had the strength?), you did not accept appointments (but none were offered)... Yet ... each is a Cain to his brother, that each of us (here I say "us" in a very broad—indeed, universal—sense) has betrayed his neighbor and is living in his place. It's a supposition, but it gnaws at you; it's nesting deep inside, like a worm. You cannot see it from the outside, but it gnaws, and it shrieks. (2466)

In the story 'The Gyspsy' (published in *Lilith and Other Stories*), Levi tells of a case in which they had been allowed to write to their relatives. Everyone knew that it was a trick, but Levi wrote a letter nonetheless. At the time, Levi shared his bunk with a slender young man by the name of Grigo, who had arrived in the camp only a few weeks earlier, on a transport from Hungary. Grigo, who was nineteen and illiterate, asked Levi to write a letter to his fiancée on his behalf, and promised to compensate him:

> I asked him for bread: half a ration seemed to me a just price. Today I am a little ashamed of this request of mine, but I have to remind the reader (and myself) that the etiquette of Auschwitz was different from ours, and, besides, Grigo, as a recent arrival, was less hungry than I was. (1376)

Of particular note here is the parenthetical addition '(and myself)', from which we learn that Levi felt the need to remind not only the reader, but above all himself, 'that the etiquette of Auschwitz was different from ours'. Levi remembers—albeit with some difficulty—that this is the way things had to be at Auschwitz, that there were no alternative courses of action, yet shame and guilt continue to gnaw at him. This guilt is so entrenched that the incident with Daniele and the water pipe leads Levi to observe that even the Kapo cannot be judged, for if the Kapo can be judged, then so can he. Thus, to Levi's mind, his own petty actions placed him in the same grey zone as the Kapo. The conclusion is obvious: inside the concentration camp, it was impossible not to be tainted. That is why Levi must constantly remind himself—above all himself—that this was the only way to survive at Auschwitz. That is not all Levi remembers, however. He is also mindful of the fact that he was not offered any appointments (fortunately perhaps),[4] for had it not been so, who can say what he might have discovered about himself. Levi felt tainted by his own, trivial actions a taint that appears in his writing in parentheses, like an infected wound in need of containment.

In these brackets, Levi reveals his worst fears. True, he did not deliver blows, but he did not show strength either. He did not accept any appointments that would have placed him deep within the grey zone, but such roles were never offered to him, so he cannot honestly say that he would have turned them down. One might say that there were two kinds of life: outside and inside the brackets. Levi's suicide was a fall *into* the brackets *and within them*—brackets [ ] that effectively expose a vacuum ([ ]); brackets that, when they appear on their own, mark a path of descent, with an entrance and an exit {([↕])}; brackets {([ ])} that *are*, at once, the grey zone and the other plant. Thus, when Levi places himself within the grey zone, within the {([ ])}, his own boundaries become blurred. As we have seen, although it is easy, on a rational level, to tell the difference between Levi and Clamence, within the {([ ])}, the story becomes more complicated, far more complicated.

Levi repeatedly asks readers to draw a clear line between oppressor and victim, but *is Levi himself capable of drawing such a line, deep within the grey zone*? To do so would appear to require considerable effort, and it is not at all clear that Levi has the fortitude to resist the grey zone—a monster too terrible even for its own creator. At times, within the grey zone, it seems as if Levi sees Clamence, when he looks at himself in the mirror. They may be little more than fleeting instants, but in those split seconds, Levi is no longer able to see himself as a victim who acted in the only way he could to survive—precisely because Clamence too, and those like him, employ the same rhetoric that the grey zone allows. Once a person has been tainted, they remain tainted, and this is what makes the encounter between oppressor and victim an ongoing tragedy: the victim continues to be a victim even after the event is over (as we have seen so clearly in the cases of Améry and Kertész). The taint cannot be cured. It is not a disease, but a state of mind.[5]

Levi, as we have seen, describes a situation in which everyone is 'a Cain to his brother', but goes a step further, and, like Clamence, shifts from 'I' to the broadest possible 'us'. In other words, he makes being prepared to enter the depths of the grey zone a human trait: we are all guilty; just like Clamence. In Levi's case, however, the sense of guilt is much greater, as Cain not only murdered his brother, but inherited from him as well. And indeed, as we shall soon see, in some ways, that is exactly how Levi felt.

As noted earlier, in Levi's opinion, 'The most substantial material for reconstructing the truth about the camps is the survivors' memories', yet 'today, many years later, we can safely say that the story of the Lagers has been written almost exclusively by people who, *like me, did not plumb the depths*' (2015, 2415–6). Levi in fact stresses that 'we, the survivors, are not the true witnesses' (2468). Thus, when Levi performs his duty and testifies, each and every time, he must grapple with the question, why did he (Levi) survive while others did not? Was it because he was a lesser person? 'We are the ones', he writes, 'who, because of our transgressions, ability, or luck, did not touch bottom' (ibid.). With great sensitivity, he continues, 'We speak in their place, *by proxy*. I could not say whether we did or are doing so out of a sense of moral obligation toward the silenced or if, rather, *it is to free ourselves of their memory*' (2469). The answer would appear to be, not to remember (or not only to remember) but, as Clamence says, also to forget ('to free ourselves of their memory'). In testifying, those who survived seem merely to add insult to injury: not only are we their Cain, but we also dare to speak in their name. These insights bring Levi no end of suffering:

> The righteous among us, whose number was neither higher nor lower than in any other human group, felt remorse, shame, and sorrow for the wrongs that were committed by others, not by them, but in which they felt implicated.... It would prove that man, the human race—we, in other words—was capable of building an infinite mass of suffering; and that suffering is the only force created from the void, with neither expense nor effort. All it takes is a refusal to see, to hear, and to act. (2470)

This suffering is a black hole orbited by Clamence and all of Europe, as well as by Levi, who is part of that same Europe, as he himself attests:

> In my family Fascism was accepted, with some annoyance. My father joined the Party reluctantly, but still he wore the black shirt. And I was a Balilla and then an Avanguardista [the Balilla and the Avanguardisti were the Fascist youth organizations; enrollment was obligatory for all Italian youths]. (xxviii)

Levi was indeed a victim—a fact he practically pleads with himself to remember—but when he recalls that he did not share a life-saving drink of water with Daniele, he is unable to forgive himself, even if he was, first and foremost, a victim in this story. Levi's omission is, of course, a drop in the ocean compared to other acts of cruelty. Nevertheless, in his eyes, this incident revealed to him the potential he too harboured within: 'They [the SS] were made from the same cloth as us, average human beings, of average intelligence and average malice' (2566). For a sensitive soul, this is more than enough to develop a sense of guilt (although of an entirely different sort).

An incident that occurred during Levi's short-lived career as a partisan reveals another source of his sense of guilt.[6] Lang (2013, 25) summarizes the incident as follows:

> On the night of December 8, four days before what would be the group's capture, in Frumy, a village close to Amay, two members of the partisan group quartered there were shot—executed—by Sergeant-Major Berto of the partisans. That punishment was imposed because of what is described as a rampage in nearby St. Vincent—"drunken looting"— by the men executed. That summary is simple, but the punishment was anything but simple for the group and arguably least of all for Levi. Apparently, he did not participate in or witness the execution; it remains unknown what part he had in the decision to punish the two men in that way. Whatever his distance from it, however, he was sufficiently involved to feel responsible for an act that brought him as close as he would come in his role as a partisan to killing another human being.

Lang stresses Levi's profound sense of guilt and shame in the wake of this incident. Could such feelings of guilt, related to specific events, explain Levi's suicide? I would argue that even if guilt and shame did play a role in Levi's suicide, they are far from its only cause. To suggest otherwise would be superficial, when more complex explanations are required—explanations that take into consideration the actual lives of survivors, both before the camps and after liberation. Consider that according to this model, anyone who was at Auschwitz feels guilt and shame, resulting either in denial or in suicide. In this sense, the model applies not only to victims, but to oppressors as well—indeed, it is the model adopted by Clamence. I believe that discourse pertaining to guilt must be precise, cautious, and clear. It must present a complex reality that places feelings of guilt on some sort of scale, taking into account not only intensity of feeling, but an entire world of causes and circumstances as well.

9.2 Levi and Semprún

By his own account, Semprún began writing *Literature or Life* (published in French in 1994 as *L'Écriture ou la vie*) on the Saturday of Levi's suicide (11 April 1987), exactly forty-two years after his own liberation from the Buchenwald concentration camp. The book opens with a scene in which a survivor from Buchenwald, Semprún himself, meets three officers and, through their gazes, begins to grasp what he has experienced. On that same day, Semprún also began writing another book—working title *Un homme perdu* (A Lost Man), later published as *Netchaïev est de retour* (Netchaïev Is Back)—which begins at the same point in time as *Literature or Life*: the day after the liberation of Buchenwald. In *Netchaïev est de retour*, Semprún tells the story of the French officer Roger Marroux (Marc, in *Literature or Life*), lover of Laurence—who would later become Semprún's own lover (at least according to *Literature or Life*). On 8 May 1945, at Laurence's home, she reads Semprún a letter sent to her by Marc (one of the three officers Semprún met on liberation day), who was killed on 12 April 1945, the day after the liberation of Buchenwald. The letter, which describes the effect that Semprún's gaze had on Marc, serves as the basis for both books. After having written the beginning of *Netchaïev est de retour*, Semprún put it aside and began to write a new book, this time from his perspective as a survivor, or perhaps more accurately, from his perspective as a victim:

> And so, on April 11, 1987, on the anniversary of the liberation of Buchenwald, I'd wound up meeting myself once again. Recovering an essential part of myself, of my memory, which I had been—and was still—obliged to repress, to restrain, in order to go on living. To simply be able to breathe. Stealthily, turning up by chance in a work of fiction that had not initially seemed to require my presence, I was appearing in the novel, equipped only with the stricken shadow of the memory.... In fact, from that moment on, the writing turned toward the first person singular.[7] Toward the extreme singularity of an experience that was difficult to share. (Semprún 1997, 228–9)

With this in mind, we may begin to examine the following story, recounted in *Literature or Life*. On 5 August 1945, the day before the dropping of the atomic bomb codenamed Little Boy on Hiroshima, after a sleepless night with Claude-Edmonde Magny, Semprún was on a wheezy, overcrowded commuter train. Just as the train was about to enter the station,

Semprún, who had been standing at the edge of the passage between two carriages, *fell out* the open door—or at least that is what the pharmacist tells him. But did he really *fall*, or did he *jump*? 'Actually, I'd fallen off a train,' he tells Lorène, but a woman who had been standing next to Semprún at the time took a different view: 'At all events, the young woman was respectful—perhaps to a fault—of the freedom of others. Of mine, in this case. Having decided that I wished to commit suicide, she declared later, she moved aside to make it easier for me.' Semprún himself is unsure: 'I had no definitive judgment on the question.... But *perhaps voluntary death is a kind of dizziness*, nothing else' (209–10). Between leaping and falling.

One might ask: was Semprún aware of where he was when he boarded the crowded train? When he wakes up, he asks the pharmacist what day it is, and the pharmacist, who does not understand the question, replies 'Monday'. When Semprún explains that is not what he meant, the pharmacist adds: 'Today is Monday, the fifth of August, nineteen hundred and forty-five,' and 'You fell from the Paris train just as it was entering the station... You've been injured!' (216–18). Semprún, as if waking from a dream, begins to process where he is:

> I was in a train that had just halted. There had been a jolt, in the grinding noise of locked brakes. There had been cries, some of anger, others of despair. I was trapped in the crush of bodies that swayed back and forth, tightly pressed against one another. I saw a face turned toward me, mouth agape, trying to breathe. The young man with the expression of suffering, his face turned toward mine, was begging me, 'Don't leave me, Gérard, don't leave me!' The sliding door of the freight car opened; there was the loud, savage barking of dogs. The harsh glare of spotlights illuminated a station platform. The nocturnal landscape was blanketed with snow. There were shouts, brief, guttural orders. And still those dogs: a dark horizon of dogs howling in front of a curtain of snow-covered trees. We jumped down onto the platform in a confused, clumsy throng. Ran barefoot across the snow. Helmets, uniforms, blows with rifle butts. And always the dogs, hoarse, slavering with murderous rage. We left the station in ranks of five, on the double. We were on a broad avenue lighted by tall lampposts. At regular intervals there were columns crowned by Hitlerian eagles.

So does Semprún fall or jump, and no less importantly, does he understand where he is and when? It is hard to say. He seems to be on the verge between dreaming and reality. Of moments such as this, Semprún wrote,

'I could not have said which was the real one, which the dream' (234). As he regains consciousness after his injury, Semprún returns to what appears to be (at least for a few moments) his only reality—Buchenwald:

> That was how I found out, in the abrupt flash of this resurgent memory, who I was, where I'd come from, where I was really going. … Because I hadn't simply fallen on my head in the station at Gros-Noyer-Saint-Prix, in a northern suburb of Paris. That wasn't the main problem, anyway. The important thing was that I'd jumped down, amid the uproar of dogs and the shouting of the SS, onto the station platform of Buchenwald. (219)

Semprún's reality, so it seems, is Buchenwald. Sometimes he dreams that he is not there, but he always wakes up to discover that at least some part of him has remained a prisoner at Buchenwald. This is illustrated even more starkly in the next story. In December 1945, at a time when Semprún was engaged in a life-and-death struggle to tell his own story, he went to see an American film based on a book by Eugene O'Neill: 'On a sunny winter's day in December 1945, I had to choose between literature or life.' The problem was not writer's block: 'Not because I couldn't manage to [write, but because I couldn't manage to] survive the writing,'[8] to which Semprún adds, 'Only a suicide could put a signature, a voluntary end to this unfinished—this unfinishable—process of mourning.' In order to live, he decides to abandon 'the work in progress' and to sink into amnesia: 'I had to choose between literature and life; I chose life. I chose a long cure of aphasia, of voluntary amnesia, in order to survive' (194–6).

Semprún arrived at the cinema and the film was preceded by a newsreel (a common practice at the time). The newsreel showed images from the concentration camps, filmed immediately after their liberation by Allied forces, including Buchenwald, which Semprún recognized:

> The camera's eye watched the American army's bulldozers pushing hundreds of wasted corpses into common graves… The camera's eye followed the slow progress of a group of deportees hobbling across the open space of a parade ground, in the sunshine, toward a place where food was being distributed.

It was not the images themselves that disturbed Semprún, but something else entirely:

> There were also images of Buchenwald which I recognized. Or rather: which I knew for certain came from Buchenwald, without being certain of

> recognizing them. Or rather: without being certain of having seen them myself. And yet I had seen them. Or rather: I had experienced them. It was the difference between the seen and the experienced that was disturbing... All of a sudden... these intimate images became foreign to me, objectified up on the screen... The gray, sometimes hazy images, filmed with the jerky motions of a handheld camera, acquired an inordinate and overwhelming dimension of reality that my memories themselves could not attain. ... I saw myself returned to reality, reinstated in the truth of an indisputable experience. Everything had been true, so, it was all still true. *Nothing had been a dream... I had not imagined Buchenwald. My life, therefore, was more than just a dream.* (198–200)

If Buchenwald truly existed in the real world (as demonstrated by the newsreel footage), the only possible conclusion from Semprún's perspective is that life itself is the dream or, put another way, the only possible reality is the concentration camp. On this point, Semprún converges with Levi. The first chapter of the third and final part of *Literature or Life* is entitled 'The Day of Primo Levi's Death'. In this chapter, Semprún discusses the last page of Levi's *The Truce*:

> And a dream filled with fear has not ceased to visit me, at intervals now close, now rare. It's a dream within another dream, varying in its details, unique in its substance. I am at the table with my family, or friends, or at work, or in a verdant countryside—in a serene, relaxed setting, in other words, apparently without tension and pain—and yet I feel a subtle, profound anguish, the definite sensation of a looming threat. And in fact, as the dream proceeds, little by little or brutally, each time in a different way, everything collapses and is destroyed around me, the scene, the walls, the people, and the anguish becomes more intense and more precise. Everything has now turned into chaos; I am alone at the center of a gray and murky void, and, yes, I *know* what this means, and I also know that I have always known it. I am again in the Lager, and nothing outside the Lager was true. The rest was a brief holiday, or a trick of the senses, a dream: the family, nature in flower, the house. Now this internal dream, the dream of peace, is over, and in the external dream, which continues coldly, I hear the sound of a well-known voice: a single word, not imperious, but brief and subdued. It is the dawn command of Auschwitz, a foreign word, feared and expected: get up, '*Wstawać*'. (2015, 397–8; emphasis in the original)

The true nightmare of the survivors, argues Semprún, influenced by Levi, is the day-to-day feeling that they are in fact living in a dream, from which they will awake, at any moment—back in the camp:

> Nothing can stop the course of this dream, says Levi; nothing can relieve the secret agony it causes, even if you turn to a loved one, even if a friendly—or a loving—hand is held out to you. ... Nothing, ever, will deflect the course of that dream. ... Nothing is true except the camp, all the rest is but a dream, now and forever. Nothing is real but the smoke from the crematory of Buchenwald, the smell of burned flesh, the hunger, the roll calls in the snow, the beatings. (Semprún 1997, 235–6)

Semprún's leap from the train also took place in a dream, or, more precisely, in a state in which he was unable to distinguish between reality and dreaming. In such circumstances, it is impossible to determine whether it was a leap or a fall, or whether it was neither reality nor a dream, neither leaping nor falling. Suicide, in this case, appears to be an attempt to awaken from a dream. The leap is an attempt to awaken from a nightmare, but it is only after the fall (if one is still alive) that the survivor realizes that he is not asleep at all, but awake. Thus, the leap that was supposed to awaken him becomes something resembling suicide. More than suicide, however, it is an attempt to awaken from a dream—except that, in the case of the survivors, the dream itself turns out to be reality:

> A dream within another dream, unquestionably. The dream of death within the dream of life. Or rather: the dream of death, sole reality of a life that is itself but a dream. Primo Levi expressed that anguish we all felt with incomparable precision. The camp was indeed our only truth (242–3).

Semprún intimates that, in his opinion, this was the reason for Levi's suicide—the understanding that 'nothing was real outside the camp, that's all. The rest was only a brief pause, an illusion of the senses, an uncertain dream. And that's all there is to say' (251).

9.3 Leaping That Is Falling, Falling That Is Leaping

Why then did Levi not just commit suicide, proclaiming, in the manner of Dostoevsky, *I have understood the rules of the game and want no part of it, thank you very much.* Levi seems to have been incapable of taking his own life without leaving room for doubt. His world was not black and white, good and evil, but grey, like ours. Levi is not only a Jew, but a European as well, and as such, understands the fall. He knows full well that had he merely been a Frenchman in Paris or an Italian in Rome, there is a real possibility that he might have sunk into indifference, like Clamence in *The Fall*. Indeed, in 'Nickel', in *The Periodic Table*, Levi writes that his was a generation too sceptical to actively oppose fascism:

> It was the ironic gaiety of a whole generation of Italians, intelligent and honest enough to reject fascism, too skeptical to oppose it actively, too young to accept passively the tragedy that was looming and to despair of tomorrow: a generation to which I myself would have belonged if the providential racial laws had not intervened to age me precociously and guide my choice. (Levi 2015, 806)

Levi himself was no exception; he was part of a generation doomed to fall endlessly. He admits as much in 'Gold': 'We proclaimed ourselves enemies of fascism, but in fact fascism had worked in us, as in almost all Italians, alienating us and making us superficial, passive, and cynical' (857). Levi thus both leaps and falls, and the leap cannot be separated from the fall—at once choice and crushing compulsion. Levi's suicide was an act of freedom, and even if it was merely an illusion of freedom, it was, under the circumstances, a choice.

The difference between leaping and falling is immense. Leaping is the choice (if only an illusion of choice) not to play the game, while falling is the culmination of a lengthy process of aversion to reality (from Camus's perspective). Levi, however, found a third way: *leaping that is falling, falling that is leaping*. Levi's suicide conveys the idea that life and death, white and black may exist outside the camp, but inside the camp, all is grey: death is not death and life is not life. In the grey zone, one cannot really live, nor can one really die; it is impossible to make a clear distinction—leaping is falling and falling is leaping. Every action is ambiguous, and, although it may try to illude us that understanding and even judgement are possible, they are not. Levi's suicide tells us that, ultimately, even his life and his writing are in the grey zone. He is not only a witness or a writer or a chemist or a historian or a victim or a judge. He is all of those things and he is none of them. Levi declares that he himself is deep within the grey zone.

In a sense, Levi's leap-fall is a repeat of Ka-Tzetnik's faint-fall during the Eichmann trial. While the latter redefined the concept of testimony in the context of public, judicial discourse, the former redefined the concept of testimony within the entire European sphere. In order to understand Levi's suicide, however, we must first understand the extent to which the grey zone tainted everyone and everything in it, which will be discussed in the next chapter.

Notes

1. Camus may have meant this as an allusion to Sartre, who was drafted into the French army in 1938 and assigned to a meteorological unit on the famous Maginot Line. Taken captive by the Germans in 1940, he spent some nine months in prison—first in Nancy and later in Trier, until his release (or escape, according to some) in April 1941, due to poor health.
2. In this context, it is worth noting Friedländer's (2007) focus on the silence of the Pope at the time of the extermination of the Jews.
3. We thus learn that at the heart of Clamence's journey lies a traumatic memory, and perhaps, as Felman suggests (Felman and Laub 1992) regarding the missing painting above the bartender's head in the Mexico City: the empty space represents absence—that which we wish to forget but cannot help but remember. In this context, it is interesting to recall Benjamin's (2006, 392) famous remark: 'There is no document of culture which is not at the same time a document of barbarism. And just as such a document is never free of barbarism, so barbarism taints the manner in which it was transmitted from one hand to another.'
4. Levi often refers to his good fortune: 'Of the 96 men who entered the camp with me 15 survived, and of the 29 women 8 survived. Thus, among the 650 deportees on our train there were 23 survivors, that is, 3.5 percent. But that was a lucky train because it left Italy a little less than a year before the liberation: almost no one survived two or three years of prison' (2015, 1298).
5. For an extensive discussion, see Ataria (2018, 2019).
6. Levi himself characterized his time as a partisan as 'undoubtedly the most opaque of my career … and it's best left among the things that are forgotten' (2015, xxx), remarking that it 'counted very little' and that he had been 'a partisan in name only' (2001, 227), and describing his group as 'ill-prepared and untrained' and therefore 'quickly captured' (24).
7. Note the similarity between this description and Ka-Tzetnik's observation that he suddenly found himself writing in the first person singular.
8. Emended following the original French text.

References

Ataria, Yochai. 2018. *Body disownership in complex posttraumatic stress disorder.* New York: Palgrave Macmillan.

———. 2019. Total destruction. In *Jean Améry: Beyond the minds limits*, ed. Yochai Ataria, Amit Kravitz, and Eli Pitcovski, 141–158. New York: Palgrave Macmillan.

Benjamin, Walter. 2006. On the concept of history. In *Selected writings, vol. 4, 1938–1940*, ed. Howard Eiland and Michael W. Jennings, 388–400. Cambridge, MA: The Belknap Press of Harvard University Press.

Camus, Albert. 1955. *The myth of Sisyphus and other essays.* Trans. Justin O'Brien. New York: Vintage Books.

———. 1956. *The rebel: An essay on man in revolt.* Trans. Anthony Bower. New York: Vintage Books.

———. 1958. *The fall.* Trans. Justin O'Brien. New York: Alfred A. Knopf.

Felman, Shoshana. 2002. *The juridical unconscious.* Cambridge, MA: Harvard University Press.

Felman, Shoshana, and Dori Laub. 1992. *Testimony: Crises of witnessing in literature, psychoanalysis, and history.* Florence: Routledge.

Friedländer, Saul. 2007. *Nazi Germany and the Jews: The years of extermination 1939–1945.* London: Weidenfeld and Nicolson.

Herzberg, Abel J. 2016. *Amor Fati: Seven essays on Bergen-Belsen.* Trans. Jack Santcross. Göttingen: Wallstein Verlag.

Kertész, Imre. 2004. *Kaddish for an unborn child.* Trans. Tim Wilkinson. New York: Vintage Books.

———. 2008. *Detective story.* Trans. Tim Wilkinson. New York: Knopf.

———. 2011. *Fiasco.* Trans. Tim Wilkinson. New York: Melville House.

Lang, Berel. 2013. *Primo Levi: A matter of a life.* New Haven: Yale University Press.

Levi, Primo. 2015. *The complete works of Primo Levi.* Ed. Ann Goldstein. Various translators. 3 vols. New York: Liveright.

Semprún, Jorge. 1997. *Literature or life.* Trans. Linda Coverdale. New York: Viking.

CHAPTER 10

The Grey Zone

The world of the camps, Levi claimed, cannot be 'reduced to two blocs'. Indeed, one of the crushing blows upon entering the camps was the 'concentric aggression at the hands of the very persons in whom you had hoped to find future allies' (Levi 2015, 2431–2). Breaking the dichotomous model of *good* and *evil* and entering the grey zone, which has 'undefined contours' and 'both separates and connects the two opposing camps of masters and servants' (2435), is an extremely complex but necessary step to understanding the ways in which different people on both sides of the divide (victims and perpetrators) act in the context of totalitarian force. To attempt to comprehend and explain the grey zone one must possess great emotional strength and extraordinary analytical ability. Levi lives up to the challenge. This chapter explores Levi's definition of the grey zone, as well as the concept's explanatory force.

It is true of every totalitarian regime, and certainly of the concentration camps, that 'the harsher the oppression, the more widespread among the oppressed is the willingness to collaborate with power'.[1] It thus comes as no surprise that 'the hybrid category of inmate-functionaries' was the 'framework' of the Lager, and although such functionaries were, on the whole, products of the system, Levi still deems them the camp's 'most disturbing feature' (ibid.). It is in this light that Levi examines the 'privileged'—the Judenrat member, the Sonderkommando, and the Kapo.[2]

The issue of the grey zone is especially sensitive, since, as Levi stresses, 'The privileged prisoners were a small minority of the camp population,

Y. Ataria, *Primo Levi and Ka-Tzetnik*,
https://doi.org/10.1007/978-3-030-76743-3_10

but they represent a large majority of the survivors' (2433). The survival of these prisoners cannot be ascribed exclusively to good fortune. It was also determined by their actions in the grey zone. Our natural tendency to judge makes this a particularly delicate point, as the grey zone 'harbors just enough to confound our need to judge' (2435). Nevertheless, we who are outside the grey zone often think that we are capable of judging those who act within the grey zone, which is why Levi cautions against 'rushing to moral judgment'. Levi also asks the reader to consider that 'the greatest fault lies with the system' and, therefore, 'We would prefer to entrust that judgment only to people who have been in similar circumstances and experienced for themselves what it means to act under coercion.' Furthermore, the fact that the victims themselves experience feelings of guilt does not mean that they can be judged for having acted as they did in the grey zone. Levi insists that he does not know and in fact finds it difficult conceive of 'a human court that could be delegated to take its measure'. Levi asserts that if he himself had to judge, 'he [I] would freely absolve anyone whose complicity in the crime was minimal and whose coercion was maximal'. Levi goes on to argue, however, that 'A more subtle and varied judgment is required for those who held senior positions: the heads—Kapos—of the work squads' (2436–7).

10.1 Collaborators

10.1.1 The Kapo

Levi distinguishes between three types of Kapos: common criminals; political prisoners 'sapped by five or ten years of suffering'; and Jews 'who saw the crumb of authority offered to them as the only way to escape the "final solution"'. Some were selected for the job, while others 'aspired to power spontaneously'. Among the Jews who served as Kapos, Levi identifies a further motive: 'There were many among the oppressed who were contaminated by the oppressors and tended to unconsciously identify with them' (2438–9). This last group, according to Levi, did not seek to escape the Final Solution or to satisfy their sadistic impulses, but had actually internalized the Nazi rationale.

Levi understands that the Kapos have only one real limit on their power: the degree of violence they must employ. That is to say that 'a lower limit was set on their violence—in the sense that they were punished or dismissed if they were not harsh enough—but not an upper limit' (2438).

Nevertheless, even the most brutal Kapos occasionally showed signs of humanity.

In the story 'The Cantor and the Veteran' (*Lilith and Other Stories*; 2015, 1379–84), Levi describes Otto, a political prisoner and true veteran of the camp ('one of the founding fathers of Auschwitz'), as witnessed by the serial number 14 he wore on his jacket: 'He had been part of the legendary patrol of thirty prisoners who were sent from Dachau to the swamps of Upper Silesia to build the first barracks.' Indeed, he commanded the respect of the other prisoners, but that was primarily 'because he had powerful fists and reflexes that were still rapid' (1379). One of the inhabitants of Barrack 48—a non-Jewish Pole by the name of Vladek, who bore the red triangle of a political prisoner—refused to wash, and it fell to the Kapo, as head of the barracks, to ensure the cleanliness of his subjects. Levi stresses how simple-minded Vladek was: 'The fact is that Vladek didn't have the brain of a chicken, poor fellow… To all appearances, Vladek … was incapable of connecting causes with effects.' Thus, on a warm and non-working Sunday in September, Otto informed the prisoners that there would be a celebration: the washing of Vladek. Otto 'had one of the soup vats carried outside, cursorily rinsed, and filled with hot water from the showers' and then 'put Vladek in it, naked and upright, and washed him personally, as you might wash a horse, scrubbing him from head to toe first with a brush and then with rags for cleaning the floor'. Levi notes that all were amused by the spectacle, but there was more to it than that: 'We went away concluding that this Otto was not among the worst: someone else, in his place, would have used cold water, or would have transferred Vladek to the Penal Squad, or would have beaten him, because certainly fools, in the Lager, do not enjoy particular indulgences' (1380–1).

On another occasion, Otto acted in a way that was completely at odds with the rules of the camp. It was Yom Kippur eve, and the prisoners had lined up for their soup, as they did every evening. Among them was Ezra, a Lithuanian watchmaker and Sabbath Cantor. When his turn came, Ezra stood before the Kapo and, instead of holding out his pail, said to Otto: 'Mr. Head of the Barrack, for us today is a day of atonement, and I cannot eat the soup. I ask you respectfully to save it for me until tomorrow evening.' Otto's jaw dropped: 'In all his years in the Lager he had never met a prisoner who refused food.' At first he could not decide whether to laugh or slap the prisoner, but told him to come and see him afterwards. Otto sat with Ezra and tried to understand the reason for his behaviour.

Was Ezra less hungry than usual? Ezra explained to the astonished Kapo, the significance of the Day of Atonement, and asked him to keep his portion of soup for him, as well as the following morning's bread ration. Furthermore, he asked that the soup be allowed to go cold, rather than keeping it hot, for reasons more practical than religious: 'The Lager soup tended to turn sour quickly, especially if it was kept warm' (1383). Otto's reaction revealed his human side and placed him within the grey zone:

> Otto grumbled something incomprehensible, in which the word *meshugge* recurred, which means "crazy" in Yiddish but is understood by all Germans; yet he took Ezra's pail, filled it, and put it in the personal closet that he, as an official, was entitled to, and told Ezra that he could come and get it the following night. To Ezra it seemed that the ration of soup was particularly generous. (ibid.)

The story of the vice Kapo Eddy, recounted by Levi in 'The Juggler' (*Lilith and Other Stories*; 2015, 1355–9), also pertains to the grey zone. Eddy was a common criminal, of the kind marked with a green triangle in the camp:

> Germans already imprisoned in ordinary jails, who had been offered, on the basis of mysterious criteria, the alternative of serving their sentence in a camp rather than in a prison. Generally they were despicable types; many of them boasted that they lived better in the camp than at home, because, besides the pleasure of giving orders, they had a free hand with the rations intended for us; many were murderers in the strict sense of the word. They made no secret of it and showed it in their behavior. (1355)

Eddy was just such a 'green triangle', although not a murderer. It is hard not to notice a certain admiration in Levi's description of him: 'He had a dazzling beauty. Fair, of average height but slender, strong, and extremely agile, he had fine [It. *nobili*, noble][3] features and skin so clear that it seemed transparent.' Eddy 'didn't give a damn about anything or anyone'—including the SS (1356). He became the vice Kapo of Levi's barracks in June 1944. Around that time, the opportunity arose for Levi to send a letter home to his family, through an Italian worker. He needed paper, a pencil, and free time—all precious commodities in the camp. Levi managed nonetheless and began to write, but was caught:

> I hadn't counted on Eddy's silent footsteps; he was already looking at me when I became aware of him. Instinctively, or, rather, stupidly, I unclasped my fingers; the pencil fell, but the paper wafted to the floor like a dead leaf. Eddy grabbed it, then he knocked me down with a violent slap. (1357)

Levi adds, however: 'And yet as I write the word "slap" *I realize that I'm lying, or at least conveying to the reader false emotions and information*,' for 'Eddy was not a brute, and didn't mean to punish me or make me suffer'. Rather, 'In the Lager a slap had a meaning very different from what it might have for us today, and here.' In the Lager, 'A slap like Eddy's was like the smack you give a dog, or the whack you give a donkey,[4] to convey to them, or reinforce, an order or a prohibition' (1358). The purpose of the slap was therefore not to cause pain or humiliate the recipient, but to educate and convey a message: 'Watch out, now you've done it—you're putting yourself in danger, maybe without knowing it, and putting me in danger, too' (1357). What Eddy should have done in a case like this is to take the letter and Levi to the Political Department, which would certainly have been Levi's undoing: 'I knew that if he reported me to the Political Department, the gallows awaited me, but before the gallows an interrogation (what an interrogation!) to discover who my accomplice was, and perhaps also get from me the address of the person I was writing to in Italy' (1358). After having ascertained the content of the letter, Eddy returns and tells Levi that he should 'thank him' for the slap, 'because it had been a good deed, of the sort that lead to Paradise'. Levi does not believe he ever thanked Eddy, and he certainly did not develop any positive feelings towards the 'green triangles'. Nevertheless, he did begin to wonder about their humanity. The grey zone is complex: it is hard to say exactly where Eddy—German, Kapo, and criminal—belongs on the continuum from white to black.

Indeed, Eddy's story becomes more complex when his own circumstances change: 'A few weeks after the incident I've recounted, he disappeared for a few days; then we saw him again one evening, standing in the alley between the barbed wire and the electrified fence; hanging around his neck was a sign with *Urning* written on it, that is, "Pederast"' (1359). At the end of the story we understand that Eddy's only crime may have been the fact that he was a homosexual—perhaps the reason he was imprisoned in the first place.

10.1.2 A Strange Hiatus Between Kapo and Sonderkommando

In the chapter on the grey zone in *The Drowned and the Saved*, Levi progresses from the low-level functionaries to the most extreme cases—from white-grey to black-grey. Just before moving on from the Kapo to the Sonderkommando, Levi uncharacteristically departs from his usual detached, analytical acuity, and places himself at the centre:

> I am no expert on the unconscious or the inner depths, but I do know that there are few experts, and that those few are more cautious. I do not know, nor am I particularly interested in knowing, whether a murderer is lurking deep within me, but I do know that I was an innocent victim and not a murderer. I know that murderers existed, and not just in Germany, and that they still exist, retired or on active duty, and that confusing them with their victims is a moral disease, an aesthetic license, or a sinister sign of complicity. Above all, it is a precious service rendered (intentional or not) to the deniers of the truth. (2439–40)

To my mind, this is one of the book's most dramatic passages—one that may offer a key to understanding Levi's emotional state, shortly before his suicide. Anyone who has even a minimal knowledge of Levi's past cannot possibly suspect that Levi himself was a functionary in the camp. Why then—in one of his most difficult chapters on the concentration and extermination camps—does he write with such vehemence, warning us not only against blurring the boundary between victim and oppressor (an understandable concern in itself), but also to remember that he too was on the side of the victims (again, could there be any doubt?).[5]

Levi exclaims, '*I do not know, nor am I particularly interested in knowing, whether a murderer is lurking deep within me, but I do know that I was an innocent victim and not a murderer*'; but no one suspects or accuses Levi of having been a criminal—with the possible exception of Levi himself. Levi does not write, *At Auschwitz, I faced impossible situations, but I* ***do know*** *that a murder* ***is not*** *lurking deep within me*, but the very opposite, that he may indeed have something of the murderer in him. Levi thus tells us that he is a victim, but he does not know whether he too could have become like one of the functionaries who, in the horrific circumstances of the camp, inflicted harm on their fellow prisoners.

Levi seems to have been frightened by the possible ethical ramifications of the grey zone, and therefore sought, first and foremost, to place himself on the side of the victims and to warn his readers, as if to say, *I have revealed the complexity of the grey zone to you, but this knowledge should by no means be used against the victims. Yes, there is a grey zone, but some boundaries are still absolutely clear.* That being said, Levi stresses that the fact that someone suffered at a concentration camp does not, in and of itself, make them a victim:

> The truth remains that most of the oppressors, during or (more often) after their actions, realized the evil they were doing or had done, and may have had misgivings, felt uneasy, or even been punished, *but their suffering is not enough for them to be counted among the victims* (2440).

10.1.3 The Sonderkommandos

In the context of the grey zone, Levi also describes the Sonderkommandos:[6] the 'special squads' charged with carrying out the process of destruction and the destruction of evidence, which were, in fact, two aspects of the same process—destroying the Jewish people, while eliminating the evidence of its destruction. It is important to stress that even the Sonderkommandos 'did not escape the common fate. On the contrary, the SS was extremely diligent in making sure that none of them would live to tell' (Levi 2015, 2441). The members of the special squads were liquidated and the first task of their replacements would be to cremate their bodies. No one had any illusions about how the story would end. 'Envisioning and organizing the squads', Levi believes, 'was National Socialism's most diabolical crime. … Through this institution, the attempt was made to shift the burden of guilt to others, that is, to the victims, so that not even the awareness that they were innocent was left to bring them relief' (2443).

Often, the Sonderkommandos were recruited in impossible circumstances or without knowing or understanding where they were going. Indeed, it is one thing to know and another to understand. Filip Müller, a Czech Jew who survived five Sonderkommando liquidations, describes it as follows:

> It was a Sunday in May. We were locked in an underground cell in Block 11. We were held in secret. Then some SS men appeared and marched us along a street in the camp. We went through a gate, and around three hundred feet away, three hundred feet from the gate, I suddenly saw a building. It

> had a flat roof and a smokestack. I saw a door in the rear. I thought they were taking us to be shot. Suddenly, before a door, under a lamp in the middle of this building, a young SS man told us: "Inside, filthy swine!" We entered a corridor... We were in the incineration chamber of the crematorium in Camp 1 at Auschwitz. From there they herded us to another big room and told us to undress the corpses... I couldn't understand any of it... I didn't even know where I was... When we undressed some of them, the order was given to feed the ovens. Suddenly, an SS man rushed up and told me: "Get out of here! Go stir the bodies!" ... At that point I was in shock, as if I'd been hypnotized, ready to do whatever I was told. (Lanzmann 1985, 57–8)

As we read Müller's testimony, it is worth bearing in mind Levi's (2015, 2443) assertion that the testimonies of the Sonderkommandos should not be taken literally:

> From men who have known this extreme destitution one cannot expect a deposition in the legal sense of the term but, rather, something between a complaint, a curse, atonement, and the impulse to justify, to rehabilitate oneself. What should be expected is a liberating outburst rather than truth with the face of Medusa.

The fact that the grey zone should remain beyond judgement does not mean that those who collaborated, even unwillingly, will be spared feelings of guilt. Nor does the fact that the Sonderkommandos cannot be judged, legally or morally, make them innocent or guilty. Either way, they will be racked with guilt.

Richard Glazar, a Treblinka survivor who had been tasked with sorting the belongings of those sent to the gas chambers, and who committed suicide in 1997, recounts:

> The trainloads came from an assembly camp in Salonika. They'd brought in Jews from Bulgaria, Macedonia. These were rich people; the passenger cars bulged with possessions. Then an awful feeling gripped us, all of us, my companions as well as myself, a feeling of helplessness, of shame. For we threw ourselves on their food. ... The trainloads from the Balkans brought us to a terrible realization: we were the workers in the Treblinka factory, and our lives depended on the whole manufacturing process, that is, the slaughtering process at Treblinka. (Lanzmann 1985, 147–8)

The grey zone that produces victims relentlessly consumed with guilt is indeed complex. The greyer the zone, it seems, the worse the sights and, consequently, the insights regarding the human race. Tadeusz Borowski, a non-Jewish Pole, was a member of the Kanada Kommando and, as such, a prisoner with special privileges. He worked mainly on the train ramp at Auschwitz-Birkenau and witnessed the process whereby Jews were taken from the trains and sent to the gas chambers:

> The train has been emptied. A thin, pock-marked S.S. man peers inside, shakes his head in disgust and motions to our group, pointing his finger at the door. '*Rein*. Clean it up!' We climb inside. In the corners amid human excrement and abandoned wrist-watches lie squashed, trampled infants, naked little monsters with enormous heads and bloated bellies. We carry them out like chickens, holding several in each hand. 'Don't take them to the trucks, pass them on to the women,' says the S.S. man, lighting a cigarette. His cigarette lighter is not working properly; he examines it 'Take them, for God's sake!' I explode as the women run from me in horror, covering their eyes. […] 'What, you don't want to take them?' asks the pock-marked S.S. man with a note of surprise and reproach in his voice, and reaches for his revolver. 'You mustn't shoot, I'll carry them.' A tall, grey-haired woman takes the little corpses out of my hands and for an instant gazes straight into my eyes. […] 'You see, my friend, you see, I don't know why, but I am furious, simply furious with these people—furious because I must be here because of them. I feel no pity. I am not sorry they're going to the gas chamber. Damn them all! I could throw myself at them, beat them with my fists. It must be pathological, I just can't understand …' […] It is impossible to control oneself any longer. Brutally we tear suitcases from their hands, impatiently pull off their coats. Go on, go on, vanish! They go, they vanish. Men, women, children. […] Here is a woman […] young, healthy, good-looking, she wants to live. But the child runs after her, wailing loudly: 'Mama, mama, don't leave me!' 'It's not mine, not mine, no!' Andrei, a sailor from Sevastopol, grabs hold of her. His eyes are glassy from vodka and the heat. With one powerful blow he knocks her off her feet, then, as she falls, takes her by the hair and pulls her up again. His face twitches with rage. 'Ah, you bloody Jewess! So you're running from your own child! I'll show you, you whore!' […] 'Here! And take this with you, bitch!' and he throws the child at her feet. (Borowski 1976, 39–43)

Accounts such as these offer some insight into Levi's state of mind when he wrote, 'dead in spirit long before our anonymous death. No one must leave here who might carry to the world, together with the mark stamped in his flesh, the evil tidings of what man's audacity made of man in Auschwitz' (Levi 2015, 52). Those who enter the grey zone are not exactly human when they emerge from it—first and foremost in their own eyes. The reason for this lies neither in their actions nor in the loss of their humanity (although that is also a possibility), but in the fact that those who have been in the grey zone and returned to everyday life no longer know what the concept 'human' means—hence the titles *If This Is a Man* (Levi), *The Human Race* (Antelme), and others. Conversely, we might argue that those who have been in the grey zone understand the concept 'human' all too well, and once it has been definitively and unequivocally explained (*This Is a Man!*), no longer wish to be associated with it, to be classified as such.

10.1.4 Rumkowski, King of the Jews

The story of 'The King of the Jews', Chaim Rumkowski—head of the Judenrat of the Lodz ghetto from its establishment in 1940 to its final liquidation in 1944—is a particularly fascinating one. Rumkowski created a cult of personality around himself, riding through the ghetto in a horse-drawn carriage, and printing stamps and New Year's cards bearing his image. He ruled as an absolute monarch, establishing what appeared to be a state within a state. As a Jewish leader who collaborated with the Nazis, Rumkowski remains a controversial figure to this day.

It is worth noting that Levi tells the story of Rumkowski, in *The Drowned and the Saved*, right after that of Muhsfeld, thus placing him within the darker areas of the grey zone. The incident involving Muhsfeld reads as follows:

> A doctor is summoned and revives the girl with an injection. No, the gas had not achieved its effect, yes, she will be able to survive, but where and how? At that moment Muhsfeld, one of the SS officers assigned to the machinery of death, arrives. The doctor takes him aside and explains the situation. Muhsfeld hesitates, then makes his decision. The girl has to die. If she were older the situation would be different, it would make more sense. Maybe she could be persuaded to keep quiet about what has happened to her, but she is only sixteen: she can't be trusted. But he does not kill her by his own hand; he summons a subordinate, who kills her with a shot to the nape of the neck. Now, this Muhsfeld was not a merciful man; his daily ration of slaughter was punctuated by arbitrary and capricious episodes, and he stood out for the refined cruelty of his inventions. He was tried in 1947, sentenced

> to death, and hanged in Kraków, and this was just. But not even he was a monolith. *Had he lived in a different place and time, he probably would have behaved like any other ordinary man.* (2446)

To Levi's mind, Muhsfeld is guilty and should be judged. In that moment of hesitation, however, Muhsfeld entered the grey zone. Let us now return to the case of Rumkowski.

More than anything else, more than being good or evil, Rumkowski was a man who 'loved authority'. According to Levi, 'He had adopted (deliberately? knowingly? or had he unconsciously identified with the model of the providential man, the "necessary hero," that was dominant in Europe at the time?) the oratorical technique of Mussolini and Hitler' (1411). Nevertheless, although he himself may have thought otherwise, Rumkowski was nothing more than a puppet. The Germans encouraged him in his delusions, 'although they were playing with him'. He had power but it did not save him. Ultimately, what Rumkowski failed to understand is that he was not a master, but a servant who believed himself to be a master: 'Although he was despised and derided by the Germans, Rumkowski probably thought of himself not as a servant but as a master' (1412). Can Rumkowski be judged? Levi asks, and answers: 'He eludes our judgment, the way a compass goes wild at the magnetic pole.' Rumkowski was indeed a tyrant, but he cannot simply be defined as an 'accomplice', since, 'to some extent, he must have gradually convinced not only others but also himself that he was a messiah, a saviour of his people, whose good he must have wanted, at least intermittently' (2452). Levi believes that Rumkowski is no different from us: 'He's not a monster, but he's not a man like other men, either; he is like many, like the many frustrated men who taste power and are intoxicated by it.' Like them, like us, he denies reality and falls prey to dreams of omnipotence, even to the point of seeing himself as being 'above the law'. Yet, we cannot judge him, nor can we know how we would have behaved in his place. In any event, Levi is of the opinion that 'this does not exempt Rumkowski from responsibility'. We thus learn that Levi ascribed great importance to individual responsibility—responsibility that transcends jurisprudence. Levi, in fact, clearly distinguishes between legal and moral judgement: 'It's likely that, had he survived his tragedy … no court would have absolved him, and we certainly cannot absolve him on the moral plane.' There are, nevertheless, 'some extenuating circumstances: a lower order, like National Socialism, exercises a frightening power of seduction, which it's hard to guard against. … To resist it, a solid moral structure is needed, and the one available to Chaim Rumkowski, the merchant of Lodz, was frail.' Rumkowski operated in the grey zone, 'between the potentates of evil and the pure victims; in this band Rumkowski should be placed', and in this sense, '*In Rumkowski we are all reflected*: his ambiguity is ours, that of hybrids kneaded of clay and spirit; his fever is ours, that of our Western civilization' (1414–15).

Now that we understand what the grey zone is, we may take a closer look at its power to explain human behaviour in inhuman conditions. I believe the story of Reserve Police Battalion 101 of the German Order Police (*Ordnungspolizei*) offers a chilling test case.

10.2 The Grey Zone as a Possible Explanation

10.2.1 Reserve Police Battalion 101 of the Order Police

Reserve Police Battalion 101 was active in Poland throughout most of the war. The unit was responsible for the mass execution of Jews, liquidation of ghettos, guarding the trains on which the Jews were deported to the extermination camps, manhunts and massacres against Polish partisans, and other atrocities. The battalion was commanded by Major Wilhelm Trapp and most of its members were from the city of Hamburg—one of the least Nazi cities in Germany (only a quarter of its inhabitants were Nazi Party members). Thus, a majority had joined the battalion to avoid being sent into battle. They were family men in their thirties and forties (the average age of the rank and file was thirty-nine), with decent jobs and relative financial security, who had not been subject to Nazi brainwashing in their formative years. Their behaviour thus cannot be explained by youthful zeal.

Reserve Police Battalion 101 was not sent to Lublin to murder Jews because its members were selected or considered particularly suited to the task. On the contrary, 'The battalion was the "dregs" of the manpower pool available at that stage of the war. It was employed to kill Jews because it was the only kind of unit available for such behind-the-lines duties' (Browning 2001, 165). Less than three weeks after their arrival in Poland, on the morning of 13 July 1942, the battalion commander, Major Trapp, gathered his troops on the outskirts of the village of Józefów, ordered them to assemble in a half-circle around him, and, according to the witnesses cited by Browning:

> Pale and nervous, with choking voice and tears in his eyes, Trapp visibly fought to control himself as he spoke. The battalion, he said plaintively, had to perform a frightfully unpleasant task. This assignment was not to his liking, indeed it was highly regrettable, but the orders came from the highest authorities. If it would make their task any easier, the men should remember that in Germany the bombs were falling on women and children. (2)

At this point, Trapp made them a rather generous offer:

> Any of the older men who did not feel up to the task that lay before them could step out. Trapp paused, and after some moments one man from Third Company, Otto-Julius Schimke, stepped forward. Captain Hoffmann, who had arrived in Józefów directly from Zakrzów with the Third Platoon of Third Company and had not been part of the officers' meetings in Biłgoraj the day before, was furious that one of his men had been the first to break ranks. Hoffmann began to berate Schimke, but Trapp cut him off. After he had taken Schimke under his protection, some ten or twelve other men stepped forward as well. (57)

Based on Browning's research, we may thus say that it would have been at least technically possible for members of the battalion to avoid actively participating in the massacre. Moreover, it seems that none of the men who chose not to take part—whether in this case or in other cases, involving other units—were punished severely: 'Quite simply, in the past forty-five years no defense attorney or defendant in any of the hundreds of postwar trials has been able to document a single case in which refusal to obey an order to kill unarmed civilians resulted in the allegedly inevitable dire punishment' (170). Browning estimates that between 10 and 20 per cent of the members of the firing squads evaded their murderous assignments.

Let us focus, for a moment, on the figure of Trapp. Trapp did not go with the men to the forest, did not witness the massacre. He was distressed, and it did not escape those around him. Some of the men even recalled him saying aloud, as if to himself, 'Oh, God, why did I have to be given these orders,' and 'Man … such jobs don't suit me. But orders are orders,' while another described 'how Trapp, finally alone in our room, sat on a stool and wept bitterly. The tears really flowed' (58). Trapp's reaction, as we shall see, is crucial, because it undermines the 'obedience to orders' explanation of behaviour like that of the Reserve Police Battalion 101 (Trapp's own statement, 'But orders are orders,' notwithstanding).

Bauman and Browning, as well as many other scholars, cite the Milgram experiment as having provided us with a better understanding of how ordinary people can become killers. Milgram's experiment (Fig. 10.1), conducted in 1962, examined the extent of participants' obedience to authority, when instructed to act in ways that conflicted with their values and conscience. Prior to the experiment, Milgram polled psychologists about the results they thought he would obtain. The consensus was that, with the exception of a handful of probable sadists (around 4 per 1000 in their estimate), most participants would refuse to administer electric shocks at the maximum voltage. Milgram himself believed that there was some specific national trait that made Germans more likely to defer to authority and therefore intended to use the American subjects merely as a control group. Ultimately, the results of the American experiment were so shocking that he decided not to proceed with a German group. Milgram's results indeed raise many questions, since, from the very first series of experiments, 65 per cent of participants administered the maximum voltage (450 V), although many did so unwillingly, some breaking into hysterical laughter as they did so. It is important to stress that *none of the participants stopped before reaching 300 V*.

Milgram argued that an uncontested authority figure is more likely to be obeyed. Accordingly, when experiments included peer confederates who challenged the experimenter, obedience to authority declined. Bauman offers the following analysis of the phenomenon of obedience to authority:

> To reveal the extent of distortion, he added to the project a number of experiments in which the subjects were confronted with more than one experimenter, and the experimenters were instructed to disagree openly and argue about the command. The outcome was truly shattering: the slavish obedience observed in all other experiments vanished without trace. The subjects were no longer willing to engage in actions they did not like; certainly they would not be prompted to afflict suffering even to the unknown victims. Out of twenty subjects of this additional experiment, one broke off before the staged disagreement between the two experimenters started, eighteen refused further co-operation at the first sign of disagreement, and the last one opted out just one stage after that. It is clear that the disagreement between the authorities completely paralyzed action. The meaning of

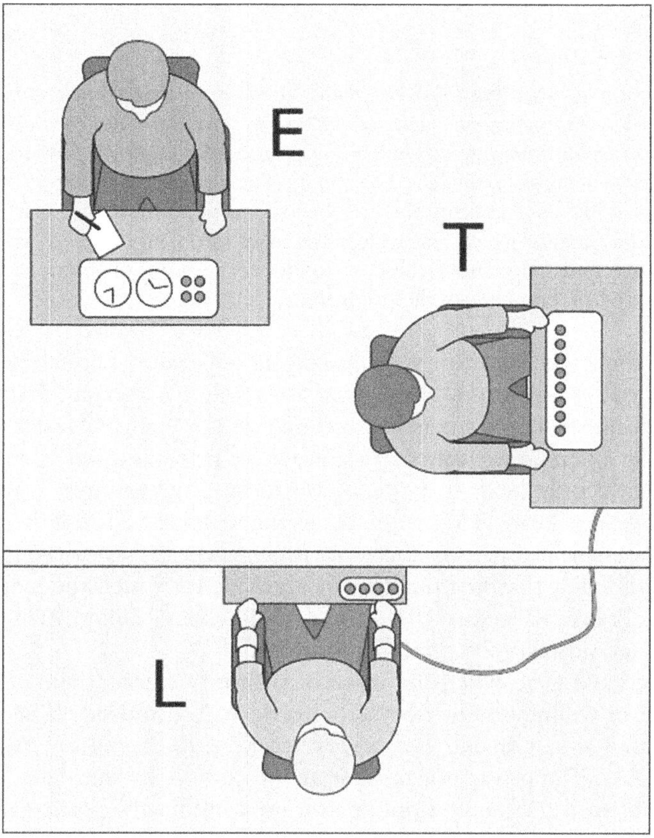

Fig. 10.1 The Milgram Experiment. The experiment began with the subject reading a list of word pairs to the learner, followed by multiple-choice questions. When the learner answered a question correctly, the subject moved on to the next one. For every incorrect answer, the subject informed the learner of the correct answer and administered an electric shock, at 15-volt increments. The learner was a confederate of the experimenter and no electric shocks were actually administered, but the subject was not aware of this. The subject would hear the learner moan, and the learner's incorrect answers would become more frequent. At 105 V, the subject would hear the learner grunt; at 120 V, shout in pain; and at 150 V, cry and plead to leave the room, complaining of a heart condition. At 200 V, the learner would continue to scream and shout, demanding that the experiment be stopped, and at 330 V, would fall silent. During the course of the experiment, the subjects would turn to the experimenter for guidance and ask whether they should halt the experiment. Some even confronted the experimenter and asked to stop. The experimenter would respond dismissively, demanding that the subjects continue: 'Please continue'; 'The experiment requires that you continue'; 'It is absolutely essential that you continue'; 'You have no other choice; you must go on.' (Image source: https://upload.wikimedia.org/wikipedia/commons/thumb/0/0d/Milgram_experiment_v2.svg/1200px-Milgram_experiment_v2.svg.png)

> correction is unambiguous: *the readiness to act against one's own better judgment, and against the voice of one's conscience, is not just the function of authoritative command, but the result of exposure to a single-minded, unequivocal and monopolistic source of authority.* Such readiness is most likely to appear inside an organization which brooks no opposition and tolerates no autonomy, and in which linear hierarchy of subordination knows no exception: an organization in which no two members are equal in power. (Bauman 2008, 164–5; emphasis in the original)

Bauman believed the most striking among Milgram's findings to be '*the inverse ratio of readiness to cruelty and proximity to its victim*', that is to say, 'It is difficult to harm a person we touch. It is somewhat easier to afflict pain upon a person we only see at a distance. It is still easier in the case of a person we only hear. It is quite easy to be cruel towards a person we neither see nor hear' (155; emphasis in the original). This, in itself, poses a serious challenge to our ability to understand the murderous process that unfolded at that first incident in Józefów, for which the members of Reserve Police Battalion 101—those middle-class family men with an average age of thirty-five—were unprepared.

As we have seen, when the voice of authority cracks, there is a drastic decrease in willingness to obey cruel orders. And indeed, 'Major Trapp represented not a strong but a very weak authority figure' (Browning 2001, 174). Trapp was not present at the site of the murders, however. The problem is further compounded if we consider the particularly gruesome method employed to commit the murders. The policemen were paired off with their victims, whom they marched to the execution site into the forest: 'Kammer then ordered the Jews to lie down in a row. The policemen stepped up behind them, placed their bayonets on the backbone above the shoulder blades as earlier instructed, and on Kammer's orders fired in unison' (61). As noted, proximity to the victim is supposed to decrease obedience.

It is important to note that even in this situation, that is, during the course of the massacre, it was still possible to refrain from participating: 'One policeman approached First Sergeant Kammer, whom he knew well. He confessed that the task was "repugnant" to him and asked for a different assignment. Kammer obliged,' and 'Another group of policemen approached Kammer and said they could not continue. He released them from the firing squad' (62). Lieutenant Drucker took a similar approach.[7] These examples are important, as they show that it is was not only the partially absent battalion commander, Major Trapp, who did not impose his authority, but, for the most part, the direct commanders at the execution site as well. This would appear to strengthen the argument that, at least in the case of Reserve Police Battalion 101, participation in horrific acts of murder cannot be explained by obedience alone. As Browning put it: 'There are some difficulties in explaining Józefów as a case of deference to authority' (174).

The absence of authority, combined with the principle whereby the greater the proximity the harder it is to commit acts of cruelty, should have led—at least according to Milgram's experimental model—to disobedience and the failure of the operation. Ultimately, however, the mission was completed *in a single seventeen-hour day*. Although a small number did ask to be released, 'it must not obscure the corollary that at least 80 percent of those called upon to shoot continued to do so until 1,500 Jews from Józefów had been killed' (74). It is worth noting at this point that the men of Reserve Police Battalion 101 'had not seen battle or encountered a deadly enemy. Most of them had not fired a shot in anger or ever been fired on, much less lost comrades fighting at their side.' They thus acted, 'not out of frenzy, bitterness, and frustration but with calculation' (161). In other words, the opposite of authority—if that is indeed what uncontrolled rage and madness are—cannot explain the reserve battalion's murderous behaviour either.

Browning, Bauman, and other scholars argue that it is far too easy to blame the German people, as uniquely capable of such atrocities. There may indeed be some relevant aspect of German culture, but this massacre cannot possibly be attributed wholly to some German biological or cultural trait. Beyond being superficial, such explanations lack scientific basis. Furthermore, the actions of Reserve Police Battalion 101 cannot be attributed to the Nazi education received by its members either, as these particular murderers were not educated under the Reich at all, nor were they ardent Nazis. The 'human nature' argument is both too general and insufficient. We know that the murderers experienced nausea and often found it difficult to carry out their assignments. Bauman suggests that Milgram's results may be explained in terms of the trap of sequential actions ('complicity after one's own act'): 'The trap is … a paradox: one *cannot get clean without blackening oneself*. To hide filth, one must forever draggle in the mud' (Bauman 2008, 158; emphasis in the original). This explanation, however, does not apply here.

The explanation of gradual progression—from a weaker electric shock to a slightly stronger one—is equally inadequate in this case, as the policemen were instructed to murder right from the start. Furthermore, even if we were to characterize the events that unfolded in Germany in the years 1933–1939 as shocks of 15 or 30 V, and what the policemen had experienced in Poland up to then as shocks of 45 or even 60 V, that is not enough to explain the sudden jump to 400 V, where the victims were not behind a wall, but shot at point-blank range. To Bauman's mind:

> There is little question that the substitution of morality of technology for the morality of substance was made much easier than it otherwise could be by the shifting of balance between the subject's closeness to the targets of his action, and his closeness to the source of authority of the action.[8] With astonishing consistency, Milgram's experiments turned evidence of the positive dependence between the effectiveness of the substitution, and the remoteness (technical more than physical) of the subject from the ultimate effects of his actions. One experiment, for instance, showed that when 'the subject was not ordered to push the trigger that shocked the victim, but merely to perform a subsidiary act ... before another subject actually delivered the shock ... 37 out of 40 adults ... continued to the highest shock level' (one marked on the control desk 'very dangerous—XX'). Milgram's own conclusion is that it is psychologically easy to ignore responsibility when one is only an intermediate link in a chain of evil action but is far from the final consequences of the action. To an intermediate link in the chain of evil action, his own operations appear technical, so to speak, on both ends. The immediate effect of his action is the setting of another technical task—doing something to the electrical apparatus or to the sheet of paper on the desk. The causal link between his action and the suffering of the victim is dimmed and can be ignored with relatively little effort.[9] Thus 'duty' and 'discipline' face no serious competitor. (161)

This description might explain the actions of men like Eichmann,[10] but in the case of Józefów, the policemen led their victims one by one. They had time to observe them, experience them, even to talk to them in some cases. They walked with them and shot them point-blank:

> Through the point-blank shot that was thus required, the bullet struck the head of the victim at such a trajectory that often the entire skull or at least the entire rear skullcap was torn off, and blood, bone splinters, and brains sprayed everywhere and besmirched the shooters... The shooters were

gruesomely besmirched with blood, brains, and bone splinters. It hung on their clothing. (Browning 2001, 64–5)

As we can see from this description, there is no remoteness here, but there is no exertion of authority either, as the witnesses quoted by Browning affirm: 'It was in no way the case that those who did not want to or could not carry out the shooting of human beings with their own hands could not keep themselves out of this task. No strict control was being carried out here' (65). Indeed, the principle of 'obedience as drill, lunacy as final outcome' (Kertész 2004, 101) would appear to be inapplicable to the massacre carried out by the reserve battalion. In any event, the end result is incontrovertible. Bauman is of the opinion that the story of Reserve Police Battalion 101 does not allow us to ignore 'the dark and dismal knowledge that many gentle people may turn cruel if given a chance', or, put another way, 'A particular disquiet and rage were caused by his hypothesis that cruelty is not committed by cruel individuals, but by ordinary men and women trying to acquit themselves well of their ordinary duties' (Bauman 2008, 153).

In the final analysis, it is hard to explain the actions of Reserve Police Battalion 101 solely on the basis of Milgram's experiment. Bauman and Browning therefore turn to Zimbardo's 1971 Stanford prison experiment. Zimbardo placed an advertisement in the newspaper, asking for volunteers to participate in a two-week study, in which they would be randomly divided into prisoners and guards. They were screened for mental disturbances and physical disabilities, as well as a history of criminal behaviour or substance abuse. The participants were assigned to their respective roles, as prisoners or guards, by flipping a coin, with nine volunteers in each group. The experiment began with the simulated arrest of the members of the prisoners group. Upon their arrival at the 'prison', they were stripped, deloused, issued stocking caps and dress-like uniforms, and chained on one ankle. Every uniform was marked, front and back, with an ID number, to be used in place of the prisoner's name. The guards, on the other hand, were instructed to establish rules and maintain order in the prison—stressing the importance of their role as well as the risks it entailed.

The first day passed uneventfully, but a rebellion broke out already on the morning of the second day. The prisoners removed their caps, tore the ID numbers off their uniforms, and barricaded themselves in one of the cells. The guards responded with anger and frustration, and called for reinforcements (experiment volunteers who had been kept in reserve), having decided to meet force with force. They attacked the prisoners with a fire extinguisher, broke into the cell, removed the beds, stripped the prisoners, and isolated the ringleader. In the aftermath of the rebellion, a deterioration in relations between guards and prisoners was observed. Over the course of the following days, the situation continued to worsen. At times, the prisoners were even prevented from going to the toilet. Before being locked in their cells at night, they were allowed to visit the common toilet one last time before lights out. With bags over their heads, their ankles shackled, and each with his hand on the shoulder of the prisoner in front of him, they were made to run to the toilet, while being shouted at by the guards. After lights out, at 10 p.m., they had to relieve themselves in a bucket left in the cells. On occasion, the guards did not allow them to empty the buckets, and the prison smelled of urine and faeces.

Three types of guards were identified: four were 'tough but fair'; two were 'good guards'; and about a third were hostile ('cruel and tough'), taking pleasure in the power they wielded and in humiliating the prisoners. Some of the guards became increasingly sadistic, especially at night, when they thought the cameras were off, engaging in abuse and sexual humiliation of the prisoners.

A further element worth mentioning is the fact that Zimbardo himself became part of the experiment. On the fifth night, he was approached by a number of the participants' parents, who sought the release of their sons from the experiment, but Zimbardo refused. In the end, although the experiment was supposed to have lasted for two weeks, all of the participants were released on the sixth day. Over the course of six days, some fifty people observed the experiment, yet only one questioned its morality. Zimbardo blamed himself and admitted that he had been swept up in his role as a prison warden. When there were rumours of a planned escape, he did not merely observe the events from the sidelines, but became concerned about the security of the prison he had built. As noted, the scientific validity of the study has been challenged, but such criticism seems to miss the main point. What is interesting about this experiment is precisely the fact that *Zimbardo himself, as someone who should have been able to maintain scientific distance, was swept up by it and became a part of it*—beginning to think and act like a prison warden.

According to Bauman (2008, 167), Zimbardo's prison experiment shows that the surprising behaviour of the guards 'stemmed from a vicious social arrangement, and not from the viciousness of the participants'.

Bauman further claims that 'what mattered was the existence of a polarity, and not who was allocated to its respective sides. What did matter was that some people were given a total, exclusive and untampered power over some other people' (167–8), and although 'there was no external, established authority ready to take the responsibility off the subjects' shoulders', terrifying authority was nevertheless generated 'by the subjects themselves' (166). Bauman seems convinced of the centrality of authority. In the case of Reserve Police Battalion 101, however, it is unclear what authority was exerted or even generated during the course of the massacre.

Browning draws a more complex picture. He notes that Milgram's experiments showed that when subjects were part of a disobedient confederate peer group, 90 per cent refused to comply. What is more, when they were given complete discretion over the level of electric shock to administer, the vast majority of subjects (with the exception of those motivated by sadistic tendencies) consistently delivered the minimum voltage, that is, they chose not to obey the rules of the experiment. In other cases, when the authority figure was absent, subjects recorded higher shocks than they actually delivered. It is worth noting, however, that none of the subjects dared to confront authority on their own. Browning thus attributes such behaviour to the ability to withstand peer pressure, rather than to the type of authority discussed by Bauman, which may or may not have influenced Reserve Police Battalion 101. Indeed, one of the experiments revealed that 'when a naive subject acting alone had been given full discretion to set the level of electric shock, the subject had almost invariably inflicted minimal pain. But when the two collaborators, always going first, proposed a step-by-step escalation of electric shock, the naive subject was significantly influenced' (Browning 2001, 175). Browning therefore suggests that, in the case of the reserve battalion, as in the Stanford prisoner experiment, a vital factor was conformity to the extreme elements of the group: 'Only the very exceptional remained indifferent to taunts of "weakling" from their comrades and could live with the fact that they were considered to be "no man",' and '80 to 90 percent of the men proceeded to kill, though almost all of them—at least initially—were horrified and disgusted by what they were doing. To break ranks and step out, to adopt overtly nonconformist behavior, was simply beyond most of the men.' As horrific as it sounds, it would indeed seem to have been 'easier for them to shoot' (184–6).

At this point I would like to reiterate something that Browning himself stresses: throughout the day, various policemen approached their commanders and were released from the firing squads. Others found passive ways to avoid participating in the massacre. The perpetrators would certainly have noticed. There was also a far from insignificant movement towards avoidance and not just by marginal figures within the battalion.

We may thus conclude that during the course of the massacre, there were a number of top-down forces (orders) at work, as well as a number of bottom-up forces (proceeding from the policemen upwards). Some of these forces pressed for the completion of the mission while others pressed for avoidance, while virtually none (with isolated exceptions) pressed for active opposition. It is hard to say exactly how matters unfolded, but the fact remains that the massacre was carried out.

The explanations provided by Bauman and Browning may afford some important insight into the behaviour of the members of the battalion, but they are by no means sufficient. It would be a fatal mistake, however, to run into the open arms of Goldhagen, whose thesis can be discerned already in the title of his book, *Hitler's Willing Executioners* (1997), and tell ourselves that such atrocities could only have been committed by Germans. I believe that Primo Levi rises to the challenge. Levi, as we shall see, provides deeper explanations—albeit explanations that may have cost him his life. The grey zone explains but, like the absurd, also becomes a prison.

10.2.2 The Black-Grey Zone as a Possible Explanation

Browning (2001) seems to acknowledge that his explanations are insufficient and therefore turns to Levi's grey zone: 'Levi focused on the spectrum of victim behaviour within the gray zone, he dared to suggest that this zone encompassed perpetrators as well' (187)—Muhsfeld, for example (mentioned earlier). Browning notes that 'The Gray Zone' is perhaps Levi's 'most profound and deeply disturbing reflection on the Holocaust', cautiously adding, without comparing victim and perpetrator, that 'the spectrum of Levi's gray zone seems quite applicable to Reserve Police Battalion 101. The battalion certainly had its quota of men who neared the "extreme boundary" of the gray zone,' and 'at the very center of the perpetrators' gray zone stood the pathetic figure of Trapp himself, who sent his men to slaughter Jews "weeping like a child"' (188).

Browning tries to explain the massacre perpetrated by the reserve battalion in terms of the grey zone but appears to do so in a unidimensional fashion—adopting the model only in part. The grey zone, however, is three-dimensional and complex and, above all, deceptive when observed from the outside. Indeed, I believe that Browning himself was deceived by the grey zone. It is not enough to say that the grey zone is a two-dimensional spectrum, stretching from light to dark grey, along which various figures may be placed. If we do decide to adopt the grey zone as an explanatory principle, we must plumb its depths and recognize the fact that it comprises a variety of opposing forces. It is this multiplicity of meaning that Browning seems to overlook. In particular, I believe that Browning fails to address the fact that *one may justify one's actions within the grey zone* not only on a pragmatic level, but from an ethical perspective as well. This is, in my view, the truly disturbing point. What is so striking about the men of Reserve Police Battalion 101 is not their obedience to orders, deference to authority, or conformity (or all three combined), but rather the fact that they managed to create a kind of ethical rationale that is possible only within the grey zone.

We are, it would appear, not built to commit murder day after day. This is not because of any particular affection for our fellow man, but because it nauseates us. In the grey zone, however, we are able to overcome that nausea and find justification for our actions—not only rational or utilitarian justification, but justification that allows us to continue to feel part of humanity, that is, moral justification. 'I made the effort', recounts a thirty-five-year-old reservist, 'to shoot only children', offering the following rationale: 'It so happened that the mothers led the children by the hand. My neighbor then shot the mother and I shot the child that belonged to her, because I reasoned with myself that after all without its mother the child could not live any longer' (73). To us, this explanation appears completely twisted, but in the grey zone, it seems, such explanations become possible.

The grey zone is characterized not only by severe cognitive distortion, but by double bookkeeping as well—two autonomous yet interdependent systems. On the most basic level, double bookkeeping—as in Orwell's

1984—signifies that every word has a dual meaning. One who is in the grey zone may thus record every event on two different maps and always speak in ambiguities. Outside the grey zone, the word 'clean' means to make a place less dirty. In the grey zone, however, it means to empty an area of unwanted objects: Jews, Roma (Gypsies), or others. Essentially, from the perspective of one who is in the grey zone, a certain area was merely 'cleaned' of dirt—'forgetting', although 'remembering' perfectly well, that 'dirt' in the grey zone equals unwanted object, 'bacillus' equals Jew, and 'disinfection' therefore equals genocide. Under such conditions, one may comfortably commit murder. Moreover, double bookkeeping creates a distorted world, in which even the word 'victim' may assume a different meaning, as it comes to designate the oppressors and the murderers, like Clamence in Camus's *The Fall*, who 'sacrificed himself' for others in the prison camp in North Africa, where he felt it was his duty to keep himself alive for them. The murderers are victims because they are constantly forced to 'clean' (or perhaps simply to clean, without quotes) entire areas—which they do because of their burning love for the Fatherland. In this context, it is worth mentioning Himmler's famous address, delivered to senior SS officers in October 1943, in which he said:

> We do not want, in the end, because we destroyed a bacillus, to be infected by this bacillus and to die. ... All in all, however, we can say that we have carried out this most difficult of tasks in a spirit of love for our people. And we have suffered no harm to our inner being, our soul, our character. (quoted in Arad et al. 1991, 345)

The understanding that the grey zone is a complex and extremely deceptive place—rather than a unidimensional axis between whiter and blacker zones—gives us greater insight into the way in which the oppressor acts within it. No less importantly, when we truly understand the complexity of the grey zone, we must discuss a further characteristic—one that is especially crucial: in the grey zone, desire disguises itself as law, and the state of emergency 'is not the exception but the rule' (Benjamin 2006, 392).

10.3 When Desire Disguises Itself as Law: Further Thoughts on the Grey Zone

10.3.1 The Insatiable Law: Perec[11]

Those in the grey zone find themselves in circumstances in which the laws are constantly changing, but there is no dispensation for ignorance of the law. A profound illustration of this idea can be found in the story of the island of W, described by Georges Perec, a French Jew born in 1936 (his father was drafted into the French army and killed in 1940, and his mother was murdered at Auschwitz in 1943), in his book, *W or The Memory of Childhood* (1988).

So what is the island of W? 'On most maps W did not appear at all or featured only as a vague and nameless blob with scarcely determined distinctions between land and sea' (66). It was founded by western colonists—outlaws or perhaps sportsmen, although 'it doesn't make much difference'—as 'a land where Sport is king' and 'life … is lived for the greater glory of the Body' (67).[12] Any infringement of the rules, 'intentional or unwitting—a meaningless distinction on W—leads to automatic disqualification' (71). Indeed, 'The rules of Sport are harsh and life on W makes them harsher still' (110). The laws of W are 'normally … laconic, and … [their] very silence is a mortal threat to the Athletes under its yoke' (152). At the same time, 'We know the world of W well enough to grasp that its most lenient Laws are but the expression of a greater and more savage irony' (154). In any event, the athletes derive no benefit from abiding by the laws, as reality on W is governed 'by arbitrary decisions, by aberrant umpiring' (112). On W, 'The Athlete must know that nothing is certain.… Decisions concerning him … are taken without reference to him' (117). Thus, for example, 'He may well believe that his task, as a sportsman, is to win … but he may come last, and still be declared the Winner: someone, somewhere, decided that that race, on that day, would be run that way', so that it is, in fact, 'more important to be lucky than to be deserving' (118). This arbitrariness is part of the desire 'to give everyone a chance'.

On W, four villages compete against one another, and the contests between them are in fact 'selections' (73)—held, it appears, on a daily basis. The precise ranking and seeding of the athletes 'reduces checking procedures to a minimum (86)', allowing the selection process to do the officials' work for them. The nature of all of the competitions on W may be understood by examining the contest known as the Atlantiad—an event 'placed under the sign of total liberty' (130), in which the best athletes would chase women brought from the women's quarters for that purpose and rape them 'right in front of the podium' (125). Due to the nature of the contest and the propensity of the contestants to conceal weapons in their clothes, 'it was decreed that the combatants, like the women they pursue, should be entirely naked' (127). Nevertheless, by the time the race begins, 'a good third of the field has already been essentially eliminated, either because they have been knocked out and are lying unconscious on the ground or because the wounds they have suffered ... have made them unable to run any distance, however short' (130). Even earlier, 'Pitched battles break out at night in the dormitories. Athletes are drowned in sinks and lavatory pans' (133).

As the story unfolds, it becomes clear that W is not an island dedicated to sport, but an extermination camp—and indeed, 'The survival of the fittest is the law of this land' (89). As expected, the results are poor, the contests a sham, the athletes 'dressed as clowns ... and each event is used as a pretext for mockery' (85). While the losers, if they survive—as the loss of a race 'may result in the death of the man who comes last' (110)—'are ... denied their evening meal' (90), the 'winners' obtain 'an extra meal' (91). It is all part of the 'dietary system of W', 'carefully designed to fulfil the athletes' dietary and caloric needs only in part'. The defeated athletes thus return 'exhausted, ashen-faced ... tottering under the weight of oaken yokes ... a little later, tearing each other to pieces for a scrap of salami, a drop of water, a puff at a cigarette' (139).

Children up to the age of fourteen are segregated from the rest of the population. At fourteen, they are sent to one of the four villages and become novices. Neither novices nor practising athletes have names. For the first six months, the novices are kept in quarantine, handcuffed and in leg irons, gagged, and chained to their beds at night: 'Initial acquaintance with W life is, in truth, a somewhat frightening spectacle' (139). The most important lesson a novice can learn is that '*the Law is implacable, but the Law is unpredictable. The Law must be known by all, but the Law cannot be known*' (117). A novice, if he is to survive, must understand that:

> What he is seeing is not anything horrific, not a nightmare, not something he will suddenly wake from.... This is life, real life.... That's what there is, and that's all. ... You have to fight to live. There is no alternative. ... It is not possible to say no. There's no recourse, no mercy, no salvation to be had

> from anyone. There's not even any hope that time will sort things out. ... There's this, there's what you've seen... Wherever you turn your eyes, that's what you will see, you will not see anything else, and that is the only thing that will turn out to be true. (139–40)

Indeed, after six months, when the novices are released from their bonds, they have but one path to survival, and that is to become a servant to one of the seeded athletes, catering to his every need, including his sexual gratification—just like Moni in Ka-Tzetnik's *Piepel* (1961). This is the essential pattern of social relations on W: 'There are two worlds, the world of the Masters and the world of slaves. The Masters are unreachable, and the slaves tear at each other' (Perec 1988, 160). This is life on W, deep within the grey zone:

> Submerged in a world unchecked, with no knowledge of the Laws that crush him, a torturer or a victim of his co-villagers, under the scornful and sarcastic eyes of the Judges, the W Athlete does not know where his real enemies are, does not know that he could beat them or that such a win would be the only true Victory he could score, the only one which would liberate him. But his own life and death seem to him ineluctable, inscribed once and for all in an unspeakable fate. (159–60)

In the grey zone, the law changes constantly and without warning, and it is up to individuals to find a way to survive. In order to do so, they must have the capacity to continuously adjust their systems of self-justification—to cast aside old principles and, like an empty vessel, adopt new principles as if they were eternal truths or Platonic Ideas, knowing full well that in an hour's time they might have to embrace new eternal truths, often at odds with the previous ones. Every new law is justified, moral, and necessary. Every new law immediately transforms the categorical imperative and the previous 'eternal' belief system. In order to survive, one must develop the ability to quickly and easily adopt new value systems.

In the grey zone, the compass needle never stops moving; it spins round and round, yet always points north—to 'the Führer's will' (Kershaw 2008). However, the Führer himself—and this is the crucial point—is constantly in motion: *both moved by the needle that spins around itself and, at the same time, moving it.* The entire system is thus perpetually in motion. It is in this context, as the following analysis of Kafka will show, that law and desire disguise themselves as one another.

10.3.2 When Desire Disguises Itself as Law: Kafka

It is no coincidence that the judges in Kafka's *The Trial* leaf through pornographic books or that the descriptions of the machine in 'In the Penal Colony' are so sensual. These are, in fact, allusions to the possible convergence of law and desire.[13] The narrowing of the gap between law and desire is characteristic of the grey zone. In the grey zone, the law adapts itself to changing desire—collapsing before power rather than curtailing it. In Kafka's seminal 'Before the Law', published both as an independent story and as part of *The Trial*, we meet a man from the countryside who wishes (or so it seems) to enter the Law. Before the gate to the Law stands a gatekeeper. The story may be interpreted in many different ways—inter alia, as a struggle between desire and law.

There is a tendency to view the man from the countryside as an innocent and the gatekeeper as the 'villain', representing power and law. The story may be understood, however, in an entirely different way. Although it is true that the man from the countryside does not enter the Law and remains seated in front of the gate until his death, speaking to the fleas in the gatekeeper's collar, it is also a situation in which there is a sort of tension between two opposing forces that exist in all of us—the forces Freud called ego and id, desire and law. Such tension may even be considered healthy, as it allows law and desire to restrain each other, resulting in a certain equilibrium.

When there is no law, desire is not restrained, and it is clear why that is dangerous. The opposite is also true: unrestrained law, as described with frightening precision in the dystopian novel *1984*, is extremely problematic. Both situations—unbridled law and unrestrained desire—are certainly alarming, but I would argue that something else happens in the grey zone. It is not merely a question of unbridled law or, alternatively, of unrestrained desire. It is a state in which both forces are still active but the gap between them has disappeared.

Ostensibly, the grey zone is controlled by orders and commands, that is, by the law. One of the law's most prominent features is its relative stability. In Nazi Germany, however, the law adapted itself to the regime or, more precisely, to the desire of the Nazi regime to exterminate—a process of pest control. *Under such circumstances, there is no tension between the gatekeeper and the man from the countryside. Law still stands guard at the gate, but it rides on desire.* This is precisely the process that Martens goes through in Kertész's *Detective Story* (2008)—we know where things begin, but we have no idea how they will end:

> Don't expect to learn what else happened that evening. It was no longer an interrogation but a poker game. I was still a new boy, as I have said; only then had I begun to see where I was and what I had taken on. I knew, of course, that a different yardstick applied in the Corps—but I believed there was at least a yardstick. Well, there wasn't... I grasped that we had now cast away everything that bound us to the laws of man; I grasped that we could no longer place our trust in anyone except ourselves. Oh, and in destiny, in that insatiable, greedy, and eternally hungry mechanism. *Were we still spinning it, or was it spinning us?* Now it all amounts to the same thing. *You think you are being very clever in riding events out, as I say, and then you find that all you want to know is where the hell they are galloping off to with you.* (103)

In the grey zone, desire is disguised as law, under the cover of which, the keeper of the law may do terrible things. Of course, this in no way absolves or justifies the oppressors, but merely offers a possible explanation of the mechanisms and logic that govern their actions. Law can limit our will to power, but when law and desire converge—or, more accurately, when desire disguises itself as law, when the tension between the gatekeeper and the man from the countryside dissipates—*the predictable result is genocide.* This is the process one undergoes in the grey zone—the pleasure of unlimited power. Few of us can refuse such power, which is why Camus (1956, 306) asserts that in order to be a man, one must 'refuse to be a god'.

In conclusion, the grey zone offers an explanation, if only a partial one, of the way in which people act in the impossible situation in which total power is exercised. It is an explanation that Levi himself, however, appears to have been unable to accept. The process came to a head when Levi agreed to translate Kafka's novel, *The Trial*, becoming irreversibly trapped in the grey zone. Levi's translation of *The Trial* and its impact on him will be discussed in the next chapter.

Notes

1. In this sense I certainly accept Arendt's (1979) generalization. As noted earlier, however, such generalizations should, as a rule, be approached with great caution.

2. In this context, it is interesting to note Milner's (2008) view that Ka-Tzetnik's writing reflects the world of the functionaries as far more complex.
3. Levi's choice of the word 'noble' here is particularly interesting, in light of his remarks on the noble gasses in *The Periodic Table*.
4. The metaphorical use that Levi makes of animals here and elsewhere would appear significant. As we have seen (in Chap. 1), animal imagery employed by Jews under Nazi occupation was not metaphorical at all, but a reflection of concrete reality.
5. The immediate context of this passage is Levi's polemic with Liliana Cavani, over her 'fine but mendacious film', *The Night Porter*, and her remarks ('We are all victims or murderers and we accept these roles voluntarily'), which may have been among the factors that motivated him to write about the grey zone in the first place—as evidenced perhaps by his oblique reference in the introduction to 'The Gray Zone': 'Many signs indicate that the time has come to explore the space that separates the victims from the tormentors (and not only in the Nazi Lagers), and to do so with a lighter touch and a less troubled spirit than has been the case, for example, *in certain movies*' (2015, 2433). See also 'Translator's Afterword' to *The Drowned and the Saved* (2571) and 'Notes on the Texts', *The Drowned and the Saved* (2872–3).
6. Initially, Levi, who was not at Birkenau, where the crematoria were located, knew little about the men who ran them, and, in the report he wrote together with Dr De Benedetti (published in October 1945), offered the following description: 'The work of operating the gas chambers and the adjacent crematorium was carried out by a special Commando which worked day and night, in two shifts. The members of this Commando lived in isolation, carefully segregated from any contact with other prisoners or with the outside world. Their clothes gave off a sickening stench, they were always filthy and they had an utterly savage appearance, just like wild animals. They were picked from amongst the worst criminals, convicted of serious and bloody crimes' (Levi 2018, 41). (In a way, this description of the Sonderkommandos comes as a relief, as it makes the question 'if this is a man' a little easier to bear.)
7. In contrast to Captain Wohlauf, who refused to accommodate those who asked to be released.
8. In this context, I cite the following passage from Levi's 'Testimony for Eichmann': 'And here are the compliant German technicians at work; here are the gas chambers being planned and constructed; here is the ideal poison, economical and effective. It is a gas originally meant to destroy rats in ships' holds, and it is ordered in bewildering quantities by an arm of the SS from IG Farbenindustrie. IG Farben diligently fulfil the orders and collect

the proceeds, without concerning themselves about anything else. Is there an invasion of rats going on? Better not to ask in order not to know. The German industrialists salve their consciences and profit from the poison' (Levi 2018, 89).

9. In this context, it is interesting to note Levi's observation in 'Nickel' (2015, 817–18): 'I thought that I had opened a door with a key and possessed the key to many doors, maybe all… I didn't think that, even if the method of extraction I had glimpsed could have found industrial application, the nickel produced would end up entirely in the helmets and bullets of Fascist Italy and Hitler's Germany.'
10. In this I have adopted Arendt's perspective in *Eichmann in Jerusalem* (2006). As I have noted, Arendt's approach is not above criticism. Some have even suggested that Arendt misunderstood and took a rather simplistic view.
11. This subsection is based, in part, on Ataria (2016).
12. This may be understood as an allusion to Germany, in light of the 1936 Munich Olympics, as well as the United States, where sport is 'king', but also to western culture in general and its Hellenic roots.
13. Brunner's (2004) analysis of Eichmann's personality shows that desire disguised as obedience offers some explanation of Eichmann's behaviour. Of course, no explanation is complete or sufficient.

References

Arad, Yitzhak, Israel Gutman, and Abraham Margaliot, eds. 1991. *Documents on the Holocaust: Selected sources on the destruction of the Jews of Germany and Austria, Poland, and the Soviet Union*. Trans. Lea Ben Dor. Lincoln, Nebr. and Jerusalem: University of Nebraska Press and Yad Vashem.

Arendt, Hannah. 1979. The origins of totalitarianism. San Diego: Harcourt Brace & Company.

———. 2006. *Eichmann in Jerusalem: A report on the banality of evil*. New York: Penguin.

Ataria, Yochai. 2016. The witness's death: Primo Levi and Georges Perec. In *Interdisciplinary handbook of trauma and culture*, ed. Yochai Ataria, David Gurevitz, Haviva Pedaya, and Yuval Neria, 195–216. New York: Springer.

Bauman, Zygmunt. 2008. *Modernity and the Holocaust*. Cambridge: Polity Press.

Benjamin, Walter. 2006. On the concept of history. In *Selected writings, vol. 4, 1938–1940*, ed. Howard Eiland and Michael W. Jennings, 388–400. Cambridge, MA: The Belknap Press of Harvard University Press.

Borowski, Tadeusz. 1976. *This way for the gas, ladies and gentlemen*. Trans. Barbara Vedder. New York: Penguin.

Browning, Christopher R. 2001. *Ordinary men: Reserve police battalion 101 and the final solution in Poland*. London: Penguin.

Brunner, José. 2004. Critique of pure banality: On Arendt's dehumanization of Eichmann (Hebrew). In *Hannah Arendt: A half-century of polemics* [Hannah Arendt: Ḥatsi me'ah shel pulmus], ed. Idith Zertal and Moshe Zuckermann, 81–106. Tel Aviv: Hakibbutz Hameuchad.

Camus, Albert. 1956. *The rebel: An essay on man in revolt*. Trans. Anthony Bower. New York: Vintage Books.

Ka-Tzetnik. 1961. *Piepel*. Trans. Moshe M. Kohn. London: Anthony Blond.

Kershaw, Ian. 2008. *Hitler, the Germans, and the final solution*. Jerusalem/New Haven: Yad Vashem and Yale University Press.

Kertész, Imre. 2004. *Kaddish for an unborn child*. Trans. Tim Wilkinson. New York: Vintage Books.

———. 2008. *Detective story*. Trans. Tim Wilkinson. New York: Knopf.

Lanzmann, Claude. 1985. *Shoah: An oral history of the Holocaust*. New York: Pantheon Books.

Levi, Primo. 1997. *Conversazioni e interviste 1963–1987*. Ed. Marco Belpoliti. Turin: Einaudi.

———. 2015. *The complete works of Primo Levi*. Ed. Ann Goldstein. Various translators. 3 vols. New York: Liveright.

Levi, Primo, with Leonardo De Benedetti. 2018. *Auschwitz testimonies, 1945–1986*. Ed. Fabio Levi and Domenico Scarpa. Trans. Judith Woolf. Cambridge: Polity Press.

Milner, Iris. 2008. The "Gray zone" revisited: The concentrationary universe in Ka. Tzetnik's literary testimony. *Jewish Social Studies* 14 (2): 113–115.

Perec, Georges. 1988. *W, or the memory of childhood*. Trans. David Bellos. Boston: David R. Godine.

CHAPTER 11

Kafka and Levi: Description of a Struggle

This chapter explores the nature of the connection between Levi and Kafka. As we will see, when Levi translated *The Trial* in the summer of 1982, he began to identify with the novel's protagonist, Joseph K. As he worked on the translation, Levi underwent a metamorphosis, ultimately conceding the necessity, even inevitability of the story's ending. I will also suggest that Levi's suicide was related to his attempt to confront Joseph K.'s miserable death, 'Like a dog!'

11.1 Translation and Identification

If we wish to understand the relationship between Levi and Kafka, it is only natural to begin with the mental process that Levi underwent while translating Kafka's *The Trial*. The translation took Levi six months, beginning in the spring of 1982. In an interview he gave to Federico De Melis on 5 May 1983 (Levi 2001, 155–60), shortly after the publication of his Italian translation of *The Trial*, Levi admits that he had been somewhat hasty in accepting the publisher's proposal. There were probably a number of reasons for this, including a desire to supplement his pension and sincere concern for the house of Einaudi, which was in financial straits at the time (Anissimov 1999).

For some reason, Levi believed he would be able to translate Kafka while maintaining a distance: 'I never thought it would involve me so deeply' (Levi 2001, 156)—an odd notion, considering the fact that Levi

Y. Ataria, *Primo Levi and Ka-Tzetnik*,
https://doi.org/10.1007/978-3-030-76743-3_11

was not unfamiliar with Kafka. 'I have to admit that Kafka has never been one of my favourite authors,' he tells De Melis, explaining the feeling as stemming less from 'disinterest or boredom' than from 'a certain defensiveness'. Levi's feelings, as he translated *The Trial*, were complicated: 'I felt *assaulted* by this book and I had to defend myself. … It … *runs through you like a spear*, like an arrow.' The idea of Kafka's writing as an 'assault' also appears in Levi's essay 'Translating Kafka' (2015, 2348–50):

> Kafka understands the world (his own, and ours today even better) with an astounding clairvoyance, which assaults you like a *light that's too bright*. Often we are tempted to interpose a shield, to take refuge; at other times we give in to the temptation to stare at it, and then are left dazzled. (2349)

Levi is aware of the fact that many of Kafka's readers feel the same way, and translating seems to escalate the problem: 'It is one thing to read the book sitting in your armchair, rapidly, without dwelling on it, and quite another *to plough through it word by word, piece by piece*, as you do when you are translating' (2001, 156). In another essay, Levi further explains the impact that translating *The Trial* had on him:

> Now, translating is more than reading, and I emerged from this translation as if from an illness. Translating is to examine under a microscope the fabric of the book, to penetrate it, to become entangled and involved with it. You take on this distorted world, where all logical expectations are in vain. You travel with Josef K. through dark mazes, on twisting paths that never lead where you expect. (2015, 2634)

As is his wont, Levi leaves no issue unresolved: 'Translating *The Trial*, I have understood the reason for my hostility towards Kafka. It is a form of defence born of fear' (2001, 156). The fear Levi describes is not generalized, but stems from 'the very particular reason that *Kafka was a Jew and I am Jew. The Trial opens with a surprise and unjustified arrest and my career, too, opened with a surprise and unjustified arrest*' (ibid.).

In his biography of Levi, Thomson (2003) argues that the more immersed Levi became in the translation of *The Trial*, the more he believed he resembled Kafka. In an interview that Levi gave to Roberto Di Caro in 1987, he says: 'At times I have portrayed myself in my books as brave, at others as cowardly, prophetic or naive, but always, I think, as a balanced individual.' Di Caro asks, 'And aren't you a balanced individual?' To which

Levi replies: 'I'm not very balanced at all. I go through long periods of imbalance, no doubt linked to my concentration-camp experience' (Levi 2001, 173). This follows Levi's admission, earlier in the interview, that he is 'living a neurotic life, with draining gaps between one book and the next' (170). These words, uttered by Levi on 1 January 1987, only four months before his suicide, reveal a far greater affinity to Kafka than one might expect.

The resemblance is not just between Levi the man and Kafka the man, but also between Levi's *If This Is a Man* and Kafka's *The Trial*. As time went on and the summer of 1982 progressed, Levi discovered ever greater commonalities with Kafka's protagonist, Joseph K.: 'Faced with Kafka I discovered unconscious defences within myself … my defences crumbled in translating him. I found myself involved in the character of Joseph K. I accused myself, as he did' (from an interview conducted by Giuseppe Bernardi, *Il Giornale*, 22 May 1983, quoted in Anissimov 1999, 358).

The translation of *The Trial* exacted a heavy price from Levi. In December of that year (1982), Levi told the Austrian historian Hermann Langbein—a survivor of the camps and recipient of Yad Vashem's 'Righteous Among the Nations' award—that he was going through his worst period since Auschwitz (Thomson 2003).[1] Levi (2001, 43), in fact, confessed to Thomson (in an interview originally published in December 1987, shortly after Levi's death) that: 'Looking back, I wish I hadn't: the undertaking disturbed me badly. I went into a deep, deep depression … And so I haven't read any Kafka since, he involves me too much.'[2] In Kafka, Levi saw a kind of prophet: 'Kafka is an author I admire—I do not love him, I admire him, I fear him, like a great machine that crashes in on you, like the prophet who tells you the day you will die' (156).

Levi was always considered an optimist, as he himself points out: 'It has been noted by many that it [*If This Is a Man*] is an optimistic and calm book in which you breathe the air rising up from the depths.' This was also how Levi saw himself. After having translated Kafka, however, he notes: 'Today, my thoughts are quite different. I think that only another Lager can be born from the fact of the Lager, that only bad can come of this experience' (158). It may be more accurate to say that Levi did not undergo any fundamental change following the translation, but that something fundamental, something that had previously been hidden and repressed, was suddenly revealed to him. In this context, it is interesting to recall the words with which Levi (2015, 1415) concludes the story 'The King of the Jews':

> Like Rumkowski, we, too, are so dazzled by power and money that we forget the fragility of our existence: we forget that we are all in the ghetto, that the ghetto is fenced in, that outside the fence are the lords of death, and a little way off the train is waiting.

This remark, which is less about Rumkowski than about western society in general, reveals Levi's inner Kafkaesque world, before ever having translated Kafka—an aspect of Levi's thinking that will be discussed at length below. With this in mind, could it be said that Levi never actually left the concentration camp (as superficial as such a statement may be)?

> And a dream filled with fear has not ceased to visit me, at intervals now close, now rare. It's a dream within another dream, varying in its details, unique in its substance. I am at the table with my family, or friends, or at work, or in a verdant countryside—in a serene, relaxed setting, in other words, apparently without tension and pain—and yet I feel a subtle, profound anguish, the definite sensation of a looming threat. And in fact, as the dream proceeds, little by little or brutally, each time in a different way, everything collapses and is destroyed around me, the scene, the walls, the people, and the anguish becomes more intense and more precise. Everything has now turned into chaos; I am alone at the center of a gray and murky void, and, yes, I *know* what this means, and I also know that I have always known it. I am again in the Lager, and nothing outside the Lager was true. The rest was a brief holiday, or a trick of the senses, a dream: the family, nature in flower, the house. Now this internal dream, the dream of peace, is over, and in the external dream, which continues coldly, I hear the sound of a well-known voice: a single word, not imperious, but brief and subdued. It is the dawn command of Auschwitz, a foreign word, feared and expected: get up, '*Wstawać*'. (397–8; emphasis in the original)

This dream could have been taken straight from one of Kafka's books. More than conveying a sense of gloom, Kafka's novels and stories heighten the idea and intensify the feeling that a system that seeks to crush the individual cannot be opposed. In Kafka's writings, the question is not *if* the individual will be crushed, but *when* and especially *how*. Furthermore, I would argue that just as Kafka's characters are crushed by the system, the reader is crushed by Kafka himself. And so, Levi too is crushed, but all the more so, as the act of translation takes him on a Kafkaesque journey of the most dangerous kind.

As we have seen, Levi always pursued order and logic, almost obsessively so. For example, in 'Hydrogen', in *The Periodic Table*, he writes: 'Like Moses, I expected from that cloud my law, order in myself, around me, and in the world' (771)—that is to say that Levi turned to chemistry out of a desire for order and logic. The struggle against Kafka is, at once, impossible and brutal—not because the Kafkaesque conclusion is that there is no order, but precisely because there is order and method; indeed, 'nothing in Germany was accidental' (870). The problem is that order and logic have nothing whatsoever to do with the idea of humanity. On the contrary, pure logic actually demands the pulverization of the human individual.

Levi's translation of *The Trial* received a number of critical reviews, but these would have come as no surprise to Levi, who had intentionally taken certain liberties with Kafka:

> I must confess that I was constantly at war with myself, split between my philological conscience that said I must respect Kafka and my personal reflexes, my own personal habits as a writer—what is called style—which are by now quite firmly fixed in me. (Levi 2001, 155)

Ultimately, Levi found it hard to overcome his natural tendency to explain and understand: 'always trying to explain, to resolve problems'; and here, just as in *If This Is a Man*, Levi sought 'to explain', if not to the reader, then at least 'to myself' (157). The contrast with Kafka, who makes no attempt to understand and may not even believe such a thing possible, could not be sharper. In an interview to Giovanni Tesio ('L'enigma del tradurre', *Nuovasocietà*, 18 June 1983), Levi remarked that '[Kafka, like] a mole, moves underground and does not even try to find a solution to the problem. Nevertheless, or perhaps for this very reason, he is a great writer' (Levi 1997, 207). Kafka cannot, in fact, be explained. Levi nevertheless sought to simplify and elucidate Kafka, thereby doing him a disservice. Indeed, the main problem with Levi's translation of *The Trial* is his inability to overcome the need to explain and to clarify, to stop asking *why*.

Although Levi himself believed that he had managed to keep this tendency in check, Prof. Sandra Bosco Coletsos, a Germanist at the University of Turin, argued that Levi's translation was, in fact, inadequate:

> It is too free a translation. The same word is at different times translated differently by Primo Levi. Occasionally Levi's word fits in better than the same word used by the author. He uses his own subjective choice, and the vocabulary he uses is much wider than that in the original and in the other translations... In our opinion, Levi's work—always excepting many happy solutions—does not find a suitable tone for what *The Trial* is and must be, with its verbal determination, essentiality and the unresolved ambiguities inherent therein. (quoted in English in Mendel 1998, 15)

Levi's decision to translate Kafka in his own way was not incidental, but a matter of survival. It was, I believe, Levi's last attempt to save himself from the Kafkaesque steamroller—a failed attempt that exacted a heavy price. Not only did Levi never return to Kafka, as he told Thomson ('I haven't read any Kafka since'), but even while translating Kafka, he rejected the Kafkaesque formula—the very same formula he refused to accept at Auschwitz. In *If This Is a Man*, Levi recounts an episode that occurred soon after his arrival at the camp: a guard snatched away an icicle that Levi had broken off to slake his thirst. When Levi asked *why* he had done so, the guard replied that '*there is no why here*'. To some extent, it is the same answer that Levi gets from Kafka, who further distils and refines it: *there is no why here*, only a system that crushes the individual; it is pointless to ask why; one must simply accept it. So too, when Levi's bunk-mate Schmulek tries to explain the selections and Levi is sceptical, Schmulek remarks, in Yiddish, '"*Er will nix verstayen*," he doesn't want to understand' (2015, 49). What Levi refuses to understand is the futility of the question *why*.

11.2 Shame

Kafka deals with a sense of extreme guilt, with which Levi was also familiar—not for any specific actions, but simply for being human, a member of the human race. In 'Chromium', in *The Periodic Table*, Levi describes it as follows: 'I felt ... guilty for being a man, because men had built Auschwitz' (876). Robert Antelme (1992, 51), who was not Jewish, describes a similar feeling: 'We provided a disdainful humanity with the means of revealing itself completely.' Indeed, if we are all *ordinary human beings*, we are all guilty. Kafka reminds Levi, however, of a far greater source of guilt and shame: the unique guilt associated with being a Jew.

In this context, the Austrian-Jewish writer and philosopher George Steiner said the following:

> The horror of the thing is we have lowered the threshold of mankind. ... We are that which has shown mankind to be ultimately bestial... Auschwitz breaks the reinsurance on human hope in a sense... And without us, there wouldn't have been Auschwitz. In a sense, an obscene statement and yet an accurate statement. (in Rosenbaum 1998, 314–15)

This quote is often interpreted rather superficially, accusing Steiner either of blaming the victim for being a victim (as victims of rape, for example, are sometimes blamed for being victims) or of making everyone a victim, thereby failing to make a sufficient distinction between perpetrator and victim. This latter accusation is related to the tendency of many scholars to view the Holocaust in terms of structural trauma, that is, trauma born of primal fear (such as castration anxiety). According to this approach, we are all part of a 'wound culture', which means that everyone is a victim (LaCapra 2014).[3] I would argue, however, that this reading of Steiner is too simplistic (and, to some extent, unfair). The problem Steiner poses is a far graver one—especially for 'a Jew'. As we have seen, the grey zone leaves no one untainted. It forces us to consider that all (or nearly all) of us could have acted like a cruel-but-not-necessarily-sadistic SS officer, a Sonderkommando, or a Kapo (for an extensive discussion, see Chap. 10). There is nothing inherent in human nature that precludes this, just as there is nothing inherent in modernity that precludes genocide. Indeed, '*The most frightening news brought about by the Holocaust and by what we learned of its perpetrators was not the likelihood that "this" could be done to us, but the idea that we could do it*' (Bauman 2008, 153; italics in the original).

The Jews are guilty, but it is a special kind of guilt. To paraphrase Robert Antelme, survivor of Buchenwald and the death march to Dachau and author of *The Human Race*, the Jews are guilty of having created conscience, and of having proven to the world that no one possesses it. The Holocaust thus creates a new kind of Jewish guilt or, some would say, revives and perfects a kind of Jewish guilt that was always there. Indeed, Levi is not guilty of having drunk from the pipe without sharing the water with Daniele (while sharing it with Alberto). This is concrete guilt that can be explained, justified, and, consequently, addressed. Beyond such concrete guilt, which Levi knew well, the guilt that Kafka evoked in him was deeper and more terrifying: guilt for being human in general and a Jew in particular or, perhaps more accurately, for being a Jew and, as such, revealing human nature.

It is important to stress here that Kafka did not tell Levi anything he did not already know. Levi knew full well, as he wrote in *If This Is a Man* (2015, 52), that 'no one must leave here who might carry to the world, together with the mark stamped in his flesh, the evil tidings of what man's audacity made of man in Auschwitz'. Kafka does not fundamentally change Levi. Nevertheless, when Levi faces Kafka's text and translates it into his own language, using his own words, he can no longer resist what he knows and has repressed.[4] Levi knows everything there is to know (or almost everything; enough, in any event) about the dark side of humanity, but flees this knowledge—which haunts him. In this sense, his decision to translate Kafka was a fatal mistake. It no longer allowed him to flee. It finally made him a member of a family to which one must not belong: 'He does not live for the sake of his own life; he does not think for the sake of his own thought. He feels as though he were living and thinking under the constraint of a family … Because of this unknown family … he cannot be released' (Kafka, quoted in Benjamin 1999, 808). Levi was imprisoned in the penal colony. A further problem from Levi's perspective was that he translated *The Trial* after he had retired from work, leaving him no refuge. The translation was thus the digging of a pit into which Levi fell/leapt a few years later.

To say that Levi's suicide was due, in part, to a general sense of guilt may be accurate, but it is also inadequate (and truth must sometimes be sought beyond literal accuracy). It was not 'the survivor's disease'. The guilt that Levi bore was not of the ordinary variety—I am alive at the expense of others. Levi's sense of guilt was far deeper and more complex: the understanding that we are all part of the same human race that is capable of conceiving, planning, and creating Auschwitz, does not allow a man like Levi to remain indifferent. In this context, it is worth mentioning Antelme, whose book, *The Human Race*, touches on many of the same points discussed in *If This Is a Man*. Antelme (1992, 218–20) explores the question of whether mankind may be separated into different species—something that would, in a sense, resolve everything:

> We have come to resemble whatever fights simply to eat, and dies from not eating; come to where we exist on the level of some other species, which will never be ours and towards which we are tending. But this other species which at least lives according to its own authentic law—animals cannot become more animal-like—appears to us as magnificent as our 'true' species, whose law may also be to lead us here to where we are. … If, facing nature, or facing death, we can perceive no substantial difference between the SS and ourselves, then we have to say that there is only one human race. And we have to say that everything in the world that masks this unity, everything that places beings in situations of exploitation and subjugation and thereby implies the existence of various species of mankind, is false and mad; and that we have proof of this here, the most irrefutable proof, since the worst of victims cannot do otherwise than establish that, in its worst exercise, the executioner's power cannot be other than one of the powers that men have, the power of murder. He can kill a man, but he can't change him into something else.

If there is any insight, beyond experience, that truly cannot be communicated, it is precisely this. That is why the survivor feels 'that he is from now on going to be prey to a kind of infinite, untransmittable knowledge' (289). This infinite knowledge is knowledge of humanity. According to Levi (2015, 1420), at Auschwitz, 'each of us could perceive distant reflections of himself and of the human race'. Levi, as one *who was there*, plays a special role in that discovery. As a Jew, he is guilty because he is part of a contaminating group—albeit involuntarily, albeit through no fault of their own (albeit, albeit ...). Indeed, in 1955, in an essay entitled 'The Deported. Anniversary', Levi (1128) writes the following:

> It is shame. *We are men, we belong to the same human family that our executioners belong to.* Before the enormity of their crime, we feel that we, too, are citizens of Sodom and Gomorrah, and cannot be exempted from the charge that an otherworldly judge, on the basis of our own testimony, would bring against all humanity.

Levi (2018, 91) himself thus maintains, in his 'Testimony for Eichmann', that the Nazis' modus operandi in the concentration camps allowed a man like Auschwitz camp commandant Rudolf Höss to say, 'We are no more dirty than you.' As we have seen, none who entered the grey zone could preserve their innocence—or, more accurately, preserve their *feeling* of innocence—as all became tainted.[5] This taint manifests itself as a sense of guilt, and although it is nothing like the guilt of the perpetrator, it also has a price: 'I sensed one thing only, but that I was sore about, which is that everybody would have a price to pay in this case, everybody' (Kertész 2008a, 51). Thus, in Kertész's surrealistic novella, *The Pathseeker* (2008b), a man sets out on a journey—one that may be construed as a concentration camp survivor's return to the camp, in order to stimulate his memory. In the course of his journey to the camp, he discovers that all of the testimonies of the horrors that occurred there have vanished (or worse, have become institutionalized—merely another attraction for tourists), to the point that the commissioner himself no longer trusts his own memory. After having failed in his mission, he returns to the town, where he meets a woman, also a survivor, and the following dialogue ensues:

> "Madam?" he said in the end, not knowing himself how he had lighted on this semi-interrogative, semi-distancing, old-fashioned mode of address.

> "Sir?" the locution was returned in similar currency by a deep-sounding female voice, and the veil seemed to flutter as though from suppressed laughter.
>
> "Can I do anything for you?" the commissioner asked.
>
> "What can anyone do for me?" the woman responded. "I saw you up on top," she added.
>
> "On top?" the commissioner asked uncertainly.
>
> "You chased off that woman inspector. You spoke about your assignment. What did you accomplish?" The commissioner flinched at the implacability of her voice.
>
> "On what ground are you asking me?" he asked, more sharply than he had intended.
>
> "On what ground would you keep it to yourself?" the woman riposted, no less rudely.
>
> "I don't know who you are, madam," the commissioner said disconcertedly.
>
> "Nor do I any longer," came the answer. The veiled face moved, turning slightly sideways from him. "My father," she said slowly, leaving a pause between each and every word. "My younger brother. My fiancé."
>
> "I'm terribly sorry," said the commissioner. "I can't be of any help."
>
> The veil turned again to face him.
>
> "My father, my younger brother, and my fiancé," the woman repeated, as if she had heard nothing.
>
> "I have done everything that I can do," said the commissioner. "You can't accuse me of anything."
>
> "You misunderstand me," the woman answered. "How could I accuse you? There is no charge that you could not refute. After all, you are here."
>
> "By chance," said the commissioner.
>
> "There is no such thing as chance," he heard dully and tremulously from behind the veil. "Only injustice." (78–80)

The book ends with the commissioner's discovery, the following day, that the woman he had spoken to killed herself—which raises the question (a rhetorical one): could it have been otherwise? The grey zone taints everyone who interacts with it. The commissioner set out to accuse and was himself accused (and if 'there is no such thing as chance', the woman's survival was not a matter of chance either). With time, testimonies falter (sometimes concealing more than they reveal) and memories fade, and survivors find it increasingly difficult to place themselves unequivocally on the side of *the victims*, in a process that stems from the tainting of those who acted in the grey zone.

In *Fiasco*,[6] Kertész describes this inevitable sullying. The context is a meeting with an editor to discuss the publisher's assessment of his novel *Fateless* (2006):

> It was now my turn to be confused: the indications were that, to the extent he might feel my novel was bitter, it would probably not be to his taste. This would obviously be a black mark and might set its publication back. Only then did I see that I was sitting opposite a professional humanist, and *professional humanists would like to believe that Auschwitz had happened only to those to whom it had happened to happen at that time and place; that nothing had happened to the majority, to mankind—Mankind!—in general.* In other words, the publishing man wanted to read into my novel that notwithstanding—indeed, precisely notwithstanding—everything that had happened to happen to me too at that time and place, Auschwitz had still not sullied me. *Yet it had sullied me. I was sullied in other ways than were those who had transported me there, it's true, but I had been sullied none the less*; and in my view this is a basic issue. I have to recognize, however—how could it be otherwise?—that anyone who takes my novel in his hand in good faith and innocently starts to read it will thereby, it is to be feared, also be dragged a little bit into the mire. (2011, 37)

This sullying creates an irreversible sense of shame. And it is precisely in this tainted and tainting space that Levi encounters Kafka, and the encounter is doomed, an accident waiting to happen. As we discover in the final scene of *The Trial*, this shame is an indelible stain:

> But the hands of one of the partners were already at K.'s throat, while the other thrust the knife deep into his heart and turned it there twice. With failing eyes K. could still see the two of them immediately before him, cheek leaning against cheek, watching the final act. "Like a dog!" he said; it was as if the shame of it must outlive him. (Kafka 1956, 286)

In 'Translating Kafka', Levi (2015, 2350) puts it as follows:

> The famous, much analyzed phrase that seals the book like a tombstone ('… it was as if the shame of it should outlive him') *does not seem at all enigmatic to me.* What should Josef K. be ashamed of, that man who had decided to fight to the death, and who at every turn in the book proclaims that he is innocent? He is ashamed of many contradictory things, because he is not consistent, and his nature (like that of most of us) consists in being inconsistent: not the same over the course of time, unstable, erratic, divided even at

the same moment, split into two or more personalities that cannot exist together.

He is ashamed of having quarrelled with the tribunal of the cathedral and, at the same time, of not having stood up to the tribunal of the garrets with sufficient force. Of having wasted his life in petty office jealousies, in false love affairs, in morbid timidity, in static and obsessive accomplishments. *Of existing when, by now, he should no longer exist: of not having found the strength to kill himself by his own hand when all was lost, before the two inept death-bearers visited him.* But I sense, in this shame, an element that I am familiar with: Josef K., at the end of his anguished journey, feels ashamed that this secret, corrupt tribunal exists, pervading everything around it; even the prison chaplain and the precociously dissolute girls who importune the painter Titorelli belong to it. In the end it is a human, not a divine, tribunal: it is made of men and by men, and Josef, with the knife already planted in his heart, is ashamed of being a man.

11.3 Inevitable Death

The Trial ends as follows:

Then one of them opened his frock coat and out of a sheath that hung from a belt girt round his waistcoat drew a long, thin, *double-edged butcher's knife*, held it up, and tested the cutting edges in the moonlight. Once more the odious courtesies began, the first handed the knife across K. to the second, who handed it across K. back again to the first. *K. now perceived clearly that he was supposed to seize the knife himself*, as it traveled from hand to hand above him, *and plunge it into his own breast. But he did not do so, he merely turned his head, which was still free to move*, and gazed around him. *He could not completely rise to the occasion, he could not relieve the officials of all their tasks*; the responsibility for this last failure of his lay with him who had not left him the remnant of strength necessary for the deed. His glance fell on the top story of the house adjoining the quarry. With a flicker as of a light going up, the casements of a window there suddenly flew open; a human figure, faint and insubstantial at that distance and that height, leaned abruptly far forward and stretched both arms still farther. Who was it? A friend? A good man? Someone who sympathized? Someone who wanted to help? Was it one person only? Or was it mankind? Was help at hand? *Were there arguments in his favor that had been overlooked? Of course there must be.* Logic is doubtless unshakable, but it cannot withstand a man who wants to go on living. Where was the Judge whom he had never seen? Where was the high Court, to which he had never penetrated? He raised his hands and spread out all his fingers.

> But the hands of one of the partners were already at K.'s throat, while the other thrust the knife deep into his heart and turned it there twice. With failing eyes K. could still see the two of them immediately before him, cheek leaning against cheek, watching the final act. "Like a dog!" he said; it was as if the shame of it must outlive him. (Kafka 1956, 285–6)

Levi (2001, 160) finds this brutal but inevitable ending hard to swallow:

> *The Trial* makes us more aware. Think of the end of the book, the final scene: the blue sky and that form of execution at the hands of two men, in essence two automata who hardly ever speak, who swap crass insults and are wholly indifferent. They are quite expert in the rules of execution and they want to do everything just so, according to their orders. But this is a death penalty, they twist the knife in his heart. Now this ending is so cruel, so unexpectedly cruel, that if I had a young child I would spare him. I fear it would disturb him, make him suffer, although of course it is the truth. *We will die, each of us will die, more or less like that.*

In 'Translating Kafka', Levi (2015, 2349–50) writes that he, an Auschwitz survivor, would never have written such a shocking description—due to a lack of ability and imagination, due to a sense of shame in the face of death that Kafka did not know, or simply due to cowardice. Although Levi claims he could not have written such an ending, it was not enigmatic to him. I believe this was a critical moment in Levi's life—the moment he understood and internalized not only that the book's ending is not enigmatic, but that it is even inexorable and necessary.

In 'Potassium', in *The Periodic Table*, Levi (800) writes: 'Distilling is beautiful ... because it includes a metamorphosis, from liquid to gas (invisible) and back to liquid again; but on this double path, up and down, it reaches purity.' I believe that during the course of the translation, Levi experienced a kind of metamorphosis, a 'distillation' that brought him into the state in which he accepted the ending of *The Trial* as the only possible ending. Before exploring the issue further, however, I would like to take a look at the story 'In Due Time' (in *Lilith and Other Stories*; 1473–82). It is important to keep in mind that this story was first published on 25 May 1980,[7] before Levi translated Kafka.

Giuseppe is a fifty-year-old fabric salesman, who is 'tired of being Giuseppe, tired of being tired'. One evening, he receives a rare telephone call at the shop and the stranger on the other end of the line asks for an appointment with him, with 'Giuseppe N., born in Pavia, October 9

1930'. Giuseppe asks whether the matter is urgent. The stranger replies that it is not, and they agree to meet on Monday morning, a day on which the shop is closed. The visitor, who is Giuseppe's age (a kind of doppelgänger), arrives and boorishly takes a chair and sits without speaking for a number of minutes. Giuseppe becomes increasingly irritated as he waits for the stranger to say something. After a while, the visitor makes a couple of ostensibly casual remarks, as if passing the time of day, including the following: 'It used to be different ... there was more certainty than there is now.' Giuseppe does not understand what the visitor wants from him and interrupts: 'You said on the phone that you had to speak to me.' The visitor then recounts a number of incidents from Giuseppe's past, proving without a doubt that he is well acquainted with the salesman's life. Giuseppe again interrupts the visitor and impatiently asks, 'Well, what do you want from me?' The visitor's response is short and to the point: 'I've come to kill you' (1473–5). This leads to the following exchange:

> Giuseppe, although he was tired of many things, was not ready to die. Someone who is tired of life, or who says he is, doesn't necessarily want to die; in general, he wants only to have a better life. He said this to the stranger, but the man answered harshly:
>
> 'You know, what you want or don't want counts only up to a certain point. Don't think it's my initiative; these things are decided elsewhere. [...]'
>
> 'And ... why me? And when? Now? In other words, since I'm the interested party, I'd like to know a little more.'
>
> 'My, you really are something! Why, when, how, where! Do you have connections? [...] Of course, we'd all like to know certain things, but we can't: people like you (or like me, in fact; when we're off duty we're just doormats, too) have to accept it,[8] settle down and wait, and live from day to day, hoping it's not the last day.' (1475–6)

Giuseppe considers bribing the visitor—just as the man from the countryside bribes the gatekeeper in *The Trial*—to allow him to die painlessly. In Kafka's story, the gatekeeper accepts the bribes, but scrupulously tells the man from the countryside that they are of no use. Like the gatekeeper, the visitor accepts Giuseppe's cheque (how much should he give, Giuseppe wonders), but unlike the gatekeeper, the visitor does so gladly, adding that 'it was money well spent' (1476). It is important to note that the visitor himself is of little importance—as he tells Giuseppe: 'people like you (or like me, in fact; when we're off duty we're just doormats, too)'. In other words, in the eyes of the system, no one is particularly important. As noted above, Levi (2001, 156) said, in an interview conducted soon after the publication of his translation of *The Trial*, that he fears Kafka 'like a great machine that crashes in on you, like the prophet who tells you the day you will die'. In the story 'In Due Time', Levi encounters just such a prophet: the visitor who is Giuseppe's contemporary. Levi, even if he is not contemplating suicide, begins to accept a different kind of logic. Améry (1999) stresses that there is a logic of life and a logic of death, and they are incompatible. When one is willing to accept the validity of the logic of death, suicide becomes a concrete possibility: 'What must not be cannot be'; '*I die, therefore I am* ... I die, therefore I *was*' (26–7; emphasis in the original).

In any event, this story shows that Levi undoubtedly knew Kafka and corresponded with him, albeit unilaterally, long before he translated him. The Kafkaesque world is not foreign to Levi. In fact, more than Kafka changed Levi, he revealed that which Levi already harboured within. In particular, the idea of inevitable death, arbitrarily and irrevocably determined by the system, a recurrent theme in Kafka's books, is familiar to Levi from his inner experience, as it is familiar to other Holocaust survivors. In this sense, Kafka is Levi's unconscious (or doppelgänger that always foretells death)—the unconscious that Levi seeks to escape. In deciding to translate Kafka, however, Levi exposes himself to all that he has repressed—above all, the death wish.

The moment that Levi accepts the ending of *The Trial* not only as the most logical outcome, but as the only possible outcome, his time begins to run out. Once again, it is not that this mode of thinking is new to Levi, but having translated *The Trial*, he can no longer repress what he has known at least since his imprisonment in the concentration and extermination camps. Perhaps this lies at the root of the visitor's remark to Giuseppe, 'It used to be different ... there was more certainty than there is now.' In a similar vein, Kertész writes:

> 'Is that what our lives are about: avoiding winding up as freight on one of those trucks?' 'That, indeed,' the pianist nodded, and by way of reassurance, as it were, patted Köves gently on the nape of the neck. 'And then you wind up on it anyway. If you're really lucky,' he qualified with an expression that Köves this time felt was malicious, almost antagonistic, 'you might even wind up at the back, at the rear end.' (Kertész 2011, 154)

Going back to the ending of *The Trial*, we may now take another look at Levi's death:

> *K. now perceived clearly that he was supposed to seize the knife himself*, as it traveled from hand to hand above him, *and plunge it into his own breast. But he did not do so, he merely turned his head, which was still free to move*, and gazed around him. *He could not completely rise to the occasion, he could not relieve the officials of all their tasks.*

K.'s death is inevitable, but K. was unable to rise to the occasion. Levi who saw himself as Joseph K. ('I found myself involved in the character of Joseph K. I accused myself, as he did') was left with only one option: *Primo Levi now perceived clearly that he was supposed to seize the knife himself.* His death was inevitable—simply because '*Thou shalt not be*' (Antelme 1992, 74; emphasis in the original). This idea is somewhat pervasive in discourse pertaining to victims of the Holocaust, in which it is often seen as a key principle:

> Survivorship, survival, being a remnant, are extreme situations, whose rarity and improbability define them. Life after a catastrophe is considered an act of grace, a gift, but this grace is two-edged, very often it is poisoned, and sometimes it can turn into a curse. Survivors bear a kind of a lifelong guilt, a guilt both self-imposed and imposed by others, because of the very fact that they have survived; the very quality of survivorship is their offense, the offense of having lived on in a place and time in which they were supposed to be dead. Only dying—that is, joining all the other dead, however late in the day—can absolve them of that guilt. (Zertal 2005, 52)

After having translated *The Trial*, Levi could no longer escape the Kafkaesque world and had no choice but to confront Kafka. True, his death was certain, but maybe, he could die like a *man* and not like a *dog*. Contrary to K., who 'could not completely rise to the occasion', Levi does rise to the occasion, defeating Kafka in the internal struggle between the two figures, the doubles, and completing the task himself. Furthermore, in taking his own life, Levi may have adopted Améry's view of suicide as an affirmation of his having lived, or even as proof of 'my independence and my new terrible freedom' (Dostoevsky 2005, 619). He is alive and he is dead—but not like a dog, not at the hands of the arbitrary machine but by his own hand.

On 27 July 1986, less than a year before his suicide, Levi's cousin, Ada Della Torre, passed away, after having suffered from Alzheimer's disease for eight years. On the day of her death, Levi published the short story 'Force Majeure' (2015, 2311–14) in *La Stampa*. The protagonist, M.[9]—probably derived from Levi's middle name, Michele—brings to mind Kafka's K., while the story itself is reminiscent of Kafka's 'Description of a Struggle' (1958), with the addition of the motif of dog from *The Trial*.

This is the story, in brief: M. rushes to a meeting in an unfamiliar part of the city, asks directions, and finds himself in a long, narrow alley. About halfway down the alley, he sees a burly young man, probably a sailor, coming towards him and, at the same time, hears the bark of a dog behind him. The slightly built M. and the sturdy young sailor continue walking towards one another until they are standing face to face. The sailor blocks the way, snatches M.'s glasses, puts them in M.'s pocket, and punches him in the stomach. M. has never been in a situation like this before, has never hit anyone (as Levi says about himself). He musters everything he has read on the subject of fighting and attempts to take the sailor by surprise, but fails miserably. At this moment, getting through the alley seems like a matter of life and death to M. As he stands there in the sailor's grasp, with the dog sniffing at him, a young woman, probably a prostitute, passes the dog, M., and the sailor, as if they are invisible, and disappears at the end of the alley. Up to this point, M. has led a normal life, never having felt the sensation of being crushed by a force majeure, of being absolutely impotent. Escape would appear to be his only option and he wonders whether it is worth dying to get through an alley. The sailor continues to apply force, pushing M. to the ground, with his hands behind his back, like a prisoner. The sailor presses down on M.'s shoulders and grabs him by the heels, until he is lying completely flat. He then chases away the dog, takes off his sandals, and walks along M.'s body. Having passed over M., he puts his sandals back on and walks away, followed by the dog. M. gets up, puts on his glasses, straightens his clothes, wonders whether he might derive some advantage from the event, and concludes that there is nothing whatsoever to be gained from it, nothing positive he might take with him from the experience. What happened to him did not correspond to any model he knew: the models are chivalrous, while life is not. What befell him *dirtied him* and, as a result, his life was changed forever.

It is hard to overstate the importance of this story, which, when read closely, seems like it could have been written by Kafka himself. Thomson (2003) suggests that the story may be an allegory of Levi's experience at

Auschwitz, treated as an encounter with a crushing force majeure. The dog represents the shame of the encounter—a stain that can never be removed, even after death. The most important part of the story, however, is Levi's admission that, in the end, despite all of his writing and research, he learned nothing from the experience of Auschwitz, which had merely left him alone and dirtied, his life forever changed. Indeed nothing good could have come of it: 'I think that only another Lager can be born from the fact of the Lager, that only bad can come of this experience' (Levi 2001, 158).

Let us now return to the idea of distillation: 'Distilling is beautiful … because it includes a metamorphosis, from liquid to gas (invisible) and back to liquid again; but on this double path, up and down, it reaches purity.' When Levi translates Kafka, he changes to a different state—from liquid to invisible gas—and when he returns to his liquid state, he is the same Levi, or perhaps he returns, in the end, to the Levi he had repressed since Auschwitz. The process of distillation that Levi underwent left him no choice but to accept that the ending of *The Trial* is not only the most logical outcome, but perhaps the only possible outcome.

Levi's time, as we have seen, is borrowed time (until the visitor's return, *in due time*). He understands that if he does not complete the task on his own, that is, take his own life, he will end up like M., dying humiliated and entirely without dignity.

11.4 When Kafka and Levi Met in the Grey Zone

Although his writing proves how sharp and aware Levi was, how clearly he saw reality, how well he understood what few others did, he was often accused of *refusing to understand*. I believe that Levi really did understand the processes at work at the concentration and death camps. I would argue, however, that he refused to understand something deeper: the idea that some things cannot be explained.

It was his obsessive search for an explanation that led Levi to one of the most important and shocking insights into the Holocaust: that the perpetrators, the executioners, were ordinary human beings. Under certain conditions, almost anyone can become a Kapo. Levi too is an ordinary human being. Although this insight opened the door to a greater understanding of the processes of genocide, from the moment this door opened, others closed. If there was nothing unique about the executioners, we may be able to explain and understand, but at what price? The loss of humanity itself. Levi thus yielded to Kafka.

Kafka is no stranger to Levi. Indeed, Levi's M., as we have seen, is none other than Kafka's K., that is, Levi's uncanny doppelgänger. Levi flees Kafka, until, in a moment of weakness, he agrees to translate him and the dam bursts. Levi sees himself as Joseph K. and, in so doing, understands that he must die and that his death like a dog is inevitable. Joseph K., however, is unable to complete the task and therefore, rather than dying 'free' (to the extent that such a thing is possible in Kafka's writings), becomes the miserable victim of a murder. In such a world—a grey, Kafkaesque world—there is only one recourse: to rewrite *The Trial*. That is what Levi did in his life, or, more precisely, sought to accomplish with his death. Unlike K., Levi does not wait for someone else to do the job for him. When his memory begins to fail, he understands that his time has *past* and that he must take action before he is overtaken by helplessness and wretchedness. As we have seen, Levi's physical condition was also deteriorating at the time.

After translating *The Trial*, Levi began to internalize what he had refused to internalize after Auschwitz: that there is no point trying to understand. The system crushes people and it is impossible to know why. In the story 'In Due Time', the visitor who came to kill Giuseppe tells him that there is little difference between them: both the man from the countryside and the gatekeeper are in the grey zone. The gatekeeper is an ordinary person who had the opportunity to acquire some power and authority in a world in which the system crushes the individual, and therefore, when he shuts the gate, it is not only the life of the man from the countryside that comes to an end, but the life of the gatekeeper as well—he himself becomes the man from the countryside.

Closing the gap between Giuseppe and the visitor who comes to foretell his death attests to the fact that the law does not limit desire, but cleaves to it—just as the yellow star adheres not only to the lapel of the coat but to very soul of the wearer. In such circumstances, the law is no more than desire in disguise. And indeed, as we have seen, this may offer the most accurate description of the grey zone: *a zone in which desire is disguised and appears as law, and words immediately become actions.* When we read Kafka, we find this motif in *The Trial*, *The Castle*, and elsewhere.

The combination of the Kafkaesque machine and the grey zone is deadly, inescapable. The Kafkaesque world is not theoretical; it became reality at Auschwitz and tainted all who were there, both murderers and victims. As usual, Levi's message leaves room for complexity. In 'Zinc', in *The Periodic Table*, he writes:

> Two opposing philosophical conclusions could be drawn: praise of purity, which protects us from evil like a hauberk; praise of impurity, which lets in change—that is, life. I threw out the first, as grossly moralistic, and paused to consider the second, which was more congenial to me. For the wheel to turn, for life to live, impurities are needed, and the impurities of impurities. ... I, too, am a Jew and she isn't: I am the impurity that makes the zinc react.

Both sides, although they must not be confounded, became impure, tainted, dirtied. Levi is part of this story, part of this contamination. Indeed, Levi understood this already in *If This Is a Man*, even before he had completely thought it through. Levi grappled with this question for forty-two years.

In a sense, the entire philosophy of existentialism may be summed up in the phrase 'We are all human'. In Camus (1956), this idea gives us a common fate and healing. In Levi, at least in his final years, it is a Kafkaesque common fate. Yes, we are all human, but we have no responsibility for one another and, when we are given absolute power, we all become Cain—our brothers' murderers and heirs. In light of our addiction to power and in keeping with the opportunities afforded to us, we will become collaborators with the system. It is impossible to synthesize an ideal figure, capable of resisting the temptation of being part of power, nor is there a vaccine or cure for it:

> Even brotherhood and solidarity, the final strength and hope of the oppressed, break down in the Lager. The struggle is all against all; your greatest enemy is your neighbour, who has designs on your bread and your shoes, and simply by his presence deprives you of a hand's-breadth of pallet. He is a stranger who shares your afflictions but is remote from you; in his eyes you do not read love, but envy if he is suffering more than you, fear if he is suffering less. The law of the camp has turned him into a wolf; you yourself must struggle not to become a wolf, to remain a man. (Levi 2018, 131)

There is no way to immunize ourselves, because Auschwitz is the height of progress, the most important achievement of the civilized world. Auschwitz is the culmination of civilization, not the exception but the rule. Or, rather, if Auschwitz is the exception, then it is the exception that proves the rule—albeit from above, not from below, that is to say that Auschwitz succeeded where others have generally failed, for technical reasons of one kind or another. After forty years of deliberation, Levi finally came to terms with this thought. Indeed, in *The Drowned and the Saved*, Levi took this idea to its logical conclusion and remained forever trapped within it. This is the Kafkaesque, totalitarian logic.[10]

After Auschwitz, Levi wondered whether *this is a man*, knowing that a positive answer to the question would lead to the rational and reasonable solution that one must end one's life in a world that cannot be changed. For a long time, it seems that Levi could imagine other alternatives to the answer *this is a man!* After translating Kafka's *The Trial*, however, no alternatives remained. This sense of hopelessness, as a state of mind, is perfectly captured in the following conversation between Kafka and his friend Max Brod:

> [Kafka:] 'We are nihilistic thoughts, suicidal thoughts that come into God's head. … Our world is only a bad mood of God, a bad day of his.'
>
> [Brod:] 'Then there is hope outside this manifestation of a world we know.' …
>
> [Kafka:] 'Oh, plenty of hope, an infinite amount of hope, but not for us.' (quoted in Benjamin 1999, 798)

It is not a coincidence that M. finds himself in a long and narrow alley, with 'no widenings or doorways'. In Kafka's world, there is one entrance and one exit. One can choose whether to go forward and pay the price or backward and pay the price, but a price must always be paid. Nevertheless, Levi found a way out. The modern world sits atop a sewer system, and the only way out of the alley is through the sewers.

Levi steps outside his door, takes the post from the concierge, smiles, and says thank you. The solution was always there. He makes sure that the nurse, there to look after his mother, is standing by the phone, so as not to disturb him. He is in alley that is closing in on him. He is crushed: 'Because what is, is. What we are, we are. And both are impossible' (Antelme 1992, 65). Levi solved Joseph K.'s problem and, by his death, sought to save us from Kafka, to begin the world from the point at which we must die, but to try, at least, to die without shame.

Notes

1. It is worth noting that this was not the first time that Levi had experienced depression; he had gone through a similar bout in 1978. It is also worth noting that Levi probably had a genetic predisposition to depression (depression cannot, of course, be explained solely in genetic terms).
2. In a similar vein, Levi told Germaine Greer in 1985 that he had finished the translation of *The Trial* 'in a deep depression that lasted six months' (Levi 2001, 10).
3. For further debate, see Ataria (2017).
4. In this sense, Levi's mode of translation (in his own words, in his own style) may actually have made things worse, since the experience afforded by this kind of translation is closer to that of writing the text yourself.
5. The initial wording 'could preserve their innocence' is a concrete example of the kind of judgement we unconsciously and uncontrollably pass on those who acted within the grey zone.
6. The book's title may be an allusion to the 'fiasco' of Kertész's own survival, since 'the totality of my experiences could convince me only of my superfluousness' (Kertész 2011, 92).
7. 'A tempo debito', *La Stampa*, 25 May 1980.
8. We can easily imagine Kafka's gatekeeper saying something very similar.
9. The protagonist of 'Force Majeure' is rendered 'M', without a point, in Anne Milano Appel's English translation (Levi 2015, 2311–14). I have chosen, however, to follow Levi's original text ('Forza maggiore', *La Stampa*, 27 July 1986; Levi 1986, 77–80), in which the protagonist is designated 'M.', particularly in light of the strong resemblance between Levi's M. and Kafka's Joseph K. (written with a point).
10. One of the most horrifying insights in Koestler's *Darkness at Noon* (1952) concerns the confession of senior Soviet officials to crimes they did not commit and often could not even imagine, not because they feared torture, but based on thoroughly logical considerations. They concluded that by confessing they would contribute more to the party than by not confessing. Their logic thus told them to confess even at the cost of losing their honour, because they believed that serving the party was in fact the highest honour. As Bauman (2008, 142) put it, 'It appeared that when God wanted to destroy someone, He did not make him mad. He made him rational.'

References

Améry, Jean. 1999. *On suicide: A discourse on voluntary death.* Trans. John D. Barlow. Bloomington: Indiana University Press.

Anissimov, Myriam. 1999. *Primo Levi: Tragedy of an optimist.* Trans. Steve Cox.

Antelme, Robert. 1992. *The human race.* Trans. Jeffrey Haight and Annie Mahler. Evanston: The Marlboro Press/Northwestern.

Ataria, Yochai. 2017. *The structural trauma of western culture: Toward the end of humanity.* New York: Palgrave Macmillan.

Bauman, Zygmunt. 2008. *Modernity and the Holocaust.* Cambridge: Polity Press.

Benjamin, Walter. 1999. Franz Kafka. In *Selected writings, vol. 2, 1927–1934*, ed. Michael W. Jennings, Howard Eiland, and Gary Smith, 794–820. Cambridge, MA: The Belknap Press of Harvard University Press.

Camus, Albert. 1956. *The rebel: An essay on man in revolt.* Trans. Anthony Bower. New York: Vintage Books.

Dostoevsky, Fyodor. 2005. *The possessed.* Trans. Constance Garnett. New York: Barnes & Noble Classics.

Kafka, Franz. 1956. *The trial.* Trans. Willa and Edwin Muir. New York: The Modern Library.

———. 1958. *Description of a struggle.* Trans. Tania and James Stern. New York: Schocken Books.

Kertész, Imre. 2006. *Fateless.* Trans. Tim Wilkinson. London: Vintage Books.

———. 2008a. *Detective story.* Trans. Tim Wilkinson. New York: Knopf.

———. 2008b. *The pathseeker.* Trans. Time Wilkinson. New York: Melville House.

———. 2011. *Fiasco.* Trans. Tim Wilkinson. New York: Melville House.

Koestler, Arthur. 1952. *Darkness at noon.* Trans. Daphne Hardy. New York: Signet Books.

LaCapra, Dominick. 2014. *Writing history, writing trauma.* Baltimore: Johns Hopkins University Press.

Levi, Primo. 1986. *Racconti e saggi.* Turin: La Stampa.

———. 1997. *Conversazioni e interviste 1963–1987.* Ed. Marco Belpoliti. Turin: Einaudi.

———. 2001. *The voice of memory: Interviews 1961–1987.* Ed. Marco Belpoliti and Robert Gordon. Trans. Robert Gordon. New York: New Press.

———. 2015. *The complete works of Primo Levi.* Ed. Ann Goldstein. Various translators. 3 vols. New York: Liveright.

Levi, Primo, with Leonardo De Benedetti. 2018. *Auschwitz testimonies, 1945–1986.* Ed. Fabio Levi and Domenico Scarpa. Trans. Judith Woolf. Cambridge: Polity Press.

Mendel, David. 1998. Primo Levi and translation. *Bulletin of the Society for Italian Studies* 31: 11–17. http://doczz.it/doc/24956/bulletin-of-the-society-for-italian-studies

Nietzsche, Friedrich. 1974. *The gay science, with a prelude in rhymes and an appendix of songs*. Trans. Walter Kaufmann. New York: Vintage Books.
Rosenbaum, Ron. 1998. *Explaining Hitler: The search for the origins of his evil.* New York: Random House.
Thomson, Ian. 2003. *Primo Levi: A life*. New York: Henry Holt and Company.
Wagner, Richard. 1907. Judaism in music. In *Richard Wagner's prose works*, vol. 3, *The Theatre*. Trans. William A. Ellis, 75–122. London: Kegan Paul, Trench, Trübner & Co.
Zertal, Idith. 2005. *Israel's Holocaust and the politics of nationhood*. Trans. Chaya Galai. Cambridge: Cambridge University Press.

CHAPTER 12

The Price of Logic (or, Lorenzo)

In this chapter, which is a reflection on the second part of the book, I will try to show that Levi was motivated by an obsession to explain Auschwitz. Although he may in fact have succeeded in explaining Auschwitz, at least to some extent, it came at a high price, too high: the inability to explain the behaviour of Lorenzo, the Italian civilian worker who helped Levi at Auschwitz. This failure, I will suggest, was unbearable to Levi, since it was not limited to a specific case, but seemed to indicate that there was no room at all in the world for people like Lorenzo. There would thus appear to be an answer to Levi's question 'if this is a man', but not one he could live with.

Levi's declared goal is to be a witness. In an interview he gave to Giuseppe Grassano in 1979, Levi spoke of the importance of avoiding the writer's perspective: 'Galileo was a very great writer precisely because he was not a writer at all. He simply wanted to expound what he had seen' (Levi 2001, 126). This comparison goes a long way to explaining the principles that guided Levi in his writing: scientists must report their observations and describe the results of their experiments as objectively as they can. Levi believed that he had acted like Galileo, or at least aspired to do so.[1]

While still a prisoner at Auschwitz, Levi already began to prepare himself to give testimony, as he told Marco Vigevani, in a 1984 interview: 'For some reason that I cannot fathom, something anomalous happened to me, almost an unconscious preparation for the task of bearing witness.' Levi

Y. Ataria, *Primo Levi and Ka-Tzetnik*,
https://doi.org/10.1007/978-3-030-76743-3_12

felt that he was able to describe things objectively, as if he were a tape recorder: 'Even today, after so many years, I have preserved a visual and acoustic memory of my experiences there that I cannot explain. … Not only that: I also still remember, as if recorded on to tape, phrases in languages I do not know, Polish or Hungarian'; and that this allowed him to 'tell the story of what I saw truthfully, with accuracy' (255).

It was important to Levi that his book, *If This Is a Man*, should be his most accurate and reliable testimony: 'I saw this book as a judicial act. I felt like a witness' (quoted in Levi 1997, 148). The purpose of testimony is to describe, not to explain, and *If This Is a Man* should be treated as testimony, not literature (on this point, Levi and Ka-Tzetnik are in complete agreement). As Levi (2001, 250) told Vigevani, 'When I wrote the book, almost forty years ago now, I had one precise idea in mind, and it was certainly not to write a work of literature. It was rather to bear witness.… I wanted to recount what I had seen.' In another interview, conducted by Ernesto Olivero, Levi (1997, 209) remarked: 'I wrote instinctively, because I felt the need to expel something, as one might throw up an undigested meal.' Levi thus claims that the material he presented was unprocessed, disgorged just as it had been taken in. We must remember, however, that what is thrown up is not identical to the food previously ingested. Even when one vomits, the digestion process has taken place; it has just not been completed. The fallacy in Levi's argument is thus inadvertently exposed by the imagery he uses: food, once eaten, cannot remain 'undigested'. The moment information enters the subject's world, it undergoes a process, which changes it. Thus, even if Levi's goal was to testify as accurately as he could, objectivity is not possible.

Levi's obsession with telling his stories caused him to repeat them over and over again to anyone willing (or unwilling) to listen. Before they were told, however, the stories were constructed, the raw material processed, edited. As Levi himself (2001, 129) remarked to Grassano: 'And on the train [viz. the editing room] I remember telling my stories to whoever I found myself with. … If you ask me why I wanted to tell the stories, I couldn't answer. Probably it was part of an understandable instinct: I wanted to free myself from them.' Thus, Levi's (162) assertion that 'almost the entire chapter "The Canto of Ulysses" was written in half an hour between 12.30 and 1 p.m. one day. I was in a sort of trance' may be true of this particular chapter, but certainly does not represent the process that Levi went through in the rest of his work.

Levi tried to turn his memories into stories that people were both *able and willing* to hear—two conditions (willingness and ability) that were important to Levi, which is why he had to make himself understood. In order to make himself understood, however, he first had to understand. This seems to be one of Levi's biggest problems. He must tell his stories and, in order to do so, he must understand, that is, make sense of them, but he himself knows that understanding and explaining are no simple tasks: 'No wonder that a philosopher, Jaspers, and a poet, Thomas Mann, gave up trying to make sense of Hitlerism in rational terms and talked, quite literally, about "dämonische Mächte": demonic power' (2018, 90).

Over the years, the need to understand became not only an existential necessity, but a malignant presence as well: 'And what one cannot understand forms a painful void; it is a thorn, a constant urge that demands fulfillment' (Levi, quoted in Rosenfeld 2011, 196). In an interview given to Roberto Di Caro in 1987, Levi (2001, 174) describes his goal, in *The Drowned and the Saved*, for example, as: 'an immense need to put things in order, to put order back into a world of chaos, to explain to myself and to others. ... Writing is a way of creating order. It's the best way I know, even if I don't know many.' Perhaps this is what Levi means, when he says that 'the only way to survive is to tell one's story' (interview given to Giorgio De Rienzo, 'In un alambicco quanta poesia', *Famiglia cristiana*, 20 July 1975). Telling one's story allows the victims to free themselves from the weight they carry, to impose order, and to establish a dimension in which they are able to exercise control over the survivor in them.

In some cases at least, the need to understand also led Levi to colour his conclusions—regarding the figure of Henri, for example, described by Levi in *If This Is a Man*. As Anissimov (1999) shows, Levi's descriptions of Henri and other figures are somewhat slanted. This is a function not only of Levi's attempts to make the characters in his stories interesting, but also of his need to place them within an overall theoretical framework—a framework that would eventually develop into the grey zone. Levi's books thus become fascinating and incisive and he becomes a successful writer. It is important to understand, however, that Levi does not merely present the results of his research.[2]

Levi is aware of the problematic nature of the witness-writer, the writer-witness, the writer-historian, the historian-writer, and, in his case, the witness-writer-historian. Despite his efforts to break the mould, Levi nevertheless remains witness, narrator, writer, and historian all at once. He thus wonders whether 'there's a clear difference between telling stories you claim are true, demanding to be believed to the letter, and telling stories like Boccaccio, for another purpose, not to record facts' (Levi 2001, 133). Although Levi would like to answer this rhetorical question in the affirmative, it is not that simple. Indeed, when it comes to Levi's own books, an affirmative answer is elusive, because Levi, as he told Federico De Melis in a 1983 interview, constantly seeks explanations: 'I began writing about the camps and I carried on writing about things that happened to me, *always trying to explain, to resolve problems.* I have been reproached for this tendency towards the didactic' (157).[3]

As Kertész (2004, 2) suggests, the obsession to explain represents a mortal danger:

> But, it would seem, there is no getting around explanations, we are constantly explaining and excusing ourselves ... and in the end we ourselves demand explanations of ourselves, until in the end we succeed in annihilating everything around us, ourselves included, or in other words explain ourselves to death.

In Levi's case, the need to provide explanations came at a particularly high price. As time passed, Levi understood that Auschwitz could be explained. The problem was that he could not explain Lorenzo, whom he describes as follows:

> An Italian civilian worker brought me a piece of bread and the remains of his ration every day for six months; he gave me an undershirt of his, full of patches; he wrote a postcard on my behalf to Italy and brought me the reply. For all this he neither asked nor accepted any reward, because he was good and simple, and did not think that one should do good for a reward... However little sense there may be in trying to specify the reasons that I, among thousands of others like me, was able to stand up to the test, I believe that I owe it to Lorenzo if I am alive today; and not so much for his material aid as for his having constantly reminded me by his presence, by his natural and plain manner of being good, that a just world still existed outside ours, something and someone still pure and whole, not corrupt, not savage, unconnected to hatred and fear: something difficult to define, a remote possibility of good, but for which it was worth surviving... Lorenzo was a man; his humanity was pure and uncontaminated, he was outside this world of negation. Thanks to Lorenzo, I managed not to forget that I myself was a man. (Levi 2015, 113–16)

Lorenzo was not an intellectual. His motives were not complicated. In a situation in which there were only 'non-men', however, he did the impossible: he was a man. People cannot be made into Lorenzos, however. They are not simple chemical compounds to which something might be added or subtracted in order to make them someone else. Although Lorenzo was a civilian worker and not a prisoner, he found it impossible to go on living after his return to Italy. It seems that he was too good for this world, and his death came as if to prove that ours is a Kafkaesque world, in which there is no place for people like him. At the end of *The Trial*, Kafka (1956, 285–6) writes:

> His glance fell on the top story of the house adjoining the quarry. With a flicker as of a light going up, the casements of a window there suddenly flew open; a human figure, faint and insubstantial at that distance and that height, leaned abruptly far forward and stretched both arms still farther. Who was it? A friend? A good man? Someone who sympathized? Someone who wanted to help? Was it one person only? Or was it mankind?

Lorenzo's death prevented Levi from answering these questions in the affirmative. If Lorenzo is gone, then there are no white zones, only shades of grey. Levi's problem became especially acute after Lorenzo's death, leaving him trapped in a dark grey zone, unable to describe the good in humankind. This is the price of logic.

Notes

1. It was important to Levi to be as accurate as possible in his testimony. See, for example, Levi's 'Deposition for the Bosshammer Trial' (Friedrich Robert Bosshammer was Eichmann's 'specialist on Jewish affairs' in Italy), given in Turin, before a German state prosecutor, on 3 May 1971: 'Our guard was composed of SS, at least in part; in fact, our psychological state during the journey was not such as to permit us to make distinctions. I have been told that in 1945 I testified that at least two of the accompanying personnel were SS from the Fossoli camp; it is possible that my memory was fresher then than it is now, and in any case at that time I tried to reply in the most truthful way possible... During the entire journey, we did not receive any hot food; simply, during the daily descent from the wagon, two or three men per wagon would be taken by the guards to the provisions wagon to collect the bread and jam for their wagon. Only once, in Vienna, were we allowed to renew the supply of water. In our wagon there was a baby who was still being breast-fed and a little girl of three years old; even for them there was nothing to eat apart from the ration of bread and jam. I have been told that there was at least one death during the journey; I do not remember whether it concerned a man or a woman. I was told this circumstance by a doctor

friend of mine who was part of the transport. I should be grateful if my deposition of 2 September 1970 could be amended in this respect' (Levi 2018, 125–6).

2. This could of course affect his trustworthiness as a witness—a problem that Levi himself was well aware of, remarking to Giuseppe Grassano in 1979: 'This problem of being a counterfeiter, of feeling false, worries me. Often I ask myself questions. For example, this subject that I want to deal with, revisiting the *Lager*, I would have to talk about events seen thirty-five years ago. But am I sure they all happened and am I obliged to tell them exactly as they were? Couldn't I, for example, change them a little to serve my purpose, or even invent them from scratch?' (Levi 2001, 133).
3. I would suggest that those who believe that Levi's attempts to explain are not obsessive, perhaps citing his use of the phrase 'There is no explanation for Auschwitz' in some of his interviews and writings, consider Kertész's (2004) assertion: '"There is no explanation for Auschwitz" itself is an explanation.' Kertész stresses that 'what there is no explanation for is that there was no Auschwitz' (36). To Kertész's mind, 'What is truly irrational and genuinely inexplicable is not evil but, on the contrary, good' (41).

References

Anissimov, Myriam. 1999. *Primo Levi: Tragedy of an optimist*. Trans. Steve Cox.

Kafka, Franz. 1956. *The trial*. Trans. Willa and Edwin Muir. New York: The Modern Library.

Kertész, Imre. 2004. *Kaddish for an unborn child*. Trans. Tim Wilkinson. New York: Vintage Books.

Levi, Primo. 1997. *Conversazioni e interviste 1963–1987*. Ed. Marco Belpoliti. Turin: Einaudi.

———. 2001. *The voice of memory: Interviews 1961–1987*. Ed. Marco Belpoliti and Robert Gordon. Trans. Robert Gordon. New York: New Press.

———. 2015. *The complete works of Primo Levi*. Ed. Ann Goldstein. Various translators. 3 vols. New York: Liveright.

Levi, Primo, with Leonardo De Benedetti. 2018. *Auschwitz testimonies, 1945–1986*. Ed. Fabio Levi and Domenico Scarpa. Trans. Judith Woolf. Cambridge: Polity Press.

Rosenfeld, Alvin H. 2011. *The end of the Holocaust*. Bloomington: Indiana University Press.

Epilogue

What was supposed to be a short article on the literary style of Ka-Tzetnik eventually became the book you see before you. At first, I thought I would dedicate a single paragraph to a comparison between the writing styles of Ka-Tzetnik and Primo Levi, but one thing led to another.

As work on the book progressed, I felt the boundary between Levi and Ka-Tzetnik melting away, discovering the Levi in Ka-Tzetnik and the Ka-Tzetnik in Levi—'another planet' within the 'grey zone'. Indeed, despite the efforts of numerous scholars to cling to the grey zone with all their might—even at the price of making Ka-Tzetnik the embodiment of the 'wrong' kind of writing about the Holocaust—the other planet demands its place. The most striking example I have encountered is Arendt's (2006, 223–4) scathing description of Ka-Tzetnik's testimony and collapse at the Eichmann trial.[1] In a later edition of her monumental work, *The Origins of Totalitarianism* (1979, 444), however, she writes:

> There are no parallels to the life in the concentration camps. Its horror can never be fully embraced by the imagination for the very reason that it stands outside of life and death. It can never be fully reported for the very reason that the survivor returns to the world of the living, which makes it impossible for him to believe fully in his own past experiences. *It is as though he had a story to tell of another planet*, for the status of the inmates

Y. Ataria, *Primo Levi and Ka-Tzetnik*,
https://doi.org/10.1007/978-3-030-76743-3

> in the world of the living, where nobody is supposed to know if they are alive or dead, is such that it is as though they had never been born. Therefore all parallels create confusion and distract attention from what is essential.

A further, more complex example is offered by Zertal (2005, 87–8), who refers to 'the very triviality of the "crimes" exposed and the banality of the people who committed them; ordinary Jews, everyday people, who might well have been us; individuals trapped in insoluble dilemmas with no way out except suicide; who, *for one brief moment outside of "normal" time*, turned into persecutors, beating, slapping, whipping, and torturing other people'. Zertal clearly adopts Levi's perspective and tries to present collaboration in grey-zone terms, yet the other planet, seemingly intractable, finds its way into a subordinate clause. Indeed, when Zertal refers to a moment outside time, not only does she employ the terms of structural trauma, but effectively accepts the theory of the other planet in full, and, crucially, not in contrast to the grey zone. Perhaps this is the main insight of the book: that the grey zone and the other planet are not nearly as different from one another as we would like to believe. If that is indeed the case, maybe the grey zone and the other planet are not opposing explanations, but in fact describe two different dimensions of the same phenomenon. While the grey zone provides a broad theoretical framework, the other planet creates a space in which it is possible to begin to describe the experience of those who were there.

Levi and Ka-Tzetnik have both shaped our thinking about the genocide of the Jewish people, each in his own way. As long as we continue to treat them as icons, however, our ability to comprehend a reality in which ordinary people wake up in the morning and murder other people will remain limited. A complex approach is, in fact, essential to our understanding of what it means to be human.

Note

1. Arendt relates to Ka-Tzetnik as the epitome of the Israeli failure to judge Eichmann: 'It was not a "pen-name," he said. "I must carry this name as long as the world will not awaken after the crucifying of the nation … as humanity has risen after the crucifixion of one man." He continued with a little excursion into astrology: the star "influencing our fate in the same way

as the star of ashes at Auschwitz is there facing our planet, radiating toward our planet." And when he had arrived at "the unnatural power above Nature" which had sustained him thus far, and now, for the first time, paused to catch his breath, even Mr. Hausner felt that something had to be done about this "testimony," and, very timidly, very politely, interrupted: "Could I perhaps put a few questions to you if you will consent?" Whereupon the presiding judge saw his chance as well: "Mr. Dinoor, please, please, listen to Mr. Hausner and to me." In response, the disappointed witness, probably deeply wounded, fainted and answered no more questions' (224).

Appendix: Ka-Tzetnik, Biographical Notes

No comprehensive biography of Ka-Tzetnik has been written to date. The following is a brief outline of his life, based primarily on Dina Porat's (2018) article 'An Author as His Own Biographer—Ka-Tzetnik'.

- Yehiel Feiner (for the sake of convenience and consistency, I will use the name Feiner in this appendix) was born in Sosnowiec, in south-western Poland, in 1909.
- Family:
  - Yehiel Feiner's father, Abraham Feiner, belonged to the Hasidic movement.
  - Feiner's mother died when he was a boy (before 1928), and he seems to have been raised by his uncle and his elder sister.
  - Feiner had a younger sister, Malka, and a younger brother, Yitzhak.
- Feiner married Sanya Goldblum. The couple had no children.
- During the Second World War, Feiner was sent to two labour camps, Zakrau and Niederwalden, and was subsequently part of a group of prisoners sent back to the Sosnowiec ghetto.
- In the spring of 1943, Feiner, along with other Jews from Sosnowiec, was sent to the Kamionka ghetto, in the Lublin district of German-occupied Poland.
- In August 1943, the Kamionka ghetto was liquidated and Feiner was deported to Auschwitz, where he was a prisoner for six months.

Y. Ataria, *Primo Levi and Ka-Tzetnik*,
https://doi.org/10.1007/978-3-030-76743-3

- In early 1944, Feiner was transferred to the Auschwitz sub-camp of Günthergrube, near the Lędziny coal mines, where he remained for a year. The prisoners at this camp appear to have been treated relatively well, due to the importance of the mines to the German war effort, and thanks to Lagerälteste (camp elder) Ludwig Wörl, later recognised by Yad Vashem as 'Righteous Among the Nations'.[1]
- In January 1945, as the Red Army approached, the prisoners at Günthergrube were taken on a death march. Feiner marched for two days, to another Auschwitz sub-camp, Gleiwitz, where he was put on a train. When the train stopped, Feiner managed to escape, together with a group of friends who had been with him since his arrival at Auschwitz.
- Feiner went back to Sosnowiec and Będzin (in Zaglembie region of southern Poland), in search of survivors. Having encountered antisemitism and not having found any survivors, he and the group of friends with which he had been to Auschwitz decided to go on to Bucharest (Romania) and from there to Palestine (the 'Bricha route').
- Feiner and his friends (five Günthergrube survivors, who came to be referred to as the 'Auschwitz group') joined the Bricha, en route to Palestine. During the course of the journey, Feiner changed his name a number of times. Among the names he adopted were Kalman and Karl.
- In Bucharest, Feiner met the poet and partisan leader Abba Kovner, who arranged for him to have a place where he could write. It is at this point that he probably wrote the poem 'Salamandra' (see Chap. 2).
- In Tarvisio (Italy), Feiner met Eliyahu Goldenberg, and the two travelled to Naples together.
- In Naples, Feiner wrote the first book in the Salamandra series—entitled *Salamandra* (*Sunrise over Hell*), like the poem he had written in Bucharest. Goldenberg took the manuscript to Palestine, where Zalman Shazar (who would later become Israel's third president) promoted its publication, by Dvir, in 1946—before Feiner himself reached Palestine.
  - As recounted in Chap. 2, the pen name Ka-Tzetnik was born when Feiner gave the manuscript to Goldenberg and the latter asked him to add the author's name.
- In early 1946, at the age of thirty-seven, Feiner set sail from Naples to Tel Aviv.

- Feiner changed (1947–1948) his surname to De-Nur ('of fire' in Aramaic), signifying one who has emerged from the flames.
  - The expression *di-nur* appears in Daniel 7:10 ('A river of fire [*di-nur*] streamed forth before Him') and in the *Zohar*.
- Also in early 1946, Feiner met Nina Asherman, daughter of a well-known Tel Aviv family, who had decided to seek out the author of *Salamandra*. The two married and had a son, Lior, and a daughter, Daniella.
- In 1961, during the course of the Eichmann trial, Yehiel Di-Nur (Feiner) was revealed to be the author Ka-Tzetnik.
- Yehiel Di-Nur died in Tel Aviv on 17 July 2001, at the age of 92.

Note

1. '[Wörl] protected the 600 Jewish prisoners from maltreatment by sadistic German Kapos and saw to it that they get their due share of food and clothing. Even prisoners with tuberculosis were able to survive because Wörl exempted them from hard work and protected them by various subterfuges from the inspection of the SS doctors. At the time of the evacuation of Auschwitz, he helped prisoners escape from the infamous death marches' ('The Stories of Six Righteous among the Nations in Auschwitz: Flickers of Light', www.yadvashem.org/yv/en/exhibitions/righteous-auschwitz/woerl.asp).

References

Agamben, Giorgio. 1999. *Remnants of Auschwitz: The witness and the archive.* Trans. Daniel Heller-Roazen. New York: Zone Books.

Améry, Jean. 1980. *At the mind's limits: Contemplations by a survivor on Auschwitz and its realities.* Trans. Sidney Rosenfeld and Stella P. Rosenfeld. Bloomington: Indiana University Press.

———. 1999. *On suicide: A discourse on voluntary death.* Trans. John D. Barlow. Bloomington: Indiana University Press.

Amir, Dana. 2016. When language meets traumatic lacuna: The metaphoric, the metonymic, and the psychotic modes of testimony. *Psychoanalytic Inquiry* 36 (8): 620–632.

———. 2019. *Bearing witness to the witness: A psychoanalytic perspective on four modes of traumatic testimony.* Milton Park: Routledge.

Angier, Carole. 2002. *The double bond: Primo Levi, a biography.* New York: Farrar, Straus and Giroux.

Anissimov, Myriam. 1999. *Primo Levi: Tragedy of an optimist.* Trans. Steve Cox.

Antelme, Robert. 1992. *The human race.* Trans. Jeffrey Haight and Annie Mahler. Evanston: The Marlboro Press/Northwestern.

Applebaum, Ann. 2004. *Gulag: A history.* New York: Anchor Books.

Arad, Yitzhak, Israel Gutman, and Abraham Margaliot, eds. 1991. *Documents on the Holocaust: Selected sources on the destruction of the Jews of Germany and Austria, Poland, and the Soviet Union.* Trans. Lea Ben Dor. Lincoln, Nebr. and Jerusalem: University of Nebraska Press and Yad Vashem.

Arendt, Hannah. 1979. *The origins of totalitarianism.* San Diego: Harcourt Brace & Company.

Y. Ataria, *Primo Levi and Ka-Tzetnik*,
https://doi.org/10.1007/978-3-030-76743-3

———. 2006. *Eichmann in Jerusalem: A report on the banality of evil.* New York: Penguin.

Arieli, Amos, and Yochai Ataria. 2018. Helplessness: The inability to know-that you don't know-how. *Philosophical Psychology* 31 (6): 948–968.

Ataria, Yochai. 2014a. Traumatic memories as black holes: A qualitative-phenomenological approach. *Qualitative Psychology* 1 (2): 123–140.

———. 2014b. Acute peritraumatic dissociation: In favor of a phenomenological inquiry. *Journal of Trauma & Dissociation* 15 (3): 332–347.

———. 2016a. I am not my body, this is not my body. *Human Studies* 39 (2): 217–229.

———. 2016b. Post-traumatic stress disorder: A theory of perception. *Body, Movement and Dance in Psychotherapy* 11 (1): 19–30.

———. 2016c. When the body becomes the enemy: Disownership toward the body. *Philosophy, Psychiatry, & Psychology* 23 (1): 1–15.

———. 2016d. The witness's death: Primo Levi and Georges Perec. In *Interdisciplinary handbook of trauma and culture*, ed. Yochai Ataria, David Gurevitz, Haviva Pedaya, and Yuval Neria, 195–216. New York: Springer.

———. 2017. *The structural trauma of western culture: Toward the end of humanity.* New York: Palgrave Macmillan.

———. 2018. *Body disownership in complex posttraumatic stress disorder.* New York: Palgrave Macmillan.

———. 2019a. Total destruction. In *Jean Améry: Beyond the minds limits*, ed. Yochai Ataria, Amit Kravitz, and Eli Pitcovski, 141–158. New York: Palgrave Macmillan.

———. 2019b. When the body stands in the way: Complex posttraumatic stress disorder, depersonalization and schizophrenia. *Philosophy, Psychiatry, & Psychology* 26 (1): 19–31.

———. 2019c. Becoming nonhuman: The case study of the GULAG. *Genealogy* 3 (2): 1–27.

———. 2020. Investigating the origins of body-disownership: The case study of the Gulag. *Journal of Phenomenological Psychology* 51 (1): 44–82.

———. Forthcoming. *Consciousness in flesh.* New York: Palgrave Macmillan.

Ataria, Yochai, and Shaun Gallagher. 2015. Somatic apathy: Body disownership in the context of torture. *Journal of Phenomenological Psychology* 46 (1): 105–122.

Ataria, Yochai, and Omer Horovitz. In press. The destructive nature of severe and ongoing trauma: Impairments in the minimal-self. *Philosophical Psychology.*

Ataria, Yochai, and Yuval Neria. 2013. Consciousness-body-time: How do people think lacking their body? *Human Studies* 36 (2): 159–178.

Bartov, Omer. 1997. Kitsch and sadism in Ka-Tzetnik's other planet: Israeli youth imagine the Holocaust. *Jewish Social Studies* 3 (2): 42–76.

Baudrillard, Jean. 2006. *Simulacra and simulation.* Trans. Sheila Faria Glaser. Ann Arbor: University of Michigan Press.

Bauman, Zygmunt. 2008. *Modernity and the Holocaust*. Cambridge: Polity Press.

Benjamin, Walter. 1999. Franz Kafka. In *Selected writings, vol. 2, 1927–1934*, ed. Michael W. Jennings, Howard Eiland, and Gary Smith, 794–820. Cambridge, MA: The Belknap Press of Harvard University Press.

———. 2006. On the concept of history. In *Selected writings, vol. 4, 1938–1940*, ed. Howard Eiland and Michael W. Jennings, 388–400. Cambridge, MA: The Belknap Press of Harvard University Press.

Bettelheim, Bruno. 1943. Individual and mass behavior in extreme situations. *Journal of Abnormal and Social Psychology* 38: 417–452.

———. 1960. *The informed heart: Autonomy in a mass age*. Glencoe: The Free Press.

Borowski, Tadeusz. 1976. *This way for the gas, ladies and gentlemen*. Trans. Barbara Vedder. New York: Penguin.

Bos, Pascal. 2018. Sexual violence in Ka-Tzetnik's house of dolls. In *Holocaust history and the readings of Ka-Tzetnik*, ed. Annette F. Timm, 105–138. London: Bloomsbury Publishing.

Browning, Christopher R. 2001. *Ordinary men: Reserve police battalion 101 and the final solution in Poland*. London: Penguin.

Brunner, José. 2004. Critique of pure banality: On Arendt's dehumanization of Eichmann (Hebrew). In *Hannah Arendt: A half-century of polemics* [Hannah Arendt: Ḥatsi me'ah shel pulmus], ed. Idith Zertal and Moshe Zuckermann, 81–106. Tel Aviv: Hakibbutz Hameuchad.

Camus, Albert. 1955. *The myth of Sisyphus and other essays*. Trans. Justin O'Brien. New York: Vintage Books.

———. 1956. *The rebel: An essay on man in revolt*. Trans. Anthony Bower. New York: Vintage Books.

———. 1958. *The fall*. Trans. Justin O'Brien. New York: Alfred A. Knopf.

Caruth, Cathy. 1996. *Unclaimed experience: Trauma, narrative, and history*. Baltimore: Johns Hopkins University Press.

DeKoven Ezrahi, Sidra. 1995. Representing Auschwitz. *History and Memory* 7 (2): 121–154.

Deleuze, Gilles, and Félix Guattari. 1986. *Kafka: Toward a minor literature*. Trans. Dana Polan. Minneapolis: University of Minnesota Press.

Dostoevsky, Fyodor. 2005. *The possessed*. Trans. Constance Garnett. New York: Barnes & Noble Classics.

Dudai, Rina. 2005. Kitsch and trauma—A case study: *The house of dolls* by Ka-Tzetnik (Hebrew). *Mikan* 6: 125–142.

Felman, Shoshana. 2002. *The juridical unconscious*. Cambridge, MA: Harvard University Press.

Felman, Shoshana, and Dori Laub. 1992. *Testimony: Crises of witnessing in literature, psychoanalysis, and history*. Florence: Routledge.

Foucault, Michel. 2000. 'Anti-retro', an interview with Pascal Bonitzer and Serge Toubiana [originally published as 'anti-retro: Entretien avec Michel Foucault', *Cahiers du Cinema* 251–2 (July–August, 1974)]. In *Cahiers du Cinema, vol. 4, 1973–1978: History, ideology, cultural struggle*, ed. David Wilson, 159–172. London: Routledge.

Friedländer, Saul. 1984. *Reflections of Nazism: An essay on kitsch and death.* Trans. Thomas Weyr. New York: Harper & Row.

———. 2007. *Nazi Germany and the Jews: The years of extermination 1939–1945.* London: Weidenfeld and Nicolson.

Glasner-Heled. 2005. Whom does Ka-Tzetnik represent (Hebrew). *Dapim: Studies on the Holocaust* 19: 167–200.

Goldberg, Amos. 2012. *Trauma in first person: Diary writing during the Holocaust* [Traumah beguf rishon: Ketivat yomanim bitekufat hasho'ah]. Or Yehuda: Kinneret, Zmora-Bitan, Dvir and Heksherim Institute, Ben Gurion University.

———. 2013a. Body, *jouissance*, and irony in representations of suffering during the holocaust period (Hebrew). In *Pain in the flesh: Representations of the body in sickness, suffering, and jouissance* [Ke'ev basar yadam: ķovets ma'amarim al haguf haḥoleh, hasovel, hamit'aneg], ed. Orit Meital and Shira Stav, 62–100, Critical Mass series. Or Yehuda: Ben Gurion University and Kinneret, Zmora-Bitan, Dvir.

———. 2013b. Introduction to *modernity and the Holocaust* [Moderniyut vehasho'ah], by Zygmunt Bauman. Trans. Yaniv Farkas. Tel Aviv: Resling.

———. 2017. *Trauma in the first person.* Trans. Shmuel Sermoneta-Gertel and Avner Greenberg. Bloomington: Indiana University Press.

Goldhagen, Daniel J. 1997. *Hitler's willing executioners: Ordinary Germans and the Holocaust.* New York: Vintage Books.

Golomb, Jacob. 2015. Introduction to Berel Lang, *Primo Levi: life as matter* [Primo levi: Haḥayim keḥomer; Hebrew ed. of *Primo Levi: The matter of a life*]. Trans. Ilit Karp. Jerusalem: Carmel.

Gradowski, Zalmen. 2017. *From the heart of hell: Manuscripts of a Sonderkommando prisoner, found in Auschwitz.* Trans. Barry Smerin and Janina Wurbs. Oświęcim: Auschwitz-Birkenau State Museum.

Gutman, Israel, ed. 1990. *The encyclopedia of the Holocaust.* 4 vols. New York: Macmillan.

Heidelberger-Leonard, Irène. 2010. *The philosopher of Auschwitz: Jean Améry and living with the Holocaust.* London: Tauris.

Herzberg, Abel J. 2016. *Amor Fati: Seven essays on Bergen-Belsen.* Trans. Jack Santcross. Göttingen: Wallstein Verlag.

Kafka, Franz. 1956. *The trial.* Trans. Willa and Edwin Muir. New York: The Modern Library.

———. 1958. *Description of a struggle.* Trans. Tania and James Stern. New York: Schocken Books.

———. 2000. *The metamorphosis, in the penal colony, and other stories.* Trans. Joachim Neugrochel. New York: Scribner.
Ka-Tzetnik. (1946) 1991. *Salamandra: Chronicle of a Jewish family in the twentieth century* [Salamandrah: Kronikah shel mishpaḥah yehudit bame'ah ha'esrim]. Tel Aviv: Hakibbutz Hameuchad.
———. 1955. *Dos hoyz fun di lyalkes.* Buenos Aires: Unión Central Israelita Polaca en la Argentina.
———. 1961. *Piepel.* Trans. Moshe M. Kohn. London: Anthony Blond.
———. 1971. *Star eternal.* Trans. Nina De-Nur. New York: Arbor House.
———. 1977. *Phoenix over the Galilee.* Trans. Nina De-Nur. New York: Pyramid.
———. 1978. *Sunrise over hell.* Trans. Nina De-Nur. London: Corgi.
———. 1989. *Shivitti: A vision.* Trans. Eliyah Nike De-Nur and Lisa Herman. New York: Harper & Row.
———. 1993. Curriculum Vitae (Hebrew). In *Guide for teachers, moderators, and students on the Holocaust and the rebirth of Israel in the books of Ka-Tzetnik* [Madrikh lamoreh, lamanḥeh, latalmid benose hasho'ah utekumat yisra'el bekitvei k. tzetnik], ed. Eran Litvin and Dorit Sharir. Tel Aviv: Ministry of Education and Hakibbutz Hameuchad.
Ka-Tzetnik 135633. 1955. *House of dolls.* Trans. Moshe M. Kohn. New York: Simon and Schuster.
Kershaw, Ian. 2008. *Hitler, the Germans, and the final solution.* Jerusalem/New Haven: Yad Vashem and Yale University Press.
Kertész, Imre. 2004. *Kaddish for an unborn child.* Trans. Tim Wilkinson. New York: Vintage Books.
———. 2006. *Fateless.* Trans. Tim Wilkinson. London: Vintage Books.
———. 2008a. *Detective story.* Trans. Tim Wilkinson. New York: Knopf.
———. 2008b. *The pathseeker.* Trans. Time Wilkinson. New York: Melville House.
———. 2011. *Fiasco.* Trans. Tim Wilkinson. New York: Melville House.
Koestler, Arthur. 1952. *Darkness at noon.* Trans. Daphne Hardy. New York: Signet Books.
Kundera, Milan. 1984. *The unbearable lightness of being.* Trans. Michael H. Heim. New York: Harper & Row.
LaCapra, Dominick. 1996. *Representing the Holocaust: History, theory, trauma.* Ithaca: Cornell University Press.
———. 1998. *History and memory after Auschwitz.* Ithaca: Cornell University Press.
———. 2014. *Writing history, writing trauma.* Baltimore: Johns Hopkins University Press.
Lang, Fritz, dir. 1927. *Metropolis.* Written by Thea von Harbou and Fritz Lang. Universum Film (UFA).
Lang, Berel. 2013. *Primo Levi: A matter of a life.* New Haven: Yale University Press.
Lanzmann, Claude. 1985. *Shoah: An oral history of the Holocaust.* New York: Pantheon Books.

Levi, Primo. 1986. *Racconti e saggi*. Turin: La Stampa.
———. 1988. *The drowned and the saved*. Trans. Raymond Rosenthal. New York. Simon and Schuster.
———. 1997. *Conversazioni e interviste 1963–1987*. Ed. Marco Belpoliti. Turin: Einaudi.
———. 2001. *The voice of memory: Interviews 1961–1987*. Ed. Marco Belpoliti and Robert Gordon. Trans. Robert Gordon. New York: New Press.
———. 2015. *The complete works of Primo Levi*. Ed. Ann Goldstein. Various translators. 3 vols. New York: Liveright.
Levi, Primo, with Leonardo De Benedetti. 2018. *Auschwitz testimonies, 1945–1986*. Ed. Fabio Levi and Domenico Scarpa. Trans. Judith Woolf. Cambridge: Polity Press.
Levin, Itamar, ed. 2005. *Lexicon of the Holocaust* [Lexikon hasho'ah]. Tel Aviv: Yediot Aharonot, Sifre Hemed.
Libsker, Ari, dir. 2008. *Stalags: Holocaust and pornography in Israel* (Hebrew). Heymann Brothers Films.
Lyotard, Jean François. 1988. *The differend: Phases in dispu*te. Trans. Georges Van Den Abbeele. Manchester: University of Minnesota and Manchester University Press.
———. 1990. *Heidegger and "the Jews"*. Trans. Andreas Michel and Mark S. Roberts. Minneapolis: University of Minnesota Press.
Mendel, David. 1998. Primo Levi and translation. *Bulletin of the Society for Italian Studies* 31: 11–17. http://doczz.it/doc/24956/bulletin-of-the-society-for-italian-studies
Milner, Iris. 2008. The "Gray zone" revisited: The concentrationary universe in Ka. Tzetnik's literary testimony. *Jewish Social Studies* 14 (2): 113–115.
Miron, Dan. 1994. Between books and ashes (Hebrew). *Alpayim* 10: 196–224.
Neumann, Boaz. 2002. *The Nazi Weltanschauung: Space, body, language* [Re'iyat ha'olam hanatsit: Merhav, Guf, Safah]. Haifa: Haifa University.
Nietzsche, Friedrich. 1974. *The gay science, with a prelude in rhymes and an appendix of songs*. Trans. Walter Kaufmann. New York: Vintage Books.
Orwell, George. (1949) 1977. *1984*. New York: New American Library.
Ozick, Cynthia. 1989. Primo Levi's suicide note. In *Metaphor and memory*, 34–48. New York: Knopf.
Perec, Georges. 1988. *W, or the memory of childhood*. Trans. David Bellos. Boston: David R. Godine.
Porat, Dina. 2018. An author as his own biographer—Ka-Tzetnik: A man and a tattooed number. In *Holocaust history and the readings of Ka-Tzetnik*, ed. Annette F. Timm, 13–36. London: Bloomsbury Publishing.
Ronen, Avihu. 1989. Jews of Zaglembie during the Holocaust, 1939–1943 (Hebrew). PhD diss. Tel Aviv University.

Rosenbaum, Ron. 1998. *Explaining Hitler: The search for the origins of his evil.* New York: Random House.

Rosenfeld, Alvin H. 2011. *The end of the Holocaust.* Bloomington: Indiana University Press.

Ryn, Zdzisław. 1990a. Between life and death: Experiences of concentration camp mussulmen during the Holocaust. *Genetic, Social, and General Psychology Monographs* 116 (1): 5–19.

———. 1990b. The evolution of mental disturbances in the concentration camp syndrome (KZ-Syndrom). *Genetic, Social, and General Psychology Monographs* 116 (1): 21–36.

Ryn, Zdzisław, and Stanisław Klodzinski. 1987. An der Grenze zwischen Leben und Tod. *Eine Studie über die Erscheinung des "Muselmanns" im Konzentrationslager'.* In *Die Auschwitz-Hefte: Texte der polnischen Zeitschrift 'Przegląd lekarski' über historische, psychische und medizinische Aspekte des Lebens und Sterbens in Auschwitz*, ed. the Hamburger Institut für Sozialforschung, vol. 1, 89–154. Weinheim/Basel: Beltz.

Semprún, Jorge. 1997. *Literature or life.* Trans. Linda Coverdale. New York: Viking.

Sofsky, Wolfgang. 1996. *The order of terror: The concentration camp.* Trans. William Templer. Princeton: Princeton University Press.

Solzhenitsyn, Aleksandr. 1975. *The Gulag Archipelago, 1918–1956.* Trans. Thomas P. Whitney. Vols. 1–3. New York: Harper & Row.

Spadi, Milvia. 2003. *Le parole di un uomo: Incontro con Primo Levi.* Rome: Di Renzo.

Szeintuch, Yechiel. 2003. *Katzetnik 135633: A series of dialogues with Yechiel De-Nur* [Kemesiaḥ lefi tumo: Siḥot im yeḥiel di-nur], ed. Carrie Friedman-Cohen. Jerusalem: Ghetto Fighters' House and Dov Sadan Institute.

———. 2007. On Katzetnik's unknown testimony at the Eichmann trial. *The Mendele Review* 11 (12), November 11. http://yiddish.haifa.ac.il/tmr/tmr11/tmr11012.htm

———. 2009. *Salamandra: Myth and history in Katzetnik's Writings* [Salamandrah: Mitos vehistoryah bekhitvei k. tsetnik: Yetsirato hadu-leshonit beyidish uve'ivrit shel k. tsetnik al reka habiografyah shelo], ed. Carrie Friedman-Cohen. Jerusalem: Dov Sadan Project, Hebrew University and Carmel.

Thomson, Ian. 2003. *Primo Levi: A life.* New York: Henry Holt and Company.

Wagner, Richard. 1907. Judaism in music. In *Richard Wagner's prose works*, vol. 3, *The Theatre.* Trans. William A. Ellis, 75–122. London: Kegan Paul, Trench, Trübner & Co.

Yablonka, Hanna. 2004. *The State of Israel vs. Adolf Eichmann.* Trans. Ora Cummings and David Herman. New York: Schocken Books.

Zertal, Idith. 2002. *Death and the nation: History memory politics* [Ha'umah vehamavet: Historiyah zikaron politikah]. Or Yehuda: Dvir.

———. 2005. *Israel's Holocaust and the politics of nationhood.* Trans. Chaya Galai. Cambridge: Cambridge University Press.

Index[1]

[1] Note: Page numbers followed by 'n' refer to notes.

Y. Ataria, *Primo Levi and Ka-Tzetnik*,
https://doi.org/10.1007/978-3-030-76743-3

The manufacturer's authorised representative in the EU is Springer Nature Customer Service Centre GmbH, Europaplatz 3, 69115 Heidelberg, Germany. If you have any concerns regarding our products, please contact ProductSafety@springernature.com

Printed and bound by CPI Group (UK) Ltd, Croydon, CR0 4YY
30/09/2026
02225455-0007